Florida A&M University, Tallahassee
Florida Atlantic University, Boca Raton
Florida Gulf Coast University, Ft. Myers
Florida International University, Miami
Florida State University, Tallahassee
University of Central Florida, Orlando
University of Florida, Gainesville
University of North Florida, Jacksonville
University of South Florida, Tampa
University of West Florida, Pensacola

The Cult of Bolívar
in Latin American Literature

Christopher B. Conway

University Press of Florida
Gainesville/Tallahassee/Tampa/Boca Raton
Pensacola/Orlando/Miami/Jacksonville/Ft. Myers

Library of Congress Cataloguing-in-Publication Data
Conway, Christopher B., 1969–
The cult of Bolivar in Latin American literature / Christopher B. Conway.
p. cm.
Includes bibliographical references and index.
ISBN 0-8130-2683-0 (alk. paper)
1. Spanish American literature—20th century—History and criticism.
2. Spanish American literature—19th century—History and criticism.
3. Bolívar, Simón, 1783–1830—In literature. 4. Spanish American fiction—
20th century—History and criticism. 5. Spanish American fiction—19th
century—History and criticism. 6. Hero worship—Venezuela. I. Title.
PQ7081.C653 2003
860.9'351—dc22   2003061693

The University Press of Florida is the scholarly publishing agency
for the State University System of Florida, comprising Florida A&M
University, Florida Atlantic University, Florida Gulf Coast University,
Florida International University, Florida State University, University
of Central Florida, University of Florida, University of North Florida,
University of South Florida, and University of West Florida.

University Press of Florida
15 Northwest 15th Street
Gainesville, FL 32611-2079
http://www.upf.com

For John Phillip Conway

and in memory of Magdalena Josephine Conway

"In my name both good and evil is sought
in Colombia, and many invoke it as the text of their madness."

Simón Bolívar, in a letter to Antonio Leocadio Guzmán, December 1829

Contents

Illustrations

Acknowledgments

Many people and institutions have provided invaluable support while I was writing this book. I first tackled the subject of the cult of Bolívar in a dissertation in the Department of Literature at the University of California, San Diego from 1991 to 1996. I give heartfelt thanks for the generous and insightful guidance of Jaime Concha, and for the continuing support of Susan Kirkpatrick, whose scholarly and personal advice I've sought out since the beginning of my career. The Center for Iberian and Latin American Studies at UCSD funded my first research trip to Venezuela.

I am grateful for the support of the University of Texas at Arlington, which funded two trips to Venezuela. My thanks for the generosity of my colleagues and friends in Arlington: Richard Francaviglia, Ruth Gross, Melissa Miner, Elizabeth Ordoñez, Becky Rosenboom, and Fred Viña. In particular, Kimberley Van Noort and Antoinette Sol read chapters and offered encouragement when the road seemed interminable. At Brown University, I would like to thank Beth Bauer, Elliott Colla, Mary Fennell, Stephanie Merrim, Julio Ortega, and Wadda Rios-Font for stepping in to help me whenever it was necessary. Thanks to Idelber Avelar and Gema Guevara for sharing impressions and much needed materials.

In the people of Venezuela I have found great warmth and encouragement. Although not all of my Venezuelan friends will agree with some of the views expressed in this study, I am lucky to have had their unwavering support. As far back as 1992, I learned a great deal about the life of Bolívar and the Wars of Independence from my friend Rafael Guillén. I cannot thank Alejandro Contreras enough, whose friendship and interest in my work has helped me in many ways. I am also grateful for the friendship of Luis Pellicer and Vanesa Benites, who generously gave me a place to stay and many long conversations. I would also like to thank Elias Pino Iturrieta, Inés Quintero, Yolanda Salas, Henry Parejo, Josefina Gavila Luna, Helen Chaderton, and Rita Parada at the Hemeroteca Nacional.

The intellectual rigor, enthusiasm, and boundless generosity of Beatriz González Stephan have been a constant source of strength since I began my career. Without her support, this book would have taken much longer to complete. I thank Amy Gorelick and Nancy Vogeley for making suggestions that substantially improved this manuscript. My research assistant, Jerelyn Johnson, did outstanding work on issues large and small and made finishing this manuscript a fun experience. I am grateful to Juan Dávila for sending me copies and catalogues of his art, as well as hard-to-get essays about his work. Douglas García gave me personal and intellectual support, and has taught me a lot about Venezuela over the years.

Finally, I thank two people whose involvement in this book's successful completion goes deeper than that of anyone else. Matthew Alan Wyszynski is a scholar of friendship as well as one of its warmest and most able practitioners. His close attention to this book, as well as his unwavering loyalty and good sense have improved it in innumerable ways. Most of all, I thank Desirée Henderson, whose steady hand and keen insights have shaped this book's progress since its inception. Without her companionship in good times and in bad, and across mountains and deserts, this book and the life that went into its writing would not be as rich.

Author's Note

Whenever possible, I have used existing English translations of the Spanish texts under discussion. Otherwise, all translations from the Spanish are my own.

Introduction

Dominant Poses, Iconoclastic Gestures

In August of 1994, the reproduction and dissemination of a single work of art plunged Chile into a cultural crisis in which issues of freedom of speech, foreign diplomacy, and sexual freedom became entangled. The catalyst of the controversy was the reproduction of Juan Dávila's painting *The Liberator Simón Bolívar* (1994), then on display at London's Hayward Gallery, on a widely distributed postcard funded by the cultural arm of the Ministry of Education, FONDART. Dávila's postcard belonged to a collaboration called La Escuela de Santiago, which was comprised of the artists Gonzalo Díaz, Eugenio Dittborn, and Arturo Duclos, whose work was also staged in the postcard format. Dávila's image portrays the equestrian Bolívar with a woman's body and a masculine face covered with makeup. Bolívar wears a sumptuously lined military coat spread open to reveal breasts, black stockings, and feminine boots. The wide hips are bare but the saddle obstructs the hero's sex. Bolívar's horse is transected in two, with one half as an abstracted grid and the other depicted mimetically. Bolívar's left arm is lowered and bent, holding in its crook a colorful floral wreath, while his hand forms a fist with a vigorous finger extended in an obscene gesture. When we turn the postcard over, we see that Dávila has signed his name as "Juana Dávila."

The image exploded onto the front pages of newspapers and into television newscasts as national and international political figures attacked the desecration of the continental hero. "Never before in the history of Chile," declared one commentator, "had a work of art or a cultural theme activated to this extent those institutions linked to power" (Donoso 28). Gabriel Valdés, the president of the Chilean senate, decried the fact that the postcard project had received state funding and called the image a detestable insult to all Chileans, Bolivarian nations, and to good taste itself ("Advierten"). In a press release, the Venezuelan Embassy in Chile affirmed the sanctity of Bolívar and declared that the Venezuelan nation had been unjustly wounded in its national honor: "In light of the libelous campaign that is being orchestrated against the most sacred value of our nationality, which presents The Liberator Simón Bolívar in publications that we consider without decorum and in violation of the immortal genius of American independence, the Venezuelan Embassy in Chile protests and deplores these manifestations that are alien to the sentiments of the Chilean people, who have always been united to the Venezuelan people by history and shared cultural values" ("Gobierno"). Six days later, the Chilean Foreign Ministry presented apologies to the governments of Venezuela, Colombia, and Ecuador. The controversy continued to rage on, however, as Chile's cultural and political establishment debated the agenda of FONDART, its use of state funds, and whether or not the organization favored gay artists and themes. The other members of La Escuela de Santiago weighed in as well, arguing that the unrelenting attacks on Dávila in the media were creating an unacceptable atmosphere of violent censorship and veiled threats (Díaz, Dittborn, and Duclos). At a time when Chile was negotiating the transition to democracy after almost two decades of military repression, the Juan Dávila affair touched many nerves. How free was Chile after all?[1]

I begin with the Juan Dávila affair because it illustrates a constellation of themes and problems that go to the center of this book. My study's focus on monumentalism, gender, national identity, and the failures of modernity is exemplified by the toppling of the mythic Bolívar in Dávila's painting. The Liberator Simón Bolívar confronts nationalist history and its authoritarian claim to ideological truth through an iconoclastic challenge to all the absolutes represented by Bolívar; in the apt words of George Alexander, Dávila "gives us a disturbing record of history on the run" (84). In the pages to follow I consider The Liberator Simón Bolívar as a way of introducing the themes, methodologies, and focus that shape this study. A critical reading of Dávila's image enables us to define and theorize the very contours of the official ideologies that reacted so vehemently against his iconoclastic representation of the hero of Latin American independence.

Monumental Poses

Russ Castronovo's definition of monumentalist narratives summarizes how I use the term here and throughout my analysis. The word *monu-*

ment is derived from the Latin word *monere*, which signifies both to re-member and to teach with authority (Castronovo 109). Monuments are thus memory infused with the exercise of power; they are personal and intimate in their bid to make a person reflect on something past, and rela-tional in their embodiment of an authoritative narrative for the individual and the collectivity. "It is indeed power that shapes the history that defines people as citizens," writes Castronovo, "and collects them in the construct of the nation" (109). The monumentalist definition of Bolívar is not lim-ited to nationalist statuary, but extends to any representation that seeks to define the hero as an unmoveable idol that stands for eternal and invio-lable values. Juan Dávila's treatment of institutions, gender, race, aesthetic codes, and gesture all undermine the monumental Bolívar, striking the bronze and marble of his authoritative contours. His revision of Bolívar reverses the dominant poses and gestures of the monumental hero and replaces them with a set of revealing questions about gender, representa-tion, and Latin American modernity. However, to better understand Dá-vila's iconoclasm we need to define the myth of Bolívar and its ideological functions.

The concepts of pose and gesture refer to the meaningful manipulation of the human body and are particularly appropriate for exploring the con-ventions of heroic statuary. My argument is that the authority of monu-ments, and by extension, monumentalist narratives about heroes, may be diagrammed through the concept of *monumental poses*, or authoritative statements about the monumentalist hero that explain his primary claim on ideological power. In the case of Bolívar, there are three monumental poses that may be used to summarize the ideological mission of the cult of Bolívar. The first pose is the concept of progress. In modern Latin America, the symbol of Bolívar has been charged with the defense of the promise of tomorrow. History is plotted through continuities and Bolívar is a power-ful wellspring of myth capable of joining the past to the present and to a providential future. Bolívar represents a democratic project that is still unfolding some two centuries after his death, and to which he still serves as an inspiration or a kind of rosetta stone for ensuring its continual growth and consummation. Thus, the Liberator encodes an authoritative claim to the past and to the future, with the power to exert influence over the political, social, and cultural realms. The equestrian statue of Bolívar in the central plaza of Caracas illustrates this desire. The monument was erected in 1876 in order to create a centralized space for the experience and performance of national memory where before there had been none. As framed by the grid of a plaza designed by a veteran of Parisian urban design, the statue marks the site of the state's will to emerge visibly and publicly from an unstable past into the community of modern nations.[2] As noted by the celebratory newspapers of the day, the monument was not only a reminder of the glories of the past, but also a vision of the nation's future glories. The equestrian statue of Bolívar, like a bronze chaperone frozen in motion, would oversee the continuing growth of Venezuela.

Another dominant pose of the monumental Bolívar is its embodiment of a patriarchal principle. In epic representations of Bolívar, the hero effectively creates independence, willing it from the fecund seed of his genius and martial prowess. The Liberator is a symbolic father whose heroism and vision have entitled him to the unswerving loyalty of his heirs, who seek his inspiration and guidance in times of crisis. In this respect, the patriarchal power of Bolívar is well served by the purposes of monumentalist statuary, which posits his body as a sealed entity, a titan of bronze or stone that represents the foundational claims and exemplary scripts of great men. The phallic power of their monuments requires that their bodies acquire the permanence that they did not possess in life. In the memorable words of Lewis Mumford, monumentalism was a form of renewal and reproduction, "a desire to wall out life, to exclude the action of time, to remove the taint of biological processes, to exclude the active care of other generations by a process of architectural mummification" (434). Despite the unforgettable images of the iconoclastic dismantling of monuments in the former Soviet Union, which attest to the fragility of statuary in times of historical crisis, these giants of stone and bronze represent the conceit that an absolute and unquestioned narrative of identity may be materialized permanently.[3]

The third and final pose is related to language and signification, and may be termed *metatextual*. The cult of Bolívar maintains itself through unquestioned faith in the authority of the words of Bolívar, which are characterized by Bolivarians as transparent and commanding, like those of a religious catechism. "The word of Bolívar," writes Luis Castro Leiva, "is the end of History and of its unfolding" (171). In other words, the mythic Bolívar is a conduit for sacred, unquestioned truths that are not meant to be relativized or interpreted. As a script of identity, Bolívar stands for a timeless alphabet that may be utilized to respond to ever-changing social and historical realities. Bolívar represents the continuity and coherence of key terms and concepts, such as *independence, liberty,* and the *nation.* Iconoclastic representations of Bolívar disrupt these terms, questioning

their coherence and underlining their constructed nature. In the conceptual worlds of Juan Dávila, for example, signs are multivalent and contradictory, and function as a challenge to the more transparent definition of
representation that is proposed by mythmakers and official culture. The
challenge to Bolívar, then, is necessarily a challenge to the authority of the
language of myth, and to the truth claims of language in general. If signs
that are commonly seen as having one meaning can be set against each
other and deconstructed, then any attempt to create an authoritative formulation through signs may be challenged and relativized. The cult of
Bolívar is thus sustained through the defense of key terms and the definition of language as a transparent, self-evident, and immutable system.
Outside of this conservative definition of language, Bolívar-the-national-
hero cannot exist. In other words, reverence for Bolívar is an investment in
the ordering and transformation of experience through authoritative representational codes. The breakdown of the authority of such systems, from
the vantage point of official culture and its definition of Bolívar as a republican deity, signals the degeneration and failure of society and its quest for
progress. The passionate response to Juan Dávila's iconoclastic representation of Bolívar, predicated in part on his playful attitude toward signs,
brought into focus the Bolivarian commitment to a monological definition
of representation.

Iconoclastic Gestures

Now that the monumental poses of the cult of Bolívar have been defined,
Juan Dávila's iconoclasm comes into clearer focus. The most apparent
manner in which Dávila assaults the sanctity of the national hero lies in
his treatment of gender. *The Liberator Simón Bolívar* questions the correspondence between sex and gender and challenges the idea that Bolívar has
a true gender. The presence of breasts and the absence of the phallus, ob-
scured by the saddle and displaced onto the profane finger gesture, destabi-
lize the notion of Bolívar as a patriarch (Richard 189). It was precisely this
aspect of Dávila's image that provoked the Colombian ambassador to
Chile, Jorge Mario Eastman, to decry the deviant and "hermaphroditic"
nature of Dávila's "blasphemy" and defend Bolívar's heterosexuality
("Hay simbologías"). The assault on Bolívar's masculinity may also be
understood in relation to how Dávila clothes and unclothes his version of
the hero. Dávila's Bolívar wears a jacket and boots but no pants, suggesting, in effect, that Bolívar has been caught with his "pants down" and may

be penetrated.[4] However, the most important aspect of Dávila's version of Bolívar vis-à-vis gender is the fact that we are in the presence of sexual identity as an arena of performance. In her analysis of corporeality and gender, Judith Butler notes that drag, cross-dressing, and butch/femme identities in the lesbian community parody the fiction of "an original or primary gender identity" (127). Whereas dominant, masculinist defini-tions of Bolívar posit his body as a fixed, masculine entity, Dávila plays with boundaries and blurs that stable category.

Further, what critics have called the transvestic nature of Dávila's image cannot be separated from the question of race. Readers will recall how Gabriel García Márquez in *The General in His Labyrinth* succinctly de-scribes the symbolic whitening of Bolívar over time: "as his glory in-creased, the painters began to idealize him, washing his blood, mythologiz-ing him, until they established him in official memory with the Roman profile of his statues" (180). Justo Pastor Mellado argues that Dávila trans-gresses the classical, sublimated model of Latin American identity by pre-senting the hero as a *mestizo* whose visage appears to have been whitened (Richard 187). In fact, the presence of makeup on the face of Bolívar serves a dual function, not only referencing the ambiguities and instabilities of gender identity but also a racialized identity that grotesquely performs the narrative of whiteness. Unlike the aristocratic and distinctly European vis-age of Bolívar by the Venezuelan painter Tito Salas, which graces the ceil-ing murals of the National Pantheon in Caracas, Dávila's Bolívar is not the triumphalist messenger of the Creole national project but rather its object. Here is a person of color caught between whiteness and the reality of eth-nic difference, between self-important, martial mythology and irreverent gender play. Yet, this social agent is not passive; like a trickster, his/her power to play with masks keeps challenge alive and sustains the obscene finger gesture as a kind of declaration of independence from dominant nar-ratives of identity.

The concept of *mestizaje* is not limited to the imbricated concepts of gender and race. In his commentary on an exhibit by Dávila titled *Juanito Laguna* (held at the Chisenhale Gallery in London in 1995), Guy Brett reminds us that Dávila's travesty, his commitment to the theme of mestizaje, moves from gender and race to aesthetic codes, to the very mo-dalities of representation that the artist works with and ultimately relativizes. Brett's broadening of the definition of mestizaje deserves cita-tion: "*Mestizaje*, again, can stand for the syncretism of cultures and artistic styles. Making a 'travesty' refers too to Dávila's practice of lifting styles

Figure 1. Juan Dávila. *The Liberator Simón Bolívar* 1994. Oil on canvas on metal, 125 X 98 cm. Copyright Kalli Rolfe Contemporary Art, Copyright Agent.

and visual codes out of their contexts and grafting them together in wild profusion, and also to what happens in Carnival the world over, when men become women, the poor become rich, the denigrated are exalted, inhibitions are cast aside, and all that is official and serious is mocked by popular laughter" (Brett 2). Nelly Richard underscores the same point in her discussion of the representation of Bolívar's horse, calling the process the "hybridization of codes" (188). She describes the image of Bolívar in terms of a component that may be associated with the avant-garde and modernity (the abstract aspect of the horse), as well as in relation to tradition and folklore (the depiction of Bolívar's body). This juxtaposition of high and low aesthetic codes adds another layer to the questions of identity raised by the image. Is Bolívar a foundational figure or a more local, native character? What vocabulary or sensibility is best suited to capture the figure of Bolívar? Dávila's visual mestizaje, the mixing of representational registers, creates an ellipsis that allows for critical reflection on the limitations of representation and the complexities of a cultural experience that is resistant to reductive interpretive models.

Finally, Dávila's iconoclasm may be read in relation to the manipulation of gesture, in which his image is freed from the fixity of Bolivarian monumentalism and redefined as a parody of the phallic claim to authority of martial, sculptural embodiments of the hero. Bolívar's obscene finger gesture signals a diversion from a very different kind of gesture that is common to martial statuary: the hand that directs the battle, finger or sword pointing toward triumph. The martial gesture enacts the virility of the hero, his power to direct others and show the way, to pierce the air with a will to triumph.[5] For example, Martin Tovar y Tovar's painting *Batalla de Carabobo* (1884–1888), which graces the ceilings of the National Capitol of Caracas, represents the Bolivarian gesture in such a martial manner. As soldiers struggle over the panoramic battlefield, Bolívar elegantly irradiates his authority with his outstretched hand. Tito Salas's painting of Bolívar swearing to liberate the New World from a hilltop in Rome, in the National Pantheon of the same city, takes the outstretched hand to signify the power of prophecy, and references classical models of gesture as a necessary part of the *pronuntiato*, or delivery of oratory. The authoritative, indexical gesture with the index finger may in fact be associated with the relationship between signifier and signified; in his *Institutio Oratoria*, Quintillian valued indexical gestures as a way of pointing at the objects represented by the words of the orator (Graf 39; Aldrete 17). The beautiful, young Bolívar in European dress swearing to liberate the New World in the National Pantheon seems leisurely as he gazes into the future and wills the materialization, in the real world, of the order of his signs. In Dávila's depiction, the bent arm that is lowered and culminates in the *digitus impudicus*, annuls the martial pitch of the hero, situating Bolívar in a colloquial realm of signs considered to be profane. The finger represents an aggressive yet intranscendent and fleeting scene of power that displaces Bolívar's masculine virility onto a gestural act. In other words, the finger indicates the presence of a performative type of masculinity that takes the form of symbolic aggression, mockery, and defiance.

New Paths in Bolivarian Studies

My study examines how the dominant poses of the cult of Bolívar (progress, patriarchy, and the authority of the sign) are challenged in nine-
teenth- and twentieth-century representations of the most famous hero of
Latin American independence. The most elementary premise of my analysis is that Simón Bolívar should not only be examined as a military and
political agent, but also as a symbol for the construction of identity. No
doubt much work remains to be done to understand the arc of Bolívar's life
as a soldier and statesman, but this study does not examine that question,
nor does it compare and contrast a gallery of fictional Bolívars to a "real"
Bolívar in order to establish that the cult distorts the historical record. Instead I explore a richly developed cultural icon that emerged after independence for the purposes of building national identity and promoting
progress. Rather than embark on the quixotic quest to recover an authentic
Bolívar, I trace and contextualize major themes and contradictions in novels and other prose texts about Bolívar and the nation. Is Bolívar a substitute for Christ? Did he father children biologically? Was he a good lover?
In light of the painful and divisive history of the continent since his death,
is Bolívar a symbol of defeat? These are the kinds of questions that shape
my study.

Despite my commitment to reading the subject of Bolívar against the
grain of nationalism, historiography, and political philosophy, I do consider my research to be connected to a domain of study with a long and
distinguished history: Estudios Bolivarianos (Bolivarian Studies). Bolivarian Studies has been and continues to be the study of anything and everything Bolívar, such as the question of when Bolívar wore a moustache and
when he did not, the byzantine search for possible biological offspring of
the hero, and the cataloguing of his amorous conquests. Yet, in its broad
focus, Bolivarian Studies has also created spaces for the writing of cultural
histories centered on Bolívar and his time. Although until recently most
scholars working in Bolivarian Studies were devout Bolivarians who believed they were contributing to the recognition of Bolívar by detailing
historical minutiae, philology, and cultural representations of the hero,
their scholarship has established that studying Bolívar could extend beyond the terrain of martial history. Texts such as Diego Carbonell's medi-
cal study of Bolívar, *Psicopatología de Bolívar* (1916), Jose Luis Busaniche's anthology of testimonials, *Bolívar visto por sus contemporáneos*
(1960), and Pedro Grases's history of Bolívar in print, *Los papeles de*

Bolívar y Sucre (1985) exemplify the generative and critical potential of moving the focus from Bolívar's well-known political and martial biography to different registers. In recent years, however, a small group of scholars have turned the focus on the cult of Bolívar itself, creating a new subject area within scholarship about Bolívar.

The foundational text of the new critical corpus about the cult of Bolívar is Germán Carrera Damas's *El culto a Bolívar: Esbozo para un estudio de la historia de las ideas en Venezuela* (1969). Carrera Damas's underlying, theoretical argument supports the case for studying representation as an ideological phenomenon, both as a historical product and as a functional, political entity in the historical present.[6] Other important historiographical statements on the cult of Bolívar include studies by Pamela Murray (2001), Inés Quintero (2001), Elías Pino Iturrieta (1999), Napoleón Franceschi González (1999), and Miguel Americo Bretos (1976). This invaluable scholarship is pioneering a field that is still in its infancy, establishing benchmarks for a periodization of the cult of Bolívar and creating awareness that the cult is an ideological phenomenon with a cultural history of its own. Notable exceptions to the historiographic approach represented by these studies include Michael Taussig's *The Magic of the State* (1997), which traces the connections between religious syncretism, political discourse, and daily life; Luis Castro Leiva's *De la patria boba a la teología bolivariana* (1991), a philosophical meditation that takes the cult to task for strengthening a "hermetic hermeneutics" that adjudicates all discussion and political action in Venezuela to a closed system of mutilated and decontextualized quotes by Bolívar (170–171); and Yolanda Salas de Lecuna's *Bolívar y la historia en la conciencia popular* (1987), which recovers the reinvention of Bolívar in oral culture through fifty-five native informants. Still, the image of Bolívar in fiction, and the conceptual understanding that we might arrive at through the study of literature, has not been explored. More importantly, we are lacking a general synthesis of the mission, constituent thematics, and contradictions of the cult of Bolívar. It is in this arena that this book makes its contribution.

Design and Key Concepts

Although containing original, archival research, the present study does not pretend to be a diachronic cultural history of the cult of Bolívar, or an intellectual history or sociological study. Rather, it defines the cult of Bolívar in relation to modernity through novels, biography, and other narrative prose about Bolívar. I wrote this book as a result of a simple question that is worth repeating here: Why is it that modern Latin American novels about Bolívar insist on wounding his symbolic body, as in the case of Gabriel García Márquez's *The General in His Labyrinth*? As I explored this question, I discovered that such treatments of Bolívar were targeting the failures of Latin American modernity. The objects of critique were the empty promises of a spent, triumphalist ideology of progress that had taken shape after Bolívar's death. In toppling the sanctity of the monumentalist Bolívar that stood for that ideology, these writers offered their readers provocative insights about the ways in which hero-worship is constructed and manipulated by nationalists in the name of progress. The analysis of the variety of ways in which the icon of Bolívar is challenged in modern Latin America enabled me to better understand the cult of Bolívar across genres and historical periods. Thus, the present study delineates the fictions that sustain the cult of Bolívar while exploring stories that chart its failure and contradictions.

My analysis is structured around two types of inquiry, one into specific texts (primarily novels), and the other into historical and cultural trends (interdisciplinary synthesis and research). The discussion of certain themes in the texts under study, such as theology, paternity, monuments, and sentimental love, allows me to explore these questions in nonliterary, Bolivarian texts as well, thus enabling a better understanding of the symbolic foundations of the cult of Bolívar.

Chapter 1, "Bolívar and the Emergence of a National Religion," lays the groundwork for the rest of the study by examining the origins and characteristics of the nineteenth-century cult of Bolívar during the Wars of Independence and the early national period in Venezuela. I explore how Bolivarian discourses of identity emerged during Bolívar's lifetime as a means to validate his role as a republican statesman. In opposition to the image of Bolívar-as-Augustus, as exemplified by José Joaquín Olmedo's "La victoria de Junín" (1825), enemies of Bolívar deployed the image of Bolívar-as-Caesar, and called for tyrannicide. The chapter focuses on how the final years and controversies of Bolívar's career resulted in his literal and symbolic banishment from the national project. In the case of Venezuela, I demonstrate how political tensions between 1830 and 1842 resulted in a growing awareness of the necessity of using Bolívar as a symbolic linchpin for the nation. I focus on two Bolivarian texts, Fermín Toro's "Honores a Bolívar" (1842), the first official expression of Bolivarian nationalism in Venezuela, and Felipe Larrazábal's *Correspondencia general del Libertador Simón Bolívar* (1865), a romantic biography. Both texts distance Bolívar from the debates that characterized the Wars of Independence, and situate the hero in a republican project deeply indebted to the beliefs and devotional practices of Christianity.

Chapter 2, "Monumentalism and the Erotics of National Degeneration," examines the concept of the monumental Bolívar in late nineteenth-century Venezuela. I discuss the creation of the Plaza Bolívar in Caracas within the context of the ubiquitous national project of architectural renewal sponsored by President Antonio Guzmán Blanco. In particular, I consider literary texts that celebrate and question the potential of Bolivarian monumentalism to consolidate the national project. One of the narratives I examine is Eduardo Blanco's "Las noches del panteón" (1865), a gothic recreation of the secret lives of statues and monuments in the National Pantheon, which suggests that the ideals of the nation exist in a fantastic space associated with personal subjectivity and dream-states. For Blanco, the historical present, so full of monumentalist statuary and progress, is devoid of life and transcendent meaning. Further, I explore *Idolos rotos* (1901) by Manuel Díaz Rodríguez, an iconoclastic novel that decries the corruption and underdevelopment of Venezuela by presenting the monument of the Plaza Bolívar as a wounded and violated body. The amorous failures of the protagonist of Díaz Rodríguez's novel enact an allegory about the failure of the nation and of Bolivarian monumentalism at the turn of the century.

Chapter 3, "The Promise of Bolivarian Paternity," frames the issue of paternity in relation to gender and modernity in nineteenth- and twentieth-century literature for children and young people. Despite his ostensible failure in fathering biological children, Bolívar has been represented in children's literature since the nineteenth century as an accessible, filial figure. In my discussion of a variety of texts that include works by José Martí, Eduardo Blanco, and the Ecuadorian journalist Manuel Calle, I underline how the monumental Bolívar is replaced by a foundational figure capable of inspiring sentimental bonds between child and hero. Moreover, I discuss how these and other Bolivarian pedagogues frame the myth of Bolívar through narratives of national crises or failure. In this vein, I consider Teresa de la Parra's novel of childhood, *Las memorias de la Mamá Blanca* (1929), as well as her essays and letters, as a critique of the monumentalist model of Bolívar. Like others before her, Parra reconstructs Bolívar through a critique of the present, yet she denies the premises of mainstream Bolivarian ideology by idealizing the colonial period that preceded Bolívar's foundational acts. The chapter ends with a discussion of the educational policies of President Hugo Chávez of Venezuela.

Chapter 4, "'A Whore in the Palace': The Poetics of Pornodetraction," examines how Denzil Romero's explicitly sexual novel about Manuela Sáenz, *La esposa del doctor Thorne* (1983), reinforces and challenges the patriarchal dimensions of the cult of Bolívar through the narration of the sexual exploits of Bolívar's most famous lover. I analyze dominant trends in the representation of Manuela Sáenz since the nineteenth century that demonstrate that nationalist writers have had difficulties in classifying this cross-dressing and politically committed woman. This analysis sets the stage for an understanding of Romero's novel, which decenters Bolívar and his masculinity through unflinching descriptions of Manuela's insatiable, transgressive, and ambiguous sexuality. Romero narrates the destruction of the Bolivarian dream through a complex allegory in which Manuela's unruly body represents the chaos of a body politic that will only bend to Bolívar's power (dictatorship), not his romantic idealism. Paradoxically, in spite of this daring purpose, Romero reifies the cult of Bolívar by defending the phallic power of the hero.

Chapter 5, "Solitude, Signs, and Power in *The General in His Labyrinth*," explores the metatextual dimensions of Bolivarian iconoclasm, as previously defined in my discussion of the dominant poses of the cult of Bolívar. I argue that the bodily decay of the protagonist of García Márquez's well-known novel expresses the failure of representation, a phenomenon consistently related in García Márquez's treatment of the solitary nature of power in his fiction. To this end, I read *The General in His Labyrinth* (1989) alongside *One Hundred Years of Solitude* (1968), *The Autumn of the Patriarch* (1975), García Márquez's short fiction, journalism, and finally his Nobel lecture, "The Solitude of Latin America" (1982). I draw parallels between "the General" and other soldiers and dictators in García Márquez's fiction, and how their solitary nature results in a disconnect between words and the things they are intended to represent. I argue that the main theme of *The General in His Labyrinth* is hermeneutic in nature, and that García Márquez recovers Bolívar as a principle of renewal that has been buried under foreign words and misunderstandings. García Márquez's meditation on the limits of representation in relation to the cult of Bolívar is a profound statement on official nationalism's dependence on monological languages and definitions.

My study closes with an afterword, "Bolivarian Self-Fashioning into the Twenty-First Century," which explores the reinvention of Bolivarian ideology at the dawn of the twenty-first century in Venezuela. I sketch a history of the Bolivarian Movimiento Quinta República, which propelled former army paratrooper and coup leader Hugo Chávez into the Venezuelan presidency in 1999. Chávez's controversial presidency has resulted in frictions with the international community, a radical rewriting of the Venezuelan constitution, and a new name for the country: the Bolivarian Republic of Venezuela. In particular, I offer some reflections on how Hugo Chávez challenges the monumentalist contours of the official cult of Bolívar by fashioning himself as Bolívar and imagining the contemporary Venezuelan scene as a restaging of the conflicts of the nineteenth-century Wars of Independence. In light of Chávez's vigorous attempt to reclaim Bolívar, once again, at the dawn of a new century, I close with some observations about Bolivarian ideology today, its inherent conservatism and the promise of breaking with almost two centuries of Bolivarian monumentalism.

My approach to the cult of Bolívar is informed by the centrality of gender to the construction of meaning. As Ludmilla Jordanova defines it, gender is not a topic or a subject, but an "analytical category" that functions both as "a way of ordering experience, a system of representation and a metaphor for particular kinds of relationships" (474). Therefore, gender is not seen here as an essential term, but as a cultural construct that interprets bodies as "masculine" or "feminine." If we accept that gender is not equal to sex, then masculinity and femininity become artificial terms that may be associated with either sex (Butler 6). In nationalist cultures, however, masculinity is indeed seen as biological, and tightly bound up with essential characteristics that are seen as springing naturally from its fixed quality. Conversely, femininity is seen in official cultures as the other of masculinity: it is lack, absence, and periphery. Because the heroism that Western culture has enshrined as foundational is associated with "great" men, and with institutional and cultural spaces that have historically been defined by men, a focus on masculinity as a cultural construct is particularly pertinent for the study of nationalist hero-worship. The representation and distribution of the concepts of the "masculine" and the "feminine" enable us to trace how different texts challenge or reaffirm dominant modes of perceiving gender. In the chapters that follow, for example, I demonstrate how texts that challenge the monumental body of Bolívar wound the nation and its scripts of identity by diminishing the phallus of Bolívar, and introducing confusion into the conceptual and hierarchical opposition between what is represented as masculine/authoritative and what is considered feminine/subordinate.

Corporeality is also central to my study. Although vital for the construction of gender, corporeality is not only understood here in relation to the culturally constructed concepts of masculine and feminine, but also as a metaphor for society and identity writ large. In the words of the cultural anthropologist Mary Douglas, the body "is a model that can stand for any bounded system" (115). The symbolic body of Bolívar may thus be read as a diagram of identity, a bounded system that stakes a powerful claim upon the lives of Latin Americans who believe their New World is hobbled by unfinished business and broken dreams. This concept is well represented by the metaphor of the monument, which constructs the body of the foundational father and the values he represents as an unmoveable idol, one that is anchored upon a superior, mythical register that demands the reverence of his subjects. The violation of the symbolic body of Bolívar violates the narrative of identity promoted by the monument, as well as its patriarchal claim to power, which is predicated on the unassailability of its body. My study examines the interplay between this monumentalism, the quest to fix and maintain identity in an authoritative pose, and iconoclasm, which topples the monumental claims of the cult of Bolívar. The centripetal impetus of monumentalism seeks to shape culture and social interactions through the primacy of the symbol of Bolívar (the body as a closed system), while iconoclastic texts and interventions represent instances of a centrifugal disruption of the power (the body as a broken system, as polluted or as chaotic).

This conceptual antagonism between the body as a closed system and the body as an open one underpins this study in my discussions of gender. If the Bolivarian ideal is conceptualized as masculine by monumentalism, iconoclasm is logically an assault on that culturally constructed masculinity. However, an important caveat is in order: Whereas the monumentalist definition of Bolívar in this study may be read as patriarchal, texts that critique that monumentalism are not necessarily feminist nor do they necessarily represent a "feminine" perspective. A case in point is the complexity of Bolivarian identity in relation to children's literature, as discussed in chapter 3. In this chapter, I underline that filial narratives for children about Bolívar are not necessarily equivalent to monumentalist definitions of masculinity, while noting that Teresa de la Parra's feminist reconstruction of Bolívar as a sentimental being akin to women does not necessarily deny the hero's foundational role. Although I part from the premise that masculinity and femininity are essential terms in the dominant culture, I believe that Bolivarian iconoclasm raises questions about the validity of this conceptual dyad for all instances of Bolivarian nationalism.

The word *modernity* appears repeatedly in this study and deserves some discussion as well. Modernity is primarily used to refer to the project for remaking and reimagining social and political realities in Latin America since the Wars of Independence. According to Stuart Hall's succinct definition, modernity is characterized by political secularism, a monetarized exchange economy, and the decline of the traditional social order and religious worldviews (8). The values of the Enlightenment (reason, universalism, progress, and so forth) and the rise of the idea of the nation at the beginning of the nineteenth century are also central to modernity. In Latin American history and culture, the quest for modernity has defined the political, economic, and cultural programs of the liberal state. The desire to be modern has promoted the idea of progress and its teleologies of identity, the nation and its demands for sacrifice and collective recognition, and dependence on the economic and cultural systems of the so-called developed world. The present study underscores how iconoclastic representations of Bolívar engage with this overarching investment in modernity, calling into question its absolute value, disclosing its erasures, and underscoring the artifice of the developmental and cultural models it espouses. My analysis is informed by symbolic moments in which the monumental Bolívar, which has embodied the drive to modernize the continent, has registered upon its sacred, inviolable body the iconoclastic traces of the contradictions or failures of the project of modernity. However, as I note in my afterword, in all of the texts I examine in this study Bolívar remains important to discussions of identity and political development. It would seem that a truly iconoclastic treatment of Bolívar, and of modernity itself, would have to dispense with Bolívar altogether.

This book is far from being the last word on the subject of the cult of Bolívar. The definition of Latin American identity requires an eternal return to the figure of Bolívar and his pan-American thought. Whether it is the unfinished business of political freedom, or the wonders of a New World that has not found its true political measure because of its internal divisions, Bolívar continues to be the starting point for discussions of the promise of Latin America. In his landmark treatise *Facundo: Civilización y barbarie* (1845), Domingo Faustino Sarmiento yoked the mystery of the Latin American continent and its potential discovery by Europe to an unwritten biography of Bolívar, a biography that would reflect his relationship to the land and the peoples of the New World. In short, he argued that what the world needed was a biography that depicted Bolívar wearing a poncho (49). A close look at the image of Bolívar in poems, novels, essays, histories, and biographies underscores that Latin American cultural history has indeed invested Bolívar with a continental meaning, but not necessarily an intended one: Bolívar is a symbol of the contradictions of an identity that is constantly in flux, and in conflict with itself. Bolívar may be an inescapable presence but the irony is that his power is more often than not measured by a sense that his utopian vision is far from being realized in Latin America. He is a monument of abundance and lack, authority and fracture, under permanent destruction and reconstruction.[7]

Bolívar and the Emergence
of a National Religion

In the Museo Sacro of Caracas, a small museum that skirts the Plaza Bolívar, visitors may discover, among other artifacts of the colonial era, some beautiful and primitive wooden mannequins. These are the *santos de vestir* [saints-for-dressing], wooden figures that the church would dress in different garments depending on the liturgy being celebrated. These mannequins provide us with a powerful metaphor for the cult of Bolívar in Venezuelan political and cultural life. Like the santos de vestir, the monumental Bolívar is an icon that is continually refashioned. He may be dressed martially, as a commander ready for battle, or in Augustan fashion, wearing a toga, with a sword in one hand and a scroll in another. The metaphor of the santo de vestir conveys both a sense of variability and stability; the santo de vestir of the church may appear on different religious holidays in different guises, and as such is variable, but its iconicity is always directed at reinforcing the religious cosmology promoted by the church, hence its stability. Similarly, within the nationalist imagination, Bolívar may be fashioned as a soldier, a statesman, or a philosopher, yet still carry out essentially the same legitimating, nationalist function. Moreover, there is historic merit to the comparison of Bolívar to a santo de vestir. Postindependence Bolivarian ideology evolved in the nineteenth century as a nationalist variant of the iconic practices and liturgies of the church. Bolívar became the centerpiece of a secular liturgy that drew much of its power from the themes of transcendence, sacrifice, and resurrection that were at the center of church theology.

The religious contexts of the cult of Bolívar have been observed by scholars who have examined the construction and dissemination of Bolivarian ideology. Besides the religiously syncretic character of the popular cult of Bolívar, the religious overtones of official nationalism itself have been present in the representation of Bolívar since the nineteenth century. Germán Carrera Damas argues that this new Bolivarian religion responded to the need to stabilize the republic in a time of historic crisis (61). Luis Castro Leiva amplifies these arguments by arguing that the liturgical impetus of this new, civic religion sought to recreate independence within the transcendental realm, substituting religious codes with new, patriotic ones.[1] He goes on to suggest that this transference of religious zeal into an Enlightenment project has resulted in the decontextualization and mythification of Bolívar's words, impoverishing political discourse in Venezuela. Thus, Bolivarian discourse maintains its sacred authority while becoming formulaic and solipsistic (Castro Leiva 170). A liberal reading of the arguments of Carrera Damas and Castro Leiva suggests that if Bolívar had not existed, the republicans of the postindependence era would have had to invent him as a principle of national identity.

The association of the republican project with religious codes enshrined Bolívar as a sacred logos. His proclamations, letters, and constitutions took on an authoritative and transcendental significance, creating a republican ideal for the nation to pursue in its continuing march toward greatness. Yet, the sacralization of Bolívar did not come about with ease in nineteenth-century Venezuela. The creation of the republican cult was a difficult question for early national thinkers because postindependence Venezuela had been born out of a conspicuous rejection of Bolívar. In 1830, Venezuelan separatists seceded from the Republic of Gran Colombia, which Bolívar had struggled to create and to defend for much of his career as a military commander and statesman. The secession was therefore as much a rejection of Gran Colombia as it was of Bolívar, who was vilified as an enemy of the nascent Venezuelan state. Anti-Bolivarian sentiment was so strong that when Bolívar died in 1830 in Colombia, his dying wish to be laid to rest in Caracas was indefinitely postponed. The decision to repatriate Bolívar's remains twelve years later was precipitated by the emergence of an opposition party that increasingly deployed the banner of Bolívar against the political establishment that had not moved on the repatriation issue since 1830. When the government ceremoniously transported Bolívar's remains from Santa Marta to Caracas, partisan representations of Bolívar gave way to a powerful new discourse of national identity. From 1842 onward, Bolívar was no longer to be considered a former president or *caudillo*, but rather the guiding spirit of the nation.

The transference of religious paradigms into the national project in this period is amply illustrated by the work of two important writers, Fermín

Toro and Felipe Larrazábal, whose foundational representations of Bolívar disclose the processes by which a community with shared values may be constructed through the exemplary life and words of one man. In 1842, the state commissioned Toro to write an official account of the elaborate funeral event it sponsored to commemorate the ceremonial return to Venezuela of Bolívar's remains. Toro's account, titled "Honores a Bolívar," is arguably the first nationalist Bolivarian text to appear in Venezuela or Latin America. Toro's task as a chronicler of the repatriation was to catalogue and preserve for posterity the elaborate plans of Bolívar's belated funeral, the sea voyage to and from Santa Marta to recover the hero's remains, and the minutiae of the funerary rituals held in Caracas. In Toro's account, Bolívar is represented as a sacred spirit capable of healing the political and social wounds of the body politic, reconciling militarist and constitutionalist agendas.

Twenty years later, Felipe Larrazábal further elaborated Toro's proposal of a republican cult of Bolívar, clarifying how the cult gathers power and legitimacy from Christian theology. In his biography, *Correspondencia general del Libertador Simón Bolívar* (1865), Larrazábal privileges hermeneutics and suggests that republican virtue springs from the acceptance of the word of Bolívar. Much in the same manner that Jesus is presented as the "living bread" that mediates between humanity and divinity in the Gospel of John, Bolívar is the locus of the individual's entry into the morality and forms of association that are identified with republicanism. Like Toro, Larrazábal removes Bolívar from the constellation of political debates that characterized the Wars of Independence, and situates him at the center of a spiritual project indebted to the beliefs and devotional practices of Christianity. In fact, Larrazábal's voluminous biography expands upon Toro's quest for order through Bolívar by specifying that social harmony results from the internalization, in each citizen, of the Bolivarian canon of letters, proclamations, and constitutions. Bolívar is thus abstracted into an order of signs capable of shaping the inner and outer life of the nation.

While others in nineteenth-century Venezuela wrote celebrations of Bolívar, none were as thorough and programmatic as Toro and Larrazábal in their treatment of how the life and writings of Bolívar could be used for the creation of a civic religion. Their foundational vision of Bolívar delineates the contours of the patriarchal and spiritual force that iconoclastic representations of Bolívar target as a means of challenging the authority of the nation and the validity of its narratives of progress. In the pages to follow, I outline the emergence of Bolivarian identity, beginning in the era of independence and culminating in the early national period, when Toro and Larrazábal theorized the characteristics of a civic religion based upon the adoration of Bolívar.

For and Against Bolívar: Augustus, Caesar, and the Exile of Bolívar, 1813–1830

In order to understand the controversies surrounding the reconstruction of Bolívar as a sign of national and republican identity after independence, a brief overview of his life is in order. By becoming Bolívar's biographer, I am mindful of the fact that I must, in essence, become the author of yet another fiction about the hero's life, like so many of the writers included in this study. In other words, to write history is to enter into the field of fiction, requiring characterization, motific repetition, a particular tone and point of view, and most importantly, the suppression of some events and the highlighting of others (White 84). In light of this definition of history-as-narrative (as opposed to objective truth), my biography of Bolívar is as schematic as possible, and eschews issues that are central to Bolivarian mythology, such as the definition of Bolívar's essential being (his "spirit"), and totalizing conclusions about the significance of his life. Thus, the sketch that follows is neither a definitive statement about Bolívar's life nor a reiteration of his greatness, but rather a brief introduction to the events and conditions that constitute the prehistory of the modern Latin American cult of Bolívar.

Until 1813, Bolívar was relatively unknown as a military and political figure. When Napoleon invaded Spain in 1808 and placed his brother Joseph on the throne, the Creole elite of Caracas responded by resisting the authority of Bonaparte. Venezuelans were at first divided on the question of self-governance, with one faction arguing for loyalty to Ferdinand, the deposed Spanish king, while the more radical faction, which included the young Bolívar, lobbied for independence. During the short-lived first Venezuelan republic of 1811–1812, Bolívar's military service was undistinguished and marred by his loss of the port city of Puerto Cabello to the Royalists. When Caracas fell, Bolívar went into exile in neighboring Nueva Granada, where the Republicans had temporarily defeated the Royalists. In 1813, Bolívar secured a small expeditionary force from Nueva Granada and defeated the Royalists during the Admirable campaign, a string of military victories that led him straight into Caracas where he declared the second republic and assumed dictatorial powers. In spite of its auspicious beginning and Bolívar's strategies, the second republic was militarily weak. A formidable force of plainsmen, the *llaneros* rose up against the republican cause and forced Bolívar to flee Venezuela within a year.

Bolívar returned to Nueva Granada, where his plans for liberating Caracas had to be postponed because of civil war between republican factions. As the patriot venture in Nueva Granada fell into disarray because of this internal conflict, Bolívar fled to Jamaica, where he wrote the "Letter of Jamaica" (1815), his most famous tract about Latin American politics and identity. In it, Bolívar provided a vision of a whole continent at war, analyzing the differences between the varied geopolitical centers of armed conflict in the continent. In the process, he also considered the great potential of a unified Latin American republic, and called for Europe's protection in the ongoing war and future period of republican reconstruction. "As soon as we are strong and under the guidance of a liberal nation which will lend us her protection," Bolívar wrote, "we will achieve accord in cultivating the virtues and talents that lead to glory" (*Selected Writings* 123).

With the backing of Alexandre Petion, Haiti's president, Bolívar launched a new offensive out of the Orinoco basin, and made significant progress in consolidating his authority over other patriot caudillos, particularly José Antonio Páez, whose llanero forces would ensure many important military victories. Although Venezuela and New Granada had not yet been liberated, Bolívar convened the Congress of Angostura (1819) and declared the third Venezuelan republic, a move that provided his continuing military campaigns with a constitutional framework. In the words of Gerhard Masur: "Bolívar was no longer a rebel leader who assumed top command on his own initiative, nor was he merely a general or a dictator. He was the President of a new nation" (360). As an extension of the patriots' new status as a republic, their official newspaper, *El correo del Orinoco*, sought to legitimate Bolívar as a statesman-warrior and countered the rhetoric of the royalist newspaper *La gaceta de Caracas*, which vilified Bolívar as a barbaric insurgent.

By 1820, Bolívar's authority was unrivaled among other Republican caudillos, whose combined bands of men constituted a large, if dispersed, Republican army that turned the tide of the war in favor of the patriot cause and Bolívar's reputation. The liberation of Nueva Granada in 1819 at the Battle of Boyacá paved the way for the Congress of Cúcuta, which declared the Republic of Gran Colombia (comprising both Nueva Granada and the yet to be liberated Venezuela) and made Bolívar its president and

Francisco Paula de Santander vice president. Upon the liberation of Venezuela at Carabobo (1821), the Colombian congress gave Bolívar the plenipotentiary powers he had requested to pursue the integration of Quito to Gran Colombia, and the expulsion of the Royalists from Perú and Alto Perú (later renamed Bolivia in his honor). In 1822, Bolívar's talented second, Antonio José de Sucre, assured the independence of Ecuador at the Battle of Pichincha and Bolívar entered Quito to great acclaim. In Perú, where independence had been declared under the banner of the Argentinian liberator José de San Martín, Bolívar was named dictator in 1824 and charged with the task of consolidating military control over the Andes. That same year, Bolívar's defeat of the Royalists at Junín was closely followed by Sucre's victory at Ayacucho, the battle that effectively sealed Latin American independence. In 1825, as the man who had led the liberation of Venezuela, Nueva Granada, Quito, Perú, and Alto Perú, Bolívar was at the peak of his power and glory.

In 1825, at the bidding of the congress of the newly formed Republic of Bolivia, Bolívar wrote a constitution that called for a lifelong president, a hereditary vice presidency, and a fourth legislative body that would oversee morality, the sciences, arts, education, and the press. The conservatism of the constitution would not have been so controversial if it had not been linked to the emergence of a new geopolitical vision. Bolívar's plans for a loose pan-American union, which met once in 1826, gave way to the idea of forming a new nation, an Andean federation composed of Gran Colombia, Perú, Bolivia, and Chile, to be ruled under his Bolivian constitution. Although the Andean federation never became a reality, many in the government of Gran Colombia who did not agree with the plan feared that Bolívar would try to force a constitutional change. Moreover, rumors swirled about Bolívar's hunger for power because it was assumed that he would be the lifelong president of a new Andean federation. The emerging conflict between Bolivarians and anti-Bolivarians was accentuated by Venezuelan plans to secede from Gran Colombia, which Bolívar settled peacefully. For Bogotanos already suspicious of Bolívar's hold on power, the conciliatory settlement of the secession suggested that their president's loyalty lay with Venezuela and not the republic as a whole. Tensions became so grave that the stability of Gran Colombia was endangered and Bolívar declared a dictatorship in 1828. In this atmosphere of crisis, Bolívar's enemies, particularly the supporters of his rival, former Vice President Santander, produced a wealth of newspaper articles and broadsides depicting the Liberator as an enemy of liberty.[2] And despite Bolívar's conciliatory resolution of the Venezuelan secession crisis, which had hurt his political capital in Bogotá, many Venezuelan notables continued to view their president as a representative of foreign interests. Bolívar hung onto power until the Convention of Ocaña elected a new president in 1830, after which he went into a self-imposed exile. Meanwhile, the Venezuelan Congress of Valencia voted to secede from Gran Colombia and passionately rejected Bolívar's authority, calling for his arrest. Bolívar died in exile on December 17, 1830, in Santa Marta.

The cult of Bolívar began during the hero's lifetime. However, representations of Bolívar during the Wars of Independence were not defined by the geopolitical and ideological questions that nationalist thought would address afterward through the cult. Whereas postindependence nationalism attempted to theorize and demarcate a nation and a people, Republicans during the Wars of Independence struggled to define how the liberated territories should be apportioned as republics, and under what constitutional systems they should be ruled. In times of war, intellectual elites were more interested in protecting the revolution's gains and instituting a regime of law and order than in theorizing the social and cultural glue that made a national people one people. Consequently, the patriot construction of the cause of independence was not expressed in terms of separate nationalisms, but rather in the political sense of a common struggle against tyranny. E. J. Hobsbawm's description of the "revolutionary" versus the "political" nation, characteristic of the emancipatory discourses of the American and French Revolutions, may be applied to Latin America: "Late eighteenth-century constructs of the 'nation' in North America and France posited a body of citizens whose collective sovereignty constituted them a state which was their political expression. . . . But it said little about what constituted a 'people.' In particular there was no logical connection between the body of citizens of a territorial state on one hand, and the identification of a 'nation' on ethnic, linguistic or other grounds or of other characteristics which allowed collective recognition of group membership" (18–19). When Bolívar used the term "nation," it was in this revolutionary register, as demonstrated by one of his seminal statements of political philosophy, the "Discourse of Angostura" (1819): "The formation of a stable government requires as a foundation a national spirit, having as its objective a uniform concentration on two cardinal factors, namely, moderation of the popular will and limitation of public authority. . . . Love of country, love of law, and respect for magistrates are the exalted emotions that must permeate the soul of a republic. . . . Unless there is a sacred reverence for country, laws, and authority, society becomes confused, an abyss—an endless conflict of man versus man, group versus group" (*Selected Writings* 191). Bolívar's emphasis is on national spirit as consent and not as a particular set of cultural traits or narratives that bind people together into a collectivity. Although a love for laws and magistrates is indeed a part of modern nationalism, it is accompanied by a sense of belonging that Bolívar only mentions in passing with the phrase "love of country." During Bolívar's military campaigns, the "revolutionary nation" was an effective formulation that addressed the dangers of a geopolitical reality in which emancipation had not yet been achieved, but in peacetime it was less effective because regional centers of power chafed under the overarching authority of Gran Colombia. Thus, the geopolitical constructs defended by Bolívar, such as the Republic of Gran Colombia, and his plans for a vast Andean federation, cut against the grain of the regional interests that eventually resulted in the formation of smaller nations in postindependence Latin America.

The first cult of Bolívar peaked from 1820 to 1825 and was a product of a complex set of factors that can be traced to the founding of the third republic through the Congress of Angostura. As the architect of the congress, Bolívar wanted to create a political structure to legitimate the union between Venezuela and Nueva Granada. Further, Bolívar sought a republican role for himself that would satisfy both his desire for political legality as a republican president and his plans to carry on as a military leader in the theater of a continuing war (Polanco Alcántara 457). Accordingly, patriot representations of Bolívar in this period drew on classical models of statesmanship that combined the rule of law with the rule of force. Because Bolívar played both the role of president and liberator, early Bolivarian texts reinscribe *caudillismo* as an Augustan phenomenon. [3] One example of this trend in republican literature may be found in the anonymous poem "Colombia constituida," published in the *Gaceta de Colombia* in 1822. Like other poems and essays celebrating Bolívar in this period, the poem characterizes Bolívar as a providential and Augustan leader who augurs a new age of peace and prosperity:

No, by all means, Bolívar, return, accept
Only for the common good, the noble command
That the homeland presents to you without a doubt
And seeing that you already gave her liberty with laws
Also give her peace and the example to the world

That your impulse guided by Astrea
Emptied out over Colombia without measure
The ripe cup of abundance.[4]

Bolívar also viewed himself in classical terms; in the "Discourse of Angostura" he privileged classical usurpers like Pisistratus as models of statesmen-soldiers to be followed in times of historical crisis. In short, when necessary, a great republican statesman must take all the reins of power: "Let us recognize, then," wrote Bolívar, "that Salomon has opened up the eyes of the world; and he has taught it how hard it is to rule men by laws alone" (*Selected Writings* 112). Elsewhere, Bolívar compared himself to Sila, Cato, and Fabius (Briceño Perozo 36).

In 1825, at the height of his military triumphs in the Andes, Bolívar commissioned an epic poem from his friend José Joaquín Olmedo (1780–1847), whose "La victoria de Junín" cast Bolívar and the continent's indigenous past into an Augustan framework. As a member of elite society in his native Guayaquil, Olmedo was a loyal subject of the crown whose neoclassical poetry celebrated the Spanish kings and their authority over the New World. During the Wars of Independence, however, Olmedo became a Republican and was befriended by Bolívar. His poem in celebration of the Liberator tethers the Battle of Junín, where patriot forces were led by Bolívar, with the more important Battle of Ayacucho, in which Sucre commanded the Republicans. The connecting thread is the spirit of the Inca Huayna Capac, who rises over the battlefield of Junín to announce the triumph of Ayacucho and to welcome the era of peace and fertility to follow under Bolívar's guiding hand. Yet, Olmedo was never entirely comfortable with his finished product, and neither was Bolívar, who was the poem's first critic. Upon completing the poem in May of 1825, Olmedo confessed to Bolívar that he considered it long and cold, and worst of all, mediocre (*Epistolario* 252–53). Bolívar offered his critique in a letter dated July 12 in which he complained that the poem was too bombastic, comparing it to *The Iliad*, an epic that begins modestly but which in the end offers much to the reader (Lecuna 38). Bolívar did not believe that the apparition of the Inca Huayna Capac was very believable, and worst of all, found him to be an irritating presence: "You will permit me the observation that this great Inca, who should be lighter than ether because he comes from the heavens, is a bit too chatty and confusing" (38). Since these initial exchanges between Bolívar and Olmedo, "La victoria de Junín" has continued to elicit ambivalent reactions from literary critics, who find the poem's neoclassical bent formal and hollow.[5]

Aesthetic judgments aside, "La victoria de Junín" is an important cultural document that shows how Bolívar's political authority was legitimated through his deification as an all-knowing heir to intangible celestial forces, which in this case are associated with the Sun and the Inca Huayna Capac, two indigenous deities. However, in crafting this hyperbolic version of Bolívar, Olmedo was treading on familiar ground, recasting the themes of some of the monarchist poetry of his youth, in which he celebrated Spanish kings and viceregal authority through the theocratic chain of command God-King-Viceroy. Thus, in spite of the political rupture that the Wars of Independence promised in relation to the previous era of colonialism, "La victoria de Junín" underlines how manifestations of the cult of Bolívar could fall into the representational trap of replacing celebrations of one theocracy with another. Although Bolívar did not say so directly, he too may have thought that Olmedo had gone too far in celebrating his person. In one of his criticisms, the Liberator had objected to the immodest opening of the poem, which evokes Horace's "Ode to Regulus," a celebration of Emperor Augustus. Horace's poem begins:

> His thunder confirms our belief that Jove
> is lord of Heaven; Augustus shall be held
> an earthly God for adding to the Empire
> the Britons and redoubtable Parthians. (Horace 136)

Similarly, Olmedo opens his poem with the thunder of God's presence over the battlefield of Junín, and with echoing songs of victory that proclaim Bolívar "the arbiter/of peace and war on earth" (12–13). Ever zealous of his reputation as Liberator and servant of the revolution, Bolívar might simply have been a bit embarrassed by "La victoria de Junín."

In 1825, Olmedo and other Bolivarians could afford the conceit that a new era of light and peace was beginning under the tutelage of Bolívar-as-Augustus. By then, Bolívar had succeeded in emancipating a large swath of territory between Venezuela in the east and Bolivia in the Andes on the western coast of the continent. Yet, the next few years would mark the end of the dream of a peaceable period of republican reconstruction under the infallible leadership of the Liberator. From 1825 to 1830 the representation of Bolívar-as-Augustus was increasingly countered by a powerful current of republican anti-Bolivarian discourses that portrayed the hero of independence as a tyrant. In Bogotá, this vehement rejection of Bolívar was a result of several factors: the suspicion that he was too indulgent of separatist tendencies in Venezuela; his endorsement of more conservative constitutional models, as exemplified by his centralist Constitution of Bolivia; and his declaration of a dictatorship in 1828. Rhetorical attacks against Bolívar in this period of his declining power and influence were framed by the idea of tyrannicide; Bolívar was the unjust Caesar against whom some valiant Brutus must strike. Among these detractions of Bolívar, the most prominent literary work was Luis Vargas Tejada's poem "Catón en Utica," published in the anti-Bolivarian paper *El conductor* in 1827, and which "became a rallying point for disaffected New Granadan intellectuals" (Americo Bretos 59). Vargas's poem calls for Bolívar's assassination in no uncertain terms by drawing an analogy between Cato the Younger's opposition to Caesar and resistance to Bolívar in the present:

It shall not be long, your fatal empire
The homeland's suffering finally drained
There still exists some breast in which
The generous soul of a Junius Brutus palpitates.[6]

The call for violence against Caesar in poems, broadsheets, and articles peaked with an attempted assassination in 1828, when several men broke into Bolívar's residence, murdered an aide-de-camp and beat his mistress Manuela Sáenz while Bolívar fled from a second story window. One of the plotters, the Venezuelan Pedro Carujo, later declared that he was driven to participate in the assassination attempt by a deep conviction that it was the virtuous and moral act of a patriotic citizen (Gil Fortoul 1:190).

Bolívar did not fare better in Venezuela. Official animosity toward the hero of independence at the beginning of the national period cannot be separated from Gran Colombia's failure in bridging the gap between the regional elites of the republic's capital, Bogotá, and those of Caracas, in the former Captaincy General of Venezuela. The Venezuelan separatist movement associated the Gran Colombia project, and by extension, its architect, defender, and leader, with the usurpation of Venezuelan sovereignty by Bogotano interests. At the secessionist Congress of Valencia (1830), the protector of Venezuelan separatism, José Antonio Páez, described Bolívar as a principle of unchecked power that had created "dark clouds" for the pursuit of liberty (Magallanes 2:17–18). The congress enshrined this rejection of Bolívar by pardoning Bolívar's would-be assassins of 1828 and portraying them as citizen-heroes: "It is not just that those citizens who by their acts and opinions attempted to liberate the Republic from the iniquitous repression that it was suffering, remain in prison or expelled, especially now that Venezuela has recovered those rights which were extinguished and usurped by the Dictator Simón Bolívar" (18). All generals, colonels, and known military followers of Bolívar were prohibited from entering Venezuela, and many Bolivarians were expelled from Venezuela (19). Some delegates argued that Bolívar should be declared an outlaw and arrested if found on Venezuelan soil.

In light of the vehement anti-Bolivarian sentiment at the Congress of Valencia, borne out of a fear that Bolívar and his followers might sweep down and force them back into the fold of Gran Colombia, it is not surprising that word of Bolívar's death was greeted with relief, if not outright celebration in Venezuela, as exemplified by the following communiqué by the governor of Maracaibo: "Bolívar, the genius of evil, the source of discord, or better said, the oppressor of his Homeland, has ceased to exist and no longer promotes evil deeds that always flowed onto his fellow citizens. His death, which in other circumstances and in the time of deceit could have caused the mourning and sadness of Colombians, will doubtlessly be the most powerful motive of their rejoicing, because from it the peace and reconciliation of all emanate" (Magallanes 20–21). Postindependence Venezuela was thus born out of a conspicuous rejection of Bolívar that would last until mid-century. Eventually, the martial and political achievements of Bolívar would prove too dramatic and compelling for emergent, nationalist memory to deny.

The Rediscovery of Bolívar, 1830–1842

How was Bolívar rehabilitated by the Venezuelan state as a symbol of the nation? The answer lies in the waning of the politics of the Wars of Independence, in which Bolívar had been a central player, and the emergence of a new, national politics. Between 1830 and 1835, the men who had convened the Congress of Valencia and created the fourth Venezuelan republic, presided over a polity united around several liberal initiatives. These first nationalists were eager to improve roads, pacify the countryside, encourage immigration, and generally speaking, create a secular, civil society. The colonial past, associated with a lack of discipline and vision, was left behind in favor of a new, Americanist vision of the potential of Venezuelan

progress. In 1831, for example, the minister of interior and justice, Antonio
Leocadio Guzmán, described the new nation as a mysterious, natural
arcadia that could be made to bear the fruits of progress by the state (Pino
Iturrieta, *Las ideas* 24–25). Disenchanted Bolivarians, defenders of church
interests, and more conservative groups actively resisted the designs of
these early nationalists. Between 1830 and 1833, several revolts were put
down by President José Antonio Páez, the titular leader and protector of
the new republic. The insurrection of Siquisique (1830), and the revolt of
José Tadeo Monagas (1831), for example, signaled regionalist disenchantment with the break from Colombia and the new Constitution's attacks on
the privileges of both the military and the church (Magallanes 2:25–35).
In this period of national reconstruction, when military revolts cloaked
themselves with the banner of Bolívar and Colombia, Bolívar continued to
be a persona non grata for the national project.

From 1835 onward, economic and political crises precipitated an accen-
tuation of divisions within the social elite. Liberal economic measures
alienated the planter class that was chafing under onerous credit rates and
stringent laws that facilitated the expropriation of the properties of those
individuals who defaulted on their loans (Pino Iturrieta, *Las ideas* 54–55).
However, the issue that polarized the elite the most emerged as a result of
the Guerra de Reformas (1835), when a coalition of federalists, Bolivarians,
and defenders of church privilege revolted and overthrew President José
María Vargas. Although the *Reformistas* represented an amalgam of contradictory interests (the anti-Bolivarian Pedro Carujo, for example, reap-
peared, alongside Bolivarians, to challenge the state), one of their manifes-
tos suggested that the former warriors of independence were experiencing
a profound sense of dislocation in the new nation: "The doors of the homeland were closed to the valiant captains of Independence. The illustrious
warriors that were cynically expelled roamed in faraway lands. The great
patriots of the Venezuelan Church have been condemned to estrangement.
The old servants, eminent patriots, are censured and oppressed" (Pino
Iturrieta, *Las ideas* 51). The ghost of the Liberator haunts these lines; who
better than Bolívar, still buried outside of Venezuela, exemplified the in-
justice of the state to the veterans of independence? Moreover, *Reformistas* anticipated nationalist discourse when they bound the theme of military service to the nation to the image of postrevolutionary Venezuela as a
church. Their proclamation suggests that the nation should not be considered a political entity, but a community united by a shared, transcendental
project.

The Guerra de Reformas came to a quick end when José Antonio Páez came out of retirement and promptly defeated the rebels. The ensuing harsh treatment of the defeated *Reformistas,* many of whom belonged to distinguished families, proved to be overwhelmingly unpopular with many notables, who called for a more measured and conciliatory approach. A movement for clemency developed among planters and liberals, whose arguments, like those of the *Reformistas,* imagined the nation as a divided entity, separated from its own revolutionary past. One of the most talented critics of the state, Tomás Lander, wrote an impassioned letter to General Páez, arguing that Venezuela had been born out of a series of revolutions and counterrevolutions like the Guerra de Reformas. To exile, execute, and imprison members of the same generation of patriots that had liberated Venezuela in the first place was not only ungrateful, but a negation of the foundational dramas of the Wars of Independence that had established the republic.[7]

By 1836, then, a coherent and impassioned opposition had developed against the liberal state. Planters who defended economic protectionism merged with disenchanted soldiers and Bolivarians and created the Partido Liberal in 1840, which despite its name, was marked by ideological tendencies commonly associated in nineteenth-century intellectual history with conservatism. Bolívar became a vital, symbolic linchpin of the Partido Liberal. For example, a patriotic play entitled *Drama patriótico en elogio y recuerdo del glorioso día 19 de abril de 1810 y de los triunfos inmortales del primer caudillo de la libertad sudamericana* was staged with great success in 1840. The protagonists of the allegory, Hercules and Mars, celebrate Bolívar's feats in front of a white temple, festooned with trophies, shields, statues, and other accoutrements representing immortality and Bolívar's war-time feats, transcendence, and glories. At the end of the brief performance, Mars asks the audience to "observe a new day," while Hercules equates Bolívar with its dawn.[8] The authorities shut the play down, and a clamor of protest ensued, giving the critics of the state fodder for further recriminations (Magallanes 2:140). A year later at the University of Caracas, Bolívar's Saint's Day (October 28) was the object of celebrations attended by luminaries of both the opposition and the state. The issue of repatriating Bolívar's remains had reached fever pitch by this time and was evident in placards displayed at the event, for example: "The Sword of Bolívar liberated a world. Will his ashes not have a HOMELAND?" (J. González, n. pag.). The published proceedings of this event also underscore how nationalism had flowered around the figure of Bolívar. "You are the symbol of liberty and equality," declared Juan Vicente González at the speech ceremony, "the symbol of Venezuela, the symbol of order" (J. González).

Bolívar's continued exile-in-death furthered attacks by the Partido Liberal on the corruption and illegitimacy of the congress, which a dozen years after the hero's death had still not acted to return the relic of his remains from Santa Marta. Although prior calls for Bolívar's return by President Páez (1833) and Vice President Soublette (1839) were turned down, by 1842 the embattled government could not resist the temptation of making Bolívar its own and silencing its critics on one powerful count. In his communication to the congress requesting the repatriation, Páez argued that the continued exile of Bolívar represented a schism between the people and its representatives: "Convenience and even political morality are invested in this, so that henceforth those acts through which the people express their appreciation to the memory of the Liberator be supported in the legitimately expressed national vote, and so that its expressions of gratitude and admiration for his great acts of patriotism and humanity not be considered contrary to the intentions of legislators" (Leal 131). Congress buckled under the pressure of public opinion and approved Páez's measure. The ensuing repatriation of Bolívar's remains proved to be the first large-scale nationalist ritual ever to be held in the city of Caracas. Fermín Toro marveled at the large crowds that peacefully lined the streets of the city and declared that a new era of peace had begun under the tutelage of the iconic Bolívar.

Toro was proven wrong, however, as Venezuela was torn by more than twenty years of civil unrest and political instability. The escalating conflict between *Conservadores* and *Liberales* led to the military dictatorships of José Tadeo Monagas and his brother José Gregorio, which in turn provoked an alliance between warring political parties to oust the autocracy. Upon the defeat of the Monagas, however, the conflict between political factions was recast in the Guerra Federal of 1859–1863 in which more than two hundred thousand people lost their lives. However, Bolívar continued to be the object of legislation and cultural production: the city of Angostura was officially renamed Ciudad Bolívar (1846), a monumental crypt for Bolívar was erected in the Cathedral of Caracas (1851), the state prize "Busto del Libertador" was instituted (1854), and several print works in praise of Bolívar appeared, such as *Bosquejo de la historia militar de Venezuela* (1855–1857) by José de Austria, and Larrazábal's biography of Bolívar

(1865). However, it would not be until after the turmoil of the Guerra Federal that an operative, state-sponsored cult of Bolívar would take shape.

Fermín Toro's "Honores a Bolívar" and the National Bolívar

Fermín Toro, the author of the first tract to link Bolívar to the Venezuelan state, and to theorize Bolívar as a principle of postwar national identity, was a statesman and talented writer who resists easy categorization. He was born in 1806 in or near Caracas, into a distinguished family well known for its ties to Simón Bolívar.[9] Between 1821 and 1829, Toro occupied a variety of administrative posts related to the treasury department inside and outside of Caracas, one of which he was appointed to by Simón Bolívar himself. During Venezuela's first five years of existence as an entity separate from Gran Colombia (1830–1835) Toro served as representative of the island of Margarita, and distinguished himself by serving on several important committees, the most important of which was a brief stint as president of the House of Representatives (Arratia 145–49). In the latter half of the 1830s, while remaining employed in the Ministry of Finance, Toro became a professor of philosophy and began publishing essays and stories in the press. From 1839 onward, Toro was ambassador to various European capitals and a congressman charged with a series of high profile committee positions, one of which was overseeing the plans for Bolívar's reinterment and public funeral ceremonies (168). When Páez's handpicked successor, General José Tadeo Monagas, became dictator in 1848, Toro resigned from public office and retired to private life. Legend has it that upon being commanded by the president to return to Congress after a disruption that had ended in the deaths of several congressmen, Toro replied: "Tell General Monagas that they may take my dead body, but that Fermín Toro does not prostitute himself" (Tosta 222). Toro survived the tumultuous instabilities of mid-nineteenth-century Venezuela and received one last diplomatic mission to Europe before dying in 1865.

Toro's career as a writer included the direction of two newspapers and the production of poetry, *costumbrista* writings (sketches of national life and social customs), essays, and a novel.[10] One of the most interesting aspects of his political thought is the radical critique of European industrialism and imperialism that appears in his writing, suggesting a tendency toward utopian socialism (Miliani 20, 52). Moreover, as an avid reader and proponent of the Christian ideas of Francois Guizot (1787–1874) and Vic-

tor Cousin (1792–1867), Toro fused Christian and republican principles. In
Cousin's own words, as quoted and italicized by Toro: "What has come out
of Christianity and Christian Society? Modern liberty, representative governments" ("Europa y América" 51). Christ was the conduit for this link-
age between celestial and terrestrial affairs, showing that the divine had a
human face (55). This elementary concept would serve as a cornerstone for
his reconstruction of Bolívar as a national symbol; like Christ, Bolívar provided an ideal horizon toward which the Venezuelan collectivity should
strive. However, Toro's deep love of science motivated him to synthesize
his religious, republican sociology with science, and to conceptualize society through the lens of the combination of different types of matter. Toro
believed that a society and its rise and fall from greatness could be understood vis-à-vis the equilibrium between its ideal, or metaphysical elements, and its material, or purely physical properties. The path to human
progress and true civilization could only be achieved by harmonizing the
material conditions of society to ideal standards. Excess of one ingredient
or another in the equation resulted in different forms of decadence: in the
case of England, the preponderance of the material had resulted in bleak
and desperate urban landscapes, while in France, an excess of idealism had
turned freedom into a drunken and destructive anarchy (43).

Toro's commitment to the equilibrium of the ideal and the material is
central to "Honores a Bolívar." The performance of Mozart's *Requiem* before Bolívar's eulogy is represented as a materialization of a divine equation that balances the spiritual and the terrestrial: "If you show yourself to
be terrestrial . . . you are also divine, oh Music!, and then more noble in
your accents, freer in your rapture, you hearken back to your origin and
inspiredly reveal the potent and supreme voice that gave order to chaos
and harmony to the Universe" ("Honores a Bolívar" 263). In another passage, Toro specifically describes this equilibrium as an emotional state in-
duced by the funeral-event, in which pain is transformed into a form of
dignity that elevates the subject into the ideal realm (256). The iconic
Bolívar—as constituted by the majestic trajectory of his extraordinary life,
his humbling, mortal end, and finally by his resurrection as undisputed
founder of the nation—acts as an experiential nexus between the divine
and the material inside of each Venezuelan. The Bolívar-Christ association
is particularly strong in Toro's eloquent account of Bolívar's death, which
underlines, in exclamatory effusions, the poetry of Bolívar's suffering, the
sublimity of his martyrdom, and the revelatory lessons of his *via crucis*
(241). The lesson in transcendence that the dead Bolívar contributes to his

homeland is a collective epiphany that erases difference and social tension and forges an ordered mass of awed acolytes.

Toro first reflected on the nature of crowds, and appropriated the crowd as a symbol of society, in his serialized novel *Los mártires* (1839). The novel, which tells the melodramatic story of a destitute English family, opens with the narrator negotiating the crowded streets of London during the celebration of Queen Victoria's wedding in 1838. The density, diversity, and order of the milling crowds give the narrator pause to marvel: "The show of carriages and cars in the center had grown to the point of impeding all movement; on the sidewalks, the accumulated multitude formed two dense and impenetrable columns, that from time to time, appeared to be waves moving in opposite directions, like the sea. Some groups left while others arrived, they met and collided, the pushing and the crushing grew, but no one emerged the victor. The floodgates unleashed, the classes confused, the crowd was boisterous and agitated, but admirable thing!, not one affront, not one abuse, not even one bad gesture was seen" (5–6). Toro's mention of the English crowd as a sea, as a moving, oceanic push and pull directed by invisible hands, and out of which no internal conflict or victor arises, reveals the ordered crowd to be a dense space in which lesser units of self-identification—whether individual, social, or political—are cast off in favor of a single fluid organism with internal coherence. As Elias Canetti writes in *Crowds and Power* (1984),[11] the sea-crowd metaphor is multiple, yet dense and cohesive, in which each individual person of the crowd is "yielding to others as though they were oneself, as though there were no strict division between oneself and them" (80). In "Honores a Bolívar" Toro recasts this oceanic image of the ordered crowd in a variety of settings, one of which is the undulatory and peaceful sea-image that figured prominently in *Los mártires*. For example, the image appears in a passage from "Honores a Bolívar" that describes the transport of Bolívar's remains on a small craft from the Venezuelan ship *Constitución* to the docks of La Guaira, and evokes the peaceful sound and fluid movement of the sea as a crowd-symbol (254). In a more literal sense, Toro is repeatedly awed by the coming together of so many people in a peaceable and reverential posture. Density and harmony are the two operative terms: "It was like no other pageantry in Caracas, none before ever produced such a sensation, nor moved such a numerous crowd; but even more impressive than the numbers was the crowd's attitude during this serious ceremony. Having not actually seen it, it will almost seem impossible to imagine a feeling so pronounced, so uniform in decorum and gravity that the occasion required, within a group so varied in age and condition" (255). The funeral procession's movement through the streets, described as solemn, ordered, and slow, is another site of order, as is the congregation of dignitaries and notables that gather in the temple of San Francisco to listen to the eulogy (263). Thus, the epiphany of the Bolívar funeral-event, as expressed in the merging of social classes into an ordered crowd, materializes a scene that predates the division between men, their gods, and nature (241). As such, it is a world ideally suited for representing a perfect integration of the masses under Bolívar, who passes from life into an iconic role that structures acts of collective reverence and submission.

Fermín Toro also argues that the Bolívar funeral addresses the wounds inflicted by the Guerra de Reformas. Until 1842, the *Reformista* movement was viewed as an extension of the Bolivarian epoch that had secured independence for Venezuela. Further, many of the *Reformistas* were old Bolivarians, as were many of their supporters in the Partido Liberal. In "Honores a Bolívar," the *Reformista* subtext is one of the most significant deployments of Toro's narrative as a document of the state. Bolívar serves as a historical continuum in which to reconcile Venezuela's tradition of revolutionary violence with the early national era of constitutional reconstruction. Toro enables this reconciliation by periodizing Bolívar's life and Venezuelan history into two distinct eras: the era of independence, which belongs to myth, and the era of constitutionalism, which belongs to the present. For the period pertaining to the Wars of Independence, Bolívar appears as an Old Testament warrior, and for the period of reconstruction, he is a Christ-like messiah that lays the foundations of the constitutional order: "BOLIVAR . . . in the days of terror can only be compared to the biblical heroes who, armed with the ire of Saboath, rolled their bloodied carriages over destroyed armies; but during the days of reparation, he was similar to the benefactor spirits that preside over creation, the sentiment of justice and the conception of beauty" (268). Through the Ur-text of this biblical frame, Toro is able to naturalize war and postindependence reconstruction into one holy narrative, while at the same time maintaining them as separate. The founding of the nation is a divinely ordained disruption of the terrestrial (age of violence) that necessarily paved the way for the celestial on Earth (the temple of republicanism) (269). Thus, there is no contradiction between Bolivarianism and the post-Colombian Venezuelan state; the worship of Bolívar is necessarily the worship of the constitutional oracle of equality, enlightenment, independence, and representative democracy. Toro argues that the time of bloodshed and human extermination, in which Bolívar had been like a warrior superior to all, was closed by the hero himself, who founded the "temple" of reconstruction.[12] By moving Bolívar and the caudillo experience into the text of myth, Toro depoliticizes them in the arena of 1842 Venezuela and appropriates them for the nationalist imagination.

The state funeral of 1842 and Toro's reimagining of Bolívar correspond to the concept of a "second funeral," in which a body already stripped of its physical trappings is ritualized in a "bony renewal of the hopes and fabulations of the group . . . recruited for the perfection of brooding mystery" (Taussig 101). The difficult nature and profound importance of Toro's "second funeral" of Bolívar should not be glossed over because Toro belonged to the same generation of lawmakers, still in power in 1842, that had railed against Bolívar in 1830, calling for his arrest, vilifying his motives, and celebrating his would-be assassins. Toro and others finally recognized that times had changed, and sought to wrest Bolívar from partisan politics and reimagine him as the very soul of the nation. As such, Toro's "Honores a Bolívar" is a transitional text that marks the waning of the politics of the Wars of Independence and the emergence of the idea of the nation in Venezuela. His text is the first to signal the connection between the symbolic body of Bolívar and the designs of a state eager to eliminate political dissent and ensure economic prosperity and the implementation of liberal programs.

Felipe Larrazábal and the Sacred Logos of Bolívar

In his 1882 lecture "What Is a Nation?," Ernest Renan described the nation as a "spiritual principle" defined by a deep sense of solidarity, a commitment to sacrifice, and an awareness of a shared past and future (Renan 19). Renan argues, in a memorable turn of phrase, that the nation is ultimately realized by "the clearly expressed desire to continue a common life" (19). By situating Bolívar in the realm of ideas, as a discursive essence that works to channel social reality into an ordered social organization, defenders of Bolivarian historical memory situate the "common life" of the modern nation in the personal adoration of Bolívar as a republican messiah. Bolívar's life and words are the sacred scripture through which the national subject acquires a desire to transcend corruption, force, and fear, and achieve moral standing through the republican ethos of civic virtue.

Fermín Toro was the first to construct Bolívar as a principle of postindependence national unity. His vision of Bolívar as the foundation of

a political subjectivity that draws on the devotional practice of worship-
ping icons (in this case, monuments or images), or treating the words of
the hero as a sacred tract, would continue to define nineteenth-century
representations of Bolívar. Moreover, Toro's description of the constructive
resonance of Bolívar's death also results in revealing parallels to Christian
spirituality. The contemplation of Bolívar's anonymous death in Santa
Marta provides individuals with a transformative, spiritual experience that
echoes the crucifixion of Christ. The mournful scene of Bolívar's death
operates as an exemplary sacrifice that can spiritually inspire citizens to
experience and maintain the republican ways that Bolívar sought to establish in Latin America.

   These symbolic foundations for the image of Bolívar as a republican
messiah were copiously elaborated on and expanded by Felipe Larrazábal's
Correspondencia general del Libertador Simón Bolívar (1865). The legitimacy of Larrazábal's extravagantly romantic biography of Bolívar was
quickly overtaken by the advent of positivism in Venezuela, which viewed
its romantic and religious enthusiasm as signs of a lack of historical rigor
and scientific discipline (Franceschi González 108–9). In 1918, Rufino
Blanco Fombona "corrected" the original by excising large sections of
Larrazábal's text, producing a version that has since been reprinted several
times (109). Larrazábal's original text, however, is a lucid example of how
Christian devotional practices may be harnessed for the republican project.
In the same manner that Toro identified Bolívar the statesman as a Christ-
like figure, Larrazábal's vision of Bolívar is predicated on an emphatic
identification of the hero with Christ, and with a series of themes that run
through his theological writings on the nature of biblical discourse, religious education, and the centrality of Christianity to the republican
project. In the analysis to follow, I examine the processes by which Larrazábal uses concepts of sacred writing to transform Bolívar-the-hero into a
holy, republican scripture.

   Larrazábal involved himself early on in the Liberal opposition to the so-
called Conservadores who held state power: he was one of the founding
members of the Sociedad Liberal in 1840, and in 1845 he founded *El
patriota*, an opposition newspaper. A distinguished musician and com-
poser, the Venezuelan-born Larrazábal acquired degrees in philosophy and
law. His writings, mostly framed by his career as a political journalist during the birth of the Partido Liberal, attest to a romantic sensibility that
combined religious and republican fervor. In *El patriota*, Larrazábal argued
passionately for freedom of the press, the overturning of *Conservador*

laissez-faire economic practices, and the abolition of the death penalty. During the presidency of José Tadeo Monagas and subsequently José Gregorio Monagas, Larrazábal was governor of Caracas, a congressman, and coauthor of the decree abolishing slavery in Venezuela (Franceschi González 106). After the Guerra Federal, in which the Liberales of the 1840s renamed themselves as Federales, Larrazábal continued his career as a journalist and a writer, founding the newspaper *El federalista*, and becoming a professor of law at the Universidad Central. In 1872, Larrazábal had a falling out with President Antonio Guzmán Blanco and went into exile, dying tragically in a shipwreck in 1873, in which thousands of letters by Bolívar were lost, along with other biographies and writings that Larrazábal had completed.

Despite the support Larrazábal received for the publication of his work by then General Guzmán Blanco, the *Correspondencia* does not push for loyalty to the Venezuelan state, or to any specific administration. Although Larrazábal's text shares many of the dimensions of nationalist writing—that is, a preoccupation with origins, the veneration of heroes, and the promotion of harmonious forms of social organization—the universalist implications of its biblical paradigm collapse any allegorical reading of it as a specific prescription for Venezuelan nation building. Yet, Larrazábal is deeply committed to republican values, the formation of good citizens, and to the liberal slogan of *Paz, Orden, y Progreso* [Peace, Order, and Progress]. In making the word of Bolívar the centerpiece of his biography (as opposed to, say, his military genius or courage) Larrazábal effectively illustrates the primacy of discourse for the project of making citizens and forming orderly, forward-moving societies.

Larrazábal's linking of religion and political theory is most explicitly argued in his 1864 *Principios de derecho político, o elementos de la ciencia constitucional*, which was meant to be an educational tract for the study of modern political science in Venezuela. Larrazábal argues that the modern, social art of politics is based on the trinity of Liberty, Equality, and Fraternity, all of which are predicated on a preexisting Christian morality.[13] Most pertinent for our discussion, however, is Larrazábal's commitment to the Bible as a holy script, which he transposes upon the life and meaning of Bolívar. According to his analysis, the principles upon which a just, modern society rests, as well as our understanding of them, all spring from the Bible (*Obras literarias* 301). Larrazábal's convictions led him to meditate on the connections between political economy and sacred writing. For example, he explains the merits of taxation by discussing a parable in which

Jesus asks Peter to pay a Roman tax by retrieving money from a fish's belly. Larrazábal extensively analyzes the parable to glean from it concepts of political economy:

> This text clarifies the difficult subject matter of contributions. Let us analyze it. First: Jesus orders that wealth be sought for the tribute, reminding his minister that he search for it in the sea, not in a poor stream, not in standing water, nor in a fountain. Very well, does this not clearly express the first rule of all Economists, the general nature of the tribute? Secondly: When He commands that the tribute be sought in the grand immensity of the sea, where the fish are innumerable, He does not order that the fishing be done with a net that impoverishes and lessens, taking that which is large and small, useful and useless, necessary and superfluous; but rather He commands that only one lure be cast. Third: When He commands that the first fish to be caught be raised, He disposes that upon opening its mouth, a coin be extracted from it; this is a command to take from the fish only that which it contains. Fourth: Upon ordering that the *stater* or coin be extracted, not only does He command that something small from the fish be removed, but rather something that is not necessary for its existence; because for the fish the money was of no importance, and in its mouth it was evidently a superfluous substance. (*Obras literarias* 306)

As this passage shows, Larrazábal sustains a close engagement with biblical discourse, which is more than a mere compendium of parables, a repository of truths to be learned. Larrazábal saw the Bible's script as a form of writing that embodied the divine and transported readers to a higher, experiential plane. In an essay titled "De la Biblia considerada bajo un punto de vista literario," he emphasizes this point by heaping praise on the Bible as a text able to survive the act of translation, which in every other case involves a disfigurement and lessening of the original text. Biblical discourse, however, was a form of expression impervious to the limitations of individual language systems and the perils of translation (*Obras literarias* 291). In effect, the word of God is not a language in a material, *representational* sense but rather an essential syntax that takes the materials of human existence and expression, whether they be acts, words, or emotions, to make manifest the existence of a higher plane of existence. This is, for Larrazábal, the sublime, which has the power to transport understanding and feeling to a transcendent realm (93, 95).

Larrazábal's investment in the social gospel, and the machinery of his theory of holy scripts, are imported into the *Correspondencia* through the representation of Bolívar's voice. As in the Bible with the "word of God," Bolívar's words embody the hero's being—his words reflect his essential being—and operate as sublime charges that enable humanity to catch glimpses of the celestial realm. These words, like those contained in the Bible, are both personally and socially transitive, affecting progress by way of directing the movement of the soul toward Good; the words of Bolívar are thus constructed as spaces for the formation of good republican citizens. In the tempests of the Wars of Independence, Bolívar stands out as a sun, radiating rays of liberty, creating nations and illuminating peoples subjugated by the dark ages of colonial tyranny. This construction of Bolívar is achieved through three imbricated concepts at the center of Larrazábal's biography of the hero: the *epistle,* the *sublime,* and a *transcendental hermeneutics.*

The organizing principle of Larrazábal's biography is the letter, or the epistle. In a telling section of a manual for seminary students that Larrazábal authored in 1856, "Del estudio de la Sagrada Escritura," Larrazábal cites Saint Gregory's description of the Bible as a "beautiful letter" sent by the Almighty for the instruction of the soul of humanity. In that letter, the faithful find an abundance of elevating sweetness, a place of rest from which the light of salvation emanates (*Historia* 48–49). The concept of biblical discourse as a divine "letter" is central to the construction of the *Correspondencia* as a biography of Bolívar. The text is so intimately identified with epistolary writing that it is constituted as a preface to a collection of letters, and not distinguished from the body to which it is appended; the life of Bolívar is not identified as a biography but as the *Correspondencia general.* The life history thus serves as an answer key of sorts, a guide, for navigating the large mass of raw material of his projected, multivolume collection of letters. The privileging of epistolary intertexts in the telling of Bolívar's life also extricates the hero from the threat of anachronism, removing him from historically bound contexts and placing him in the realm of transcendent and invariable truths that emanate from his writings. Like the Bible according to Saint Gregory, Bolívar's writing is an experience capable of educating, inspiring, and moving readers through the intimacy of a script that is like a letter to each and every human soul.[14]

The defining characteristic of the use of language in the holy letter of Bolívar is that the signs of the hero's words are one and the same with Bolívar: "His correspondence is HE HIMSELF, such as he existed in all the instants of his life. . . . With singular mobility of projects and ideas, the Liberator had an inconceivable fixity of sentiment and impressions. What came out of his soul never changed: it was the lava transformed into granite" (Larrazábal, *Correspondencia* xxviii). The fusion of man and expression achieves several ends. For one thing, Bolívar is elevated above the terrestrial realm of politics and force, and situated in a realm of ideas, where he can be distinguished from and privileged over the more specialized role of statesman and/or the less honorable role of a victorious warlord. Further, Bolívar's extraordinary success is not seen as a function of courage, cunning, or some specialized martial prowess, but rather as springing naturally from the power of his words, which are equal to his essential, spiritual superiority over his foes. These two points are dramatically driven home by a passage in volume 2 in which Larrazábal constructs the Wars of Independence, and Bolívar's participation in them, as a triumphant instance of an illuminated word over the darkness of ignorance, tyranny, and the rule of force:

> In Arequipa Bolívar expedited the decree "creating the Republic of Alto Perú". . . . This is a monumental act. Create a Nation by decree! To take a quill to give an enslaved people the magnificent present of sovereignty! A few years before the world watched as Napoleon and Alexander sought a way to divide the geographic letter of the world between them! BOLIVAR, the father of liberty, the man of the most unencumbered virtue, did not open his mouth but to proclaim independence, to scatter rights amongst men, and if he spread his gaze upon the map it was to decide where the flags of civilization would be hoisted, where he would take the guarantees and gifts of equality, the benefits of peace and the treasure of republican institutions. Happy contrast, in which, the excesses of vanity belong to others, and the privilege of virtue, which even enamours the spirits of the perverse, belongs to Bolívar. (2:308)

By way of the map, which Larrazábal equates with terrestrial division, and by extension, with a lower and lesser order of historical activity, Alexander the Great and Napoleon are classified as mere conquerors. Bolívar, however, escapes the spatial-temporal cartography of power for power's sake, and occupies a higher plane of civilizing activity, spreading the light of liberty, equality, and fraternity.

Larrazábal's theory of the Bolivarian sublime is predicated on a particular hermeneutics or theory of reading. Throughout the biography, the writings of the hero are treated with the same veneration as the voice of Jesus in the Bible; they are articulations of truth that benefit from the critical activity of analysis, in the same way the parables of Jesus are reconstructed elsewhere in Larrazábal's work as relevant to political economy and republicanism. For example, in his essay "Del sublime," Larrazábal wrote of how biblical discourse might shorten the great distance that separates the human from the divine by sparking experiential events in the reading subject. The Book of Job is isolated as exemplar. Passages are cited and followed by an effusion of praise directed at the language, style, imagery, and truths of the sacred writing, which awaken in the spirit lofty ideas and deep sentiments (*Obras literarias* 111). A comparison of the commentary that this kind of biblical discourse provokes with the reactions inspired by Bolívar's words drives home the point that Larrazábal grants the same ontological status to both texts. On the Book of Job, he writes: "What vigor, what fiery style! What living and what lovely images! What grandiosity and what terrible figures! It seems as if Job has possessed the secrets of the Lord, and knows his designs and the unfathomable ocean of his perfections. . . . And what sublimely pathetic ideas we stop transcribing so as not to be diffuse! Oh immense book in which everything is great and elevated with simple expressions . . ." (*Obras literarias* 111). On Bolívar's writing, Larrazábal writes: "He wrote his thoughts to his friends and fellow travelers, in a language of fire, that even the most beautiful spirits of the world would envy. . . . His proclamations, his messages, his official or family letters are treasures of beauty and truth which reveal a man nurtured by important readings. . . . All is noble, proud and elegant, falling from his quill, with profusion, discrete and healthy . . ." (*Correspondencia* 1:xiv–xv). If the words of Bolívar are not mere language, but a kind of superior, sacred script with a greater claim on the intangible forces of creation, then the reading-act that is dictated by that kind of script is not singular-finite; reading is an act of worship and communion with the sacred word and the truths it embodies. For Larrazábal, in short, sacred writing is inexhaustible. It creates spaces of engagement for rest, for edification, and for higher understanding outside of the realm of language and the linear apprehension of meaning. To achieve access to such a space, the reader must return, again and again, to the text to reexperience the divine.

The *Correspondencia general del Libertador Simón Bolívar* expresses themes and motifs that permeate the cult of Bolívar up to the present. Despite the ambivalent reactions of nineteenth-century historians and writers to this biography, Larrazábal succeeded in articulating the primary

contours of a republican cult of Bolívar, one that substituted the temple of
the church with the temple of the nation. Subsequent, mythic representations of Bolívar would hit on the same themes, fleetingly, as in the case of
José Martí's volcanic vision of Bolívar as energy, José Enrique Rodo's
providential view of the hero on a divine errand, and Eduardo Blanco's
version of Bolívar as a celestial event, a comet in a firmament of heroes.
Larrazábal's text, however, uncovered and explained the underlying theology of such a mythic vision. In a letter to Antonio Guzmán Blanco,
Larrazábal described his biography as a monument that would bring
Bolívar and Venezuela to the attention of the world. His monument was a
theological vision, which deprived the historical agent of a body and conferred upon him the iconicity of holy scripture. Like all monument build-
ers, Larrazábal wanted his subject to be eternal.

The Quest for Order

In his collection of lectures, *On Heroes, Hero-Worship, and the Heroic in
History* (1840), Thomas Carlyle calls every "Great Man, every genuine
man" a "missionary of Order" (175). Like his contemporary Fermín Toro,
Carlyle was responding to profound historical changes, particularly the
French Revolution, and Europe's tentative entry into a new, republican
age. His description of heroes as principles of order aptly summarizes the
rise of the cult of Bolívar as a prescription for order in times of historical
turmoil: "While old false Formulas are getting trampled everywhere into
destruction, new genuine Substances unexpectedly unfold themselves in-
destructible. In rebellious ages, when Kingship itself seems dead and abol-
ished, Cromwell, Napoleon step forth again as Kings. The history of these
men is what we have now to look at, as our last phasis of Heroism" (176).
The concept of the return of the king is a useful one. In 1819, as Bolívar's
patriot forces approach Bogotá, the painter Pedro Figueroa hurriedly
painted a portrait of Bolívar onto the same canvas that held a portrait of a
Spanish commander, hiding the older image beneath a new coat of paint
and a new leader (Pineda 5). Similarly, Olmedo's "La victoria de Junín" not
only restaged Horatian odes to Augustus, but also reproduced the thematic
structure Olmedo had used in poems celebrating viceroys and the Spanish
Empire. In an analogous example, coins with the profile of King Ferdinand
were adapted to mint new ones of Bolívar in Bolivia in 1826 (37). For Toro
and Larrazábal, the model of the returning king was presented from a biblical point of view: their reimagining of Bolívar was predicated on the im-

age of Jesus. As in the santos de vestir, the play of identity is signaled by dressing the same body (in this case, divine power) in different clothes.

Toro and Larrazábal's representation of Bolívar as a "missionary of order" synthesizes the most salient characteristics of the Latin American cult of Bolívar. The hero is an agent of a higher power, the republic, and is best represented through the image of a sacred, harmonizing scripture. Through the republican script of Bolívar, societies could be ordered and most importantly, pacified. The new subjectivity promoted by these republican theologians of Bolívar was predicated on the consent that sprang from a sense of spiritual connection to the nation and its values, as embodied by the iconic image of the hero. Despite their different political affiliations, Toro and Larrazábal concurred in this quest for order through the mythification of Bolívar. It is worth noting, however, that both lived before the foundation of an operative and visible cult of Bolívar. In their lifetime, for example, the central plaza of Caracas was only a marketplace. Despite the sincere devotion to Bolívar among many, there were no physical markers or cultic spaces to accommodate the republican liturgy of national identity. Bolivarian nationalism was an ideology without monuments, a disembodied idea yet to find material expression. Toro and Larrazábal did not live long enough to witness the monumental embodiment of Bolívar during the presidency of Antonio Guzmán Blanco, nor the subsequent ambivalence this kind of material presence would provoke in the national imaginary. Theirs was a time when monuments were ideal forms, and not physical markers that might signal contradiction, decay, or failure.

2

Monumentalism and the Erotics
of National Degeneration

What good are statues consecrated to heroes if lazy, illiterate and
miserable multitudes throng around them?
Carlos Pellicer

In October of 1874, crowds gathered to watch men work on the vacant
pedestal in the central plaza of Caracas. A replica of Lima's equestrian
statue of Bolívar by the Italian sculptor Adamo Tadolini was on its way
from Europe, promising a renewal of the city and of the nation. Variously
known as the Plaza Principal, del Mercado, de Armas, and de la Catedral,
the plaza had served as a public market in the eighteenth century and the
nineteenth century, much to the consternation of image and class conscious governors.[1] Attempts to associate Bolívar with the city center began
in 1825 but did not succeed until the presidency of Antonio Guzmán
Blanco, who began an ambitious program of public works in the last quarter of the century.[2] The French architect Alfredo Roudier was hired to redesign the space, creating symmetry and combining garden landscapes
with tile surfaces. The placement of allegorical figures representing Art,
Commerce, Agriculture, and Industry in the corners of the plaza effectively summarized the economic and cultural dimensions of the prevailing
ideology of progress. The culmination of the redesign was the arrival and
placement of the statue of Bolívar, which would imbue this elegant garden
within a city with a reminder of the nation's martial glories.[3]

Disaster struck when the ship transporting the pieces of the bronze
Bolívar floundered off the coast of Venezuela. News of the accident created
a national panic and the Venezuelan military immediately embarked on a
self-consciously historic mission of rescue in the name of both Bolívar and
President Antonio Guzmán Blanco. The pieces of the hero were rescued
within a week and horror was transformed into collective pride at the success of the salvage operation. The state-controlled press announced that

Guzmán Blanco had effectively *liberated* the "Liberator" from watery defeat.[4] When the statue was inaugurated on November 7, commentators marveled at the massive yet peaceful forms of congregation that took place in the city center, which seemed to model the very ideal of national harmony. For the promoters of the monument, the bronze Bolívar was central to charging the landscape with historical meaning and promoting a collective, national memory in citizens. One journalist wrote, for example: "When contemplating the great Man [sic] every Venezuelan will be able to say: there is my brother; he was born here; he crossed our forests: he had our same youth: he was a boy in these places, and played in the same fields where the sons of our sons will walk and inhale his air" (*La opinión nacional*). The monument thus channeled a vital connection to the past and contributed to the construction of the "imaginary community" of the nation.[5]

The symbolic function of the statue of Bolívar was also fraught with contradictions. While it is the function of official monuments to inhabit and structure the sense of self of the national subjects they address, by their very act of political presence as physical objects raised up by governments, monuments are prone to historical contingency. In this respect, the statue of the Plaza Bolívar seemed to invite desecration from the beginning since it was closely associated with a sitting president who was fond of publicly cultivating parallels between himself and Bolívar, and whose name decorated one of the pedestal's inscriptions: EL GRAL ANTONIO GUZMAN BLANCO PRESIDENTE DE LA REPUBLICA ERIGE ESTE MONUMENTO EN 1874. [GENERAL ANTONIO GUZMAN BLANCO PRESIDENT OF THE REPUBLIC ERECTS THIS MONUMENT IN 1874.] In 1889, President Juan Pablo Rojas Paúl surrounded the statue with infantry, fearing that mobs of Guzmán Blanco's enemies would vandalize it because of its inscription. As anti-Guzmán Blanco crowds gathered in the plaza, and tensions escalated, the explosive situation was simply defused by placing a white cloth on the incriminating words. The writing on the cloth read: LA NACION AGRADECIDA A SU LIBERTADOR, ERIGE ESTE MONUMENTO EN 1874. [A GRATEFUL NATION ERECTS THIS MONUMENT TO ITS LIBERATOR IN 1874.] Bolívar now belonged to the people, not to Guzmán Blanco. Later, the stone of the pedestal was sanded down to replace the original inscription with the new one, but to this day that side of the pedestal shows a pale, horizontal discoloration.

I begin with these reflections on the Plaza Bolívar because the plaza and its monument are at the center of one of the first critiques of the modern

Figure 2. H. Neun. *Plaza Bolívar* 1877–1878. Lithograph. *Album de Caracas y Venezuela* by H. Neun (1878–1879). Reprinted by Instituto Nacional de Cultura y Bellas Artes (1968).

cult of Bolívar, Manuel Díaz Rodríguez's *Idolos rotos* (1901). Díaz Rodríguez's powerful novel uses idols, sculptures, and the monument of the Plaza Bolívar as vehicles for challenging the artifice and demagoguery of institutionalized Bolivarian nationalism. Díaz Rodríguez associates political and cultural underdevelopment with bodily degeneration and charts the decay of the nation upon the body of the monumental Bolívar. Ultimately, as the possibility of national regeneration is lost, the bronze Bolívar becomes a pathologized, feminine body. The mythic Bolívar loses the inviolable contours of its body and becomes a victim. In this chapter, I examine how Díaz Rodríguez explores Venezuelan underdevelopment through his representation of the life and loves of a young artist who returns to his native Caracas after years in Europe. In particular, I examine how the national project is linked to the promise of masculine virility, and its failure to castration and penetration. These sexual themes are framed through telling references to the monument of Bolívar in Caracas, and to patriotic statuary in general, which become objects of commerce, degeneration, and ultimately, homosexual rape.

Monuments, Dolls, and Phantoms

Díaz Rodríguez was not alone in his critique of monuments at the turn of the century. It is helpful to frame his iconoclastic novel within a more generalized ambivalence toward monumentalism during the presidency of Antonio Guzmán Blanco. I begin with a simple yet necessary axiom: the critique of monumentalism cannot be separated from its prior emergence as a vehicle for official culture. In the case of Venezuela, official Bolivarian nationalism, and the monumentalist urban renewal that accompanied it, did not arise until the presidency of Guzmán Blanco, and as such could not become an object of suspicion and critique until the end of the century. In 1874, the same year as the creation of the Plaza Bolívar, La Iglesia de la Trinidad was converted into the National Pantheon. Two years later Bolívar's remains were ceremoniously moved, in a golden sarcophagus shaped like a temple with ornate turrets, from the Cathedral to the Pantheon where they rest under ceremonial guard to this day.

However, Bolivarian public works were only one aspect of a more generalized program of urban renewal that Guzmán Blanco believed would remake Caracas into a modern city to be respected by provincials and by foreign investors (Lombardi 195). More than any previous president before him, he believed in the theatrical power of the image and in its ability to immortalize him as benefactor of the nation (Silva Beauregard 22). Guzmán Blanco's portrait and name saturated public life completely, as states, villages, aqueducts, schools, trains, and even a brand of wine were named after him (21). Many of his initiatives created architectural facades and enclosures for the liturgical celebration of national identity, while simultaneously symbolizing his personal monomania. In short, Guzmán

Blanco's identification with monumentalism made his sculptural and architectural projects visible targets for attacks against his persona. Thus,
when Guzmán Blanco fell out of favor in 1889, university students tore
down the equestrian statue of the former president and the pedestrian
statue of his father, Antonio Leocadio Guzmán. The fallen bodies were
smashed to pieces and dragged through the streets of Caracas in festive
processionals. Two newspapers of the day, sympathetic to the iconoclasm of
the masses, diminished the victimized monuments in a rhetorical act of
iconoclasm by calling them "muñecos" [dolls] (Rondón Márquez 309).

No other writer exemplifies the ambivalent role of monumentalism in
late nineteenth-century Venezuela better than Eduardo Blanco, the most
celebrated and enduring author of Bolivarian historical episodes. Despite
his popularity and his commitment to nationalist, historical memory,
Blanco's best-selling *Venezuela heroica* (1881) and his subsequent and
lesser-known *Las noches del panteón* (1895) reveal some ambivalence toward monumentalism. The first edition of *Venezuela heroica* was comprised of accounts of five famous battles of the Wars of Independence: La
Victoria (February 12, 1814), San Mateo (February and March 1814), Las
Queseras (April 3, 1819), Boyacá (August 7, 1819), and Carabobo (June 24,
1821). Blanco's episodes presented a panoramic and colorful canvas depicting patriot leaders in an epic, bloody struggle against the Royalists. The
power of the text, and its astonishing popularity in Venezuela, resulted
from its commitment to presenting the writing of history as a spectacle. In
the words of Beatriz González Stephan: "In this case, writing has the
power of plasticity. It competes with other mediums that are imposed at
the time, like painting, oratory, music, and, in a different category, fire-
works, parades, martial bands, and speeches. It must have impact. The ver-
bal sonority almost demands that it be read out loud. . . . The epic of Independence in *Venezuela heroica* is written in light of operatic decoration, of
ceremonial offerings to Guzmán Blanco, and the funerary honors in com-
memoration of the remains of national heroes in the National Pantheon"
(41). Moreover, Blanco's narrative combined temporal coordinates (dates
of battles) with spatial ones (specific places) and transformed specific landscapes into sacred spaces for the national subject. In these sacred places the
Venezuelan subject is capable of sensing the glory of the past without the
presence of commemorative markers. In other words, although Blanco
shows an awareness of the nationalist purpose of monuments, he does not
define them as the catalyst of national feeling; the monumentality of place
precedes the placement of commemorative monuments. In his evocation

of the battle site of San Mateo, Blanco defines the original inhabitant of these sacred places as memory itself (88). In short, a close look at *Venezuela heroica* reveals that its understanding of monumentalism is nuanced and tempered by its commitment to a more intangible concept of historical memory.[6]

Blanco's treatment of monuments evolved and became more pessimistic over time, culminating in his gothic tract, "Las noches del panteón." The pamphlet was commissioned as an homage to José Antonio de Sucre whose victory over the Royalists at the Battle of Ayacucho brought an end to the Wars of Independence. "Las noches del panteón" combines the gothic with martial history, resulting in a mix of shadow and patriotic nostalgia. In rejecting monumentalism in favor of a withdrawal from society into the fantastic recesses of the self, Blanco was responding to the excesses and crises of Guzmancismo, which had collapsed by 1895 in a series of coups, record unemployment, and widespread, general unrest. The illusion of stability and progress promoted by Guzmán Blanco faded, leaving a sense of disenchantment in Blanco, who now turned to phantasmagoria to describe historical memory.

"Las noches del panteón" opens with the nameless narrator wandering the streets of Caracas at night, depressed by the state of his homeland. The city is described as a vast, silent sepulcher, full of frightening and disorienting shadows that perturb the narrator, who absent-mindedly walks toward the National Pantheon. In the silence and the darkness, the narrator enters into a nebulous dimension of perception in which he cannot easily distinguish between his imaginary fears of ghosts, vampires, and dark angels and what is real. He feels alone in the world, abandoned inside a city he can only apprehend in broken-down parts: a door, a shut window, walls, and echoes. Near the National Pantheon, the ghost of a veteran of the Wars of Independence accosts the narrator. In the conversation between the narrator and this shadow, the otherworldly spirit decries the lack of patriotism and historical memory in Venezuela, and questions the notion of progress. The conversation is cut short, however, when the ghost reminds the narrator that a special celebration of the Battle of Ayacucho will be taking place in the Pantheon. The shadow guides the narrator toward the Pantheon, stopping in its plaza to reveal terrible visions of the sacrifices of the past, particularly the execution of Gual y España in 1799, the decapitation and mutilation of General José Felix Ribas in 1815, and the deaths of General Pedro María Freites and Francisco Rivas in 1817. The ghost ushers the narrator into the Pantheon and locks him into the darkness, prompting vertigo and more confusion. The Pantheon becomes illuminated in gold light, and the narrator witnesses the statue of Bolívar come to life. He watches in awe as an army of ghosts, all veterans of the Wars of Independence, heed Bolívar's call to gather in the Pantheon. As the thousands of spirits congregate, the narrator has complex visions of faraway lands and places, battlefields and events. The last to arrive is José Antonio de Sucre, upon whose head Bolívar places the crown of immortality. The text ends with the narrator waking up before dawn to find the Pantheon populated with dead marble and sepulchral silence again. Outside, in the tenuous darkness that precedes dawn, the narrator feels nostalgia for the glorious, fantastic visions that he has experienced. "Oh day!" He exclaims, "The shadows that have disappeared are better than your sun!" (74).

In "Las noches del panteón," memory is no longer a transaction between the glory of the past and the potential of the present and the promise of the future, but merely a descent into a distinctly separate and ideal realm of perception. Patriotic, historical memory has unmoored itself from an undesirable reality and taken flight into the shadowy recesses of the imagination. Monumentalism is singled out as the site of this disconnection between the mythic past and the disappointments of the present. In a revealing exchange between the narrator and the ghostly guard, the guard implies that the excess of monumentalism in modern Caracas is unsettling:

> "that which yesterday did not exist but minimally is so abundant today that it causes fright."
> "What do you allude to?" I asked him, surprised by the tone and gesture that accompanied his words. "Is it perhaps the profusion of light and monuments that the city exhibits? I presume it must be that which most surprises you."
> "Among other things, I cannot deny it. . . . Presuming to advance you have stepped backwards. . . ." (16)

The narrator's immediate association of monumentalism with decay, and the ghost's claim that Venezuela is moving backward, explains the cityscape of Caracas in the story: rather than embodying a monumental city that announces its civilization with its architectural edifications, it is a dark cemetery haunted by shadows of the dead. Caracas is not progress but the superstitious language of shadows and ghosts. Only by withdrawing from the failures of the present and surrendering to the sensory confusion provoked by melancholy is the narrator able to extricate himself from the necropolis of the nation and experience the sublimity of the Olympian past.

Eduardo Blanco's meditations on monumentalism were not the only ones of this kind. In 1884, José Martí published a description of the Plaza Bolívar that also presented the sculptural Bolívar stirring into life as a loving admirer contemplates him. In Martí's case, the scene is intended to mobilize the pan-American spirit of young people, and lacks the pessimistic overtones of Blanco's text. Another text, José Gil Fortoul's novel, *Pasiones*, which appeared the same year as "Las noches del panteón," describes the destruction of the tyranny of Guzmán Blanco in relation to the destruction of statues. Yet, Blanco's meditations on monuments in *Venezuela heroica* and his peculiar mix of gothic and martial history in "Las noches del panteón" represent the most profound challenge to nationalist monumentalism before the publication of *Idolos rotos* in 1901.

Statuary in *Idolos rotos*

Idolos rotos tells the story of Alberto Soria, who travels to France to study engineering at the turn of the century. Upon taking a grand tour of Italy and falling under the spell of Florence and Michelangelo's *Night* in the Mausoleum of the Medici, Soria decides to become a sculptor. He is moderately successful and sculpts a well-received work titled *Fauno robador de ninfas*. The beginning of Soria's artistic career is interrupted by news of his father's failing health, which compels him to leave his life in Paris behind. In Caracas, Soria quickly comes into conflict with the cultural and political establishment centered in the Plaza Bolívar, and which views all transatlantic Venezuelans as foreign and arrogant. While he becomes part of a group of fellow expatriates intent on restoring Venezuela to its past glories, Soria grows closer to a childhood friend, María. However, the promise of marriage and integration into Venezuelan society fades as Soria becomes suspicious and jealous. In a state of anomie, he succumbs to the seductive Teresa, a married woman who becomes a model for an unfinished sculpture titled *Voluptuosidad*. The novel ends with a revolution that overthrows the Venezuelan Caesar and installs a new one in his place.[7] Simultaneously, the novel closes with two moments of rupture relating to Soria's sentimental life and art. María discovers the unfinished *Voluptuosidad* in Soria's studio and flies into a blind range. Meanwhile, Soria visits the Palace of Fine Arts, a building that has been taken over by the triumphant army of the revolution, to check on his sculptures. He is horrified to see that his replicas of Antinoos, Apollo, and Venus have been thrown down and manhandled, mauled, and raped by soldiers armed with bayonets. The novel closes with Soria writing the words "FINIS PATRIA" on his heart.

True to its title, sculptures in crisis, or broken idols, abound in the novel. On the one hand, we have Soria's sculptures: the *Fauno robador de ninfas*, which represents the healthy sensuality of his Parisian love, Juliet; the *Venus criolla*, a sculpture he undertakes during the brief interregnum of happiness provoked by his love affair with María; and *Voluptuosidad*, which represents the world of unbridled desire represented by Teresa, who is a kind of Medusa. Patriotic statuary also figures prominently in the story, complementing and echoing the themes of personal redemption and degeneration that are associated with Soria's sculpture. Most importantly, the monument to Bolívar appears, as well as a projected statue of José Antonio Sucre that has been commissioned by the government. Rather than serving as sites of inspiration and power as they were intended, these monuments become broken idols that allegorize Soria's moral degeneration as well as the corruption of a nation ruled by base instincts.

Although he does not explore official monumentalism, Aníbal González's analysis of the sculptures that appear in the novel provides us with a starting point for a discussion of the many "idols" that appear in the text. González suggests that Soria's sculptures may be read as a critique of late nineteenth-century Neoplatonism, as exemplified by the Uruguayan essayist José Enrique Rodo (124). González observes how Soria's statues or "idols" represent different aspects of fin-de-siècle Latin American modernism: the *Fauno* as Hellenic symbolism; the *Venus criolla* as aesthetic Americanism; and *Voluptuosidad* as sensualism (125). González's argument suggests that these sculptures are not only different modalities of modernism, but modalities of the self that Soria explores as alternatives for the definition of his own identity (130). What remain to be clarified are the ways in which the sculptural aesthetics that González defines become the basis of a political critique.

At the very outset, Díaz Rodríguez establishes a Neoplatonic theme that explains his subsequent treatment of art, politics, and the personal development of Soria as a man. During his grand tour of Italy, Soria contemplates Michelangelo's *Night* and is fascinated by the possibility of penetrating the secret of the master's work and finishing it. The narrative voice steps back, however, to observe that many years later, Soria would come to realize that such designs would violate the purity of Michelangelo's masterpiece: "'They are best like that,' he thought. 'They are best like that, in their painful dawn; perhaps more beautiful, certainly more pure. Like open flowers, partly living the glorious life of a completed work, partly hidden in the impenetrable piece of unpolished marble, it was as if those creations of the greatest of artists had felt, for a moment, an awareness of their future perfection, and, in the supreme pride of their beauty, had stayed in the portals of life, fearful of being profaned, disdaining contact with the restless ugliness and vanity of man'" (59). In their unfinished state, Michelangelo's forms capture a moment of flight, the purest spark of a creation that has not been desecrated by completion. To complete them would be to give them a material fixity that would separate them from the ideal realm. This is the chaste mystery of *Night*, the feminine timidity and virginity of perfection, which is juxtaposed with the desecrating touch of man. Throughout *Idolos rotos*, in his plotting of Venezuelan political and social life, Díaz Rodríguez focuses on the promise and failure of achieving this delicate mediation between ideal and material forms.

The promise of achieving in the political realm what Michelangelo achieved in *Night* is explored through descriptions of political reforms that will ultimately not come to fruition. For example, Soria's younger brother Pedro states the difference between himself and his brother in relation to their deceased uncle, who is also named Alberto: Alberto Soria the younger is all ideals, Pedro is all political expediency, while the deceased Uncle Alberto crystallized a kind of idealistic, political commitment that is only possible in a moment of origins, of projection, before the corruption of having to subordinate ideals to reality (166). Uncle Alberto, a "poet of the cause" died poor, suggesting that this founder successfully resisted the corrupting temptations of the terrestrial realm (166). Although Díaz Rodríguez does not hint that Uncle Alberto should be read as an echo of Bolívar, it is worthwhile to consider that Alberto the elder's glory resonates with the glory of Bolívar: both were foundational figures who died poor, before their designs could be realized.

The parallel between Uncle Alberto and Simón Bolívar is accentuated when we consider how certain characters in the novel explore the possibility of political reform. A group of foreign educated bohemians, known in Caracas as the *inconformes*, meet in Soria's studio to plan a new political party. The details of their analysis of Venezuelan underdevelopment and their utopian plans for the future are predicated on a sophisticated awareness of the problem of cultural and economic dependence. Emazábel, the young doctor who leads the group of foreign educated cosmopolitans, evokes the sincerity of conviction and purity of spirit of Soria's uncle; although deprived of the status and dynastic ties to the foundational names of nineteenth-century Venezuela, Emazábel has inherited from his father a repository of "moral" riches. He opens the meeting with a detailed analysis of the corrupting force of Paris upon young Latin Americans, who are seduced and devoured by the city and returned to their homelands in a more primitive state, their souls made monstrous and their appetites hungry for government jobs and more money to return to the sybaritic life of Europe (223–24).

According to Emazábel, the trap of Parisian seduction for the Latin American intellectual incapacitates him upon his return to the homeland. He becomes a foreigner among his own, and wastes away his precious cultural capital in "sterile" nostalgia for the boulevards, cafés, and theaters of Paris. The task at hand, argues Emazábel, is to harness the potential of the inconformes and transform them into a new political vanguard. The inconformes can be the ones to constitute a national sense of shared interests and aspirations by spreading the word through print, the public lecture, and the art exhibition. "A luminous and beautiful word of science or art, pronounced at the right time," says Emazábel, "has an incalculable reach for he who pronounces it and sows it like a line of gold" (228). Emazábel returns to the gendered subtext of his prior condemnation of Parisian degeneration by declaring that the nationalizing of culture will result in the reinvention of the homeland as a virgin trunk, "dressed in foliage, crowned with flowers" (229). Further, this national program is allegorized as an insemination of the land, suggesting that political commitment channels the male virility lost in Paris toward a more reproductive end. The theme of recovered masculinity is echoed as the meeting breaks up into the cool January night, when the inconformes note that they, like the apostles, will be "planting the seed of redemption" in their homeland (232).

Struck by the momentousness and glory of their project, Díaz Rodríguez tellingly pauses to describe the overseeing spirit of the whole affair as the shadow of Bolívar, whom he does not name directly but rather references through the myth of his feats: "that great shadow, of that hero that was the thunder of the peaks and the marvel of volcanoes" (233). Emazábel's plans, like Michelangelo's *Night* and Uncle Alberto's time of political foundations, represent a gesture toward a pure, Bolivarian ideal that is presented as an unfinished and incomplete gesture, one that has not yet been desecrated by materiality. The sculptural connection to Michelangelo's *Night* is also underlined by the effects Emazábel's words have on Soria, who envisions the nation of tomorrow as a block of marble in which Soria sees a prodigious statue-in-waiting (219). Emazábel himself invokes the image of sculpting the nation, referring to the masses as a "hard bronze" that needs to be shaped by a national program. In both cases, these monuments to be share the sublimity of *Night* in their intangibility; the inconformes recognize that they are embarking upon a long-term, utopian project, the results of which are distant. Thus, Díaz Rodríguez reiterates a previous passage in which Pedro tells his brother that, in politics, as in religion, the moment of birth is the moment of perfection. Like Uncle Alberto, Emazábel and his followers have entered into the blessed age of foundations. Their monument, half-sculpted by their commitment to action, remains shrouded in the shapelessness of stone and bronze, and as such remains pure.

The actual statue of Bolívar in the Plaza Bolívar, as well as a projected one of Marshall José Antonio de Sucre, clarify how the nationalism of the inconformes differs from the ideology of the state, which has desecrated Venezuela's heroes by subordinating them to material self-interest. One of Soria's friends, Romero, gives Díaz Rodríguez pause to examine explicitly the disjunction between the ideal cult of Bolívar and the official cult. Romero is an avid Bolivarian whose veneration of the hero of independence is so great that he considers it his duty to serve the memory of the Liberator. As a student in Paris, Romero produced an insightful and ambitious study of how Venezuela's educational system could be transformed by European-style reforms. This encapsulated national project is received with a deadening silence in Caracas, where it passes virtually unnoticed in official and educational circles. Similarly, Romero is unable to make his mark, in the name of Bolívar, through a position at the Ministry of Education. Instead, he finds work as a copy editor at an official newspaper while contributing literary compositions to other newspapers in his free time. One day while Romero and Soria are walking through the Plaza Bolívar, Romero's bitterness overflows into an impassioned plea for the disappearance of the statue of Bolívar: "And talking, talking, with the same bitter desperation, Romero ended up wishing that the Bolívar of the monument in the plaza and his bronze horse would disappear suddenly, one afternoon, in the rain of the twilight's roses, in a flash of lightning, so that they would not honor any longer that piece of damned soil with their glorious weight" (215–16). The destruction of the monument of Bolívar through an act of nature or divine retribution does result in an iconoclastic scene, but its target is ultimately the Venezuelan state. The symbol of Bolívar remains a principle of the ideal, one that must be protected by separating it from the materialism and opportunism of the political establishment.

The divorce of national heroes from their monumental, official versions is also played out through a projected statue of Sucre that is repeatedly mentioned as a possible commission for Soria from the government. The statue is continuously trapped in a series of strategic moves and counter-moves by Pedro, who is trying to secure the commission for his brother, and whose conception of the stakes and ultimate meaning of the statue is prescient: "The statue is a pretext. Neither in it nor in its erection will there be even a hint of the apotheosis of the hero. It won't be anything more than a deal, one of many deals intended to distract the poor of spirit. Don't get your hopes up Alberto" (168). The statue finally slips through Alberto's hands when he withdraws from the political economy of bribery and material self-gain that a government minister tries to impose on him. "Even the president will want a piece of the statue!" exclaims the minister as he advises Soria to be less selfless (321). The statue of Sucre clearly represents the potential and corruption of monumental heroes; potential insofar as in the hands of Soria the statue would become an object of the selflessness of art and patriotism, and corruption in the sense that the re-gime cannot reconcile such ideal standards within the formula of govern-ment as a business venture.

The Work of Gender in *Idolos rotos*

The full impact and import of Díaz Rodríguez's critical assessment of Bolivarian nationalism and Venezuelan underdevelopment cannot be un-derstood without examining the romantic relationships that constitute the novel's melodrama. Alberto Soria's relationships with Juliet, María, and Teresa document his continual struggle to situate himself in the world: as a man, as an artist, and as a Venezuelan national. Juliet, his Parisian love, represents the creative and romantic zenith Soria reaches in Europe. Soria's relationship with María charts his struggle to reconcile with a homeland that he cannot bring himself to believe in entirely. Finally, Soria's descent into the chaos of the sexual desire embodied by Teresa re-veals his surrender to the debased, oriental instincts that make the home-land a feverish and violent stage for cyclical and sterile revolutionism. The debasement of self that results from Soria's liaisons with Teresa, and which allegorizes the failure of the nation itself, leads the text back into the symbolic logic of statues, and to the Plaza Bolívar as a site of disease, seduction, and corporeal degeneration. Hence, the novel focuses its political and moral critiques through an "erotics" of national degeneration that ultimately contaminates the space occupied by the monumental Bolívar.

Juliet is maligned as a monstrous seductress several times, beginning with an unnamed Latin American in Paris who complains to Emazábel that Soria has become yet another victim of the pleasures of the city, as embodied by Juliet and her perverse and infinitely curious mouth (62). In turn, Emazábel recasts these arguments—without mentioning Juliet by name—in his meeting with the inconformes: "The starting point of many adulteries in the bosom of Cosmópolis . . . was an error that was very analogous to that of every American student recently arrived to Paris, believing himself to be in the presence of a fine lady upon seeing the first flirt dressed in gems, lace, and rubies" (223). Further, Soria's own ambivalence toward his experiences in France and his attempts to reintegrate himself back into Venezuelan life make him accept the misogynist argument that his relationship with Juliet was merely a function of sensuality and corruption. The narrative voice, however, subtly frames these judgments as a product of a narrow, Catholic upbringing, establishing that Juliet is not impure but rather a pliable and obedient partner in a sensual love relationship that nurtures Soria's artistic quest for transcendence (156). The sculpture Fauno robador de ninfas, which may be read as allegorizing both his days in Paris and his first love, is Soria's most successful engagement with woman and his surrounding environment.

The novel's praise for Juliet as a collaborator of Soria, then, may be read in relation to her as a model, as a lover capable of maintaining Soria's purity of vision while surrendering her body. In this light, it is hardly coincidental that Díaz Rodríguez's description of the artist-model relationship that resulted in the creation of Soria's second sculpture, Venus criolla, suggests a violation. The artist's ensuing dissatisfaction with the resulting sculpture represents his dissatisfaction with the intranscendence of carnality. Soria finds a poor mulatto woman recently arrived to the city to be his model, and in order to sculpt her, has to overcome considerable "difficulty and resistances" (188). Díaz Rodríguez displaces the fear of this young woman onto the sculpture, the posture of which is "chaste and timid" and describes the act of sculpting as an impregnation: "The clay, between Soria's fingers, impregnated itself with the soft languidness and grace of movement of living forms, like the clay of an amphora impregnated with perfume" (emphasis added, 188). The resulting sculpture, the product of pleasure and domination, drives a wedge between love and creation, elements that had been harmonized together in the *Fauno robador de ninfas*. Far from being the monstrous embodiment of the temptress that depletes man's creative virility, Juliet's symbolic body promotes the expression of that virility. When Soria struggles to negate his desire for women toward the end of the novel, he fantasizes about never surrendering his name to "Woman," the "instinctive female" that threatens his art and his glory (252). Undoubtedly, Juliet's submission, inspiration, and protectiveness, to say nothing of the ensuing public success of *Fauno robador de ninfas*, mark her as distinct from this category of "instinctive female" that Soria cannot reconcile. In the gallery of idols contained in the novel, Juliet is the only image of wholeness, but hers is an image and experience that never is articulated to the national project that Soria and the inconformes embark upon. In this respect, Juliet's role in the novel is inaccurately represented by Emazábel's disparagement of Paris. Juliet energizes the equilibrium between sensuality (materiality) and purity (the ideal) without threatening Soria's masculinity. In fact, the artistic program embodied by Juliet is a model for a successful, transformative engagement with reality. However, this model, and the promise it holds as a deep structure for national reform and a national aesthetic, will go unfulfilled in Venezuela, as Soria's affairs with María and Teresa demonstrate.

In *Foundational Fictions: The National Romances of Latin America*, Doris Sommer argues that nineteenth-century novels sought to transform class and regional divisions to achieve a "national" synthesis through the union of lovers. The erotic nexus in these fictions, she argues, becomes politicized and charged with national transcendence, laying the symbolic foundations of identity.[8] Soria's second lover, María Almeida, may be read as representing a failed attempt at this kind of symbolic foundation. She briefly tames the European excess and cosmopolitan snobbishness of Soria. At first, his love for María causes him to conform to his native environment. He rejects the memory of Juliet and softens his attitudes toward his family, including his brother-in-law Uribe, who represents the impoverished state of intellectual and cultural life in Caracas. Soria's relationship to the cityscape changes as he begins to perceive it as a well-delineated, Hellenic space. In this moment of peace, he experiences something akin to "pure water" flowing out from the dirty streets, "lusty" gardens, poor neighborhoods, construction zones, and the faraway coffee plantations sprayed with red fruit (157). This is the moment and possibility of conformity for the Europeanized Soria, who is now able to negate the disarray of the city and treat it from a distance, containing its unruly body through an aesthetic that makes it available to him as something picturesque, rather than something menacing. Díaz Rodríguez narrates the idyll of this moment as a transport to an alternate experiential space, and shades it like a fairy-tale: Soria and María find in each other's love the way back into a pristine landscape of trust and purity through memory, which sculpts and re-sculpts the self in ever-increasing, beautiful forms (236). Soria and María become children on a path lined with the daisies of memory, until a menacing shadow emerges to destroy that world and innocence.

The passing mention of María's former lover, Vásquez, a man associated with the social and political cells of power that Soria disdains, changes everything. Soria becomes obsessed with Vásquez and in the process loses the ability to believe in María, his art, and the nation. The pastoral mode is eclipsed by a dark and controlling passion that begins to sculpt Soria in its own image (Aníbal González 128). He loses agency, distance, and control, and finds his idols of pure love broken at the hands of this apparition, which says to him: "From now onwards memories don't flower for you. If despite my admonishing counsel you do not retreat and pass, in vain you will seek ideal daisies on the edges of routes and paths: once there were many and their petals were plucked by another's hands. Instead of daisies you will find asphodels, a great field of asphodels, an interminable field of asphodels, the flowers of which will bring to you, like a perfume, the most mortal of sadnesses to disturb your reason, dirty your life and eat away at your insides" (240). The striking passage recasts the narrative of the end of Eden, and highlights how the knowledge of María's past love destroys not only Soria's trust in her as a woman, but also the possibility of imagining underdevelopment beneficently and aesthetically; there has been a shift from the "pure waters" of the picturesque tropicality of an edenic Caracas, to the other Caracas, a shadow world of corruption that negates the foundational union between Soria and María. The apparition now consumes Soria, who is incapable of fully possessing María and the nation through his art. This paralysis is described in a passage in which Soria searches for a nickname for María that will allow him to possess her in a way that she has never been possessed before; when Soria finds that name (María Luisa) he is overjoyed at his renewed ability to "own" her. This drive to possess María is tied to the need to recover her virginity, and by extension, the idealized contours of the homeland. Thus, the success of Soria's love relationship and the possibility of reimagining Venezuela along more idealized lines is predicated on the ability to seed them in an originary fashion.

When the pretense of María's virginal image is annulled, Soria loses the drive to enact the grandiose plans for national regeneration that Emazábel had exhorted his inconformes to pursue. Like María, the patria has been sullied, and cannot be restored to an ideal realm.

At this point, Soria is driven into the arms of Teresa Farías, his final love interest, who embodies the primitive forces of the homeland. The relationship with Farías will set the stage for the final, impassioned pages of the novel, which present Soria's descent into pleasure as an allegory of the revolution that violates Soria's sculptures, and by association the monument of Bolívar. The connection between Soria's surrender to Teresa and the failure of the nation is made clear at the outset of the novel, before both characters catch a glimpse of each other at sundown. Soria contemplates the sunset one evening during one of his walks, watching with awe the "soft, phantasmagoric fire" of "rose petals" descending upon the city skyline (88). In a "flash of lightning" he notices a shrouded woman at the entrance of a chapel, veiled like a Turkish woman in Istanbul, looking at him in a way that unnerves him. "Little coquette, Alberto told himself, and continued home, agitated by the thousands of confusing sensations of that day. He thought of the new neighborhood, seen from atop the hill of the Calvario, built on arid land the color of ochre; he thought of the unclean streets; he saw, again, upon those dirty streets, the unflowering of the infinite rose petals of sunset. And inside him flashed the vision of the native city as an oriental city, disgusting and beautiful" (90). Caracas is thus presented as a dancing Salomé, simultaneously attracting and repulsing Soria. The chromatic elements of the description of the sunset are also significant, for they clarify Romero's vision of the monument of Bolívar disappearing in a "twilight of roses" and in a "flash of lightning" (216). Teresa's gaze, framed in the same colors as Romero's despairing vision, suggest that she and her seduction of Soria represent a moment of destruction parallel to the unmooring of the statue of Bolívar. Soria's surrender to Teresa is ultimately a surrender to a social reality defined by moral turpitude, political opportunism, and barbaric revolution. While he is with María, Soria resists, but the power of his self-doubt in the wake of learning about Vásquez leads him astray into the arms of Teresa and defeat.

As an object of carnal desire, Teresa is as memorable a femme fatale as any other in nineteenth-century Western literature. The motif of attraction and repulsion is repeated throughout the novel as Díaz Rodríguez presents her body as maddeningly multiple, shapeless, and pleasurable. He describes her body surrendering to sensory experiences that resist con-

tainment and clear definition, like desire itself. For example, Díaz Rodríguez shows her merging with the body of the sea in her daily baths, as if
pleasurably collecting the countless kisses of innumerable mouths in the
arms of a "monstrous and lascivious" lover (288). This image of a body
surrounded, enclosed, and awash in seductive caresses is in turn recast
when we see how Teresa's oceanic body overwhelms Soria. Her hands are
separate creatures, white butterflies that flutter across his body, pleasuring
him into exhaustion, and giving him the sensation that his own body is
being broken down (286). The rush of voluptuosity is like an inundation
in Soria's studio, washing away his transcendent designs, including Emazábel's national project, and leaving in its place the turbulent and agitated
fog of carnal pleasure.

Another aspect of Teresa as a deity of pleasure that assaults order, transcendent art, and Soria's virility is her religious mysticism, which leads the
lovers to rendezvous in darkened churches and participate in mysterious,
devotional ceremonies. The refraction of the religious experience through
the prism of her eroticism transforms her religiousness into an "other"
Christianity, a shadow religion made up of pagan ritual and oriental sensualism. Religious practice becomes yet another physical, sensory ablution:
Teresa cleanses herself in an exotic bath of incense and church gloom in
order to return to her adulterous affair with renewed passion. The poten-
tially civilizing force of religion is thus inverted in the shadow world of
Teresa, for whom it becomes a measure of her instinctive desires. For
Teresa, love, art, and religion are not ideal projections, but dark, magical
forces to be had for pleasure. For instance, when Teresa agrees to model for
Soria, she does so out of a primitive fascination with the powerful creative
forces of his sculptural art (298). Nevertheless, she soon tires of watching
Soria caress her replica-in-progress and urges him to confer upon her body
all of his caresses. Trapped in Teresa's pleasure, Soria's art becomes a
shadow of its former self and becomes entangled in the representational
quicksands of trying to delineate the pleasure that washes over him when
he is with her. In short, he cannot sculpt her body because he cannot sub-
vert the hold it has over his senses. His unfinished sculpture *Voluptuosidad* is ultimately an attempt to sculpt pleasure and as such, is an uncontrolled, formless mass.

In her disdain for the ideal, Teresa symbolizes the temptation of the
baser instincts within Soria and within the Venezuelan landscape and body
politic. In falling into the abyss of this landscape, Soria leaves behind the
generative nationalizing project of Emazábel, the foundational promise of

his union with María, and the possibility of a regenerative artistic expression. In falling into Teresa's arms, Soria has allowed his relationship to himself, his art, and his nation to hit bottom; if Juliet embodied the transcendent potentiality of Soria's identity abroad and María the attempt to construct a viable image of the self in the nation, Teresa is undoubtedly the monstrosity of the homeland tearing Soria apart as he surrenders to it. His ultimate failure to engage in a nationally redemptive project is not a result of the monstrosity of Paris, as Emazábel's analysis indicates, but the paralyzing effect of the "oriental" degeneracy and attraction of a whorish homeland on his agency as a man, an intellectual, and an artist.

Soria's failure is not his alone, but characterizes all the members of his family as well, drawing attention to a generalized dimming of a seigniorial principle based upon the foundational origins and genealogies of a liberal, patrician class (Salas de Lecuna, *Ideología y lenguaje* 18). Although the novel does not dwell too much on the proprietary elements of the Soria family, it does suggest that its single, remaining agricultural possession is not a source of wealth and production but rather a residual status symbol (Díaz Rodríguez 162). The loss of the landed estates that defined the power of the Sorias in the past is also echoed in Soria's reaction to a government minister who had once been an agricultural laborer: "That man? He is just a poor devil of a peasant who doesn't know his place, ignorant of everything" (94). The Soria family's access to privilege and political power is clearly in a process of disintegration as Don Pancho the patriarch dies and the new generation fails to propagate the clan through successful, reproductive unions. These failures may in turn be viewed as symptomatic of a crisis of masculinity. Rosa, Soria's sister, is not only married to an impotent and dependent Uribe, but she is also the focal point of a family folding in upon itself in the absence of a mother figure. Soria's feelings for his sister are tinged with a lover's desire and jealousies, as well as by nostalgia for his mother. Further, because she has been forced into the role of primary caregiver to her father, who decries her union with Uribe, Rosa is also structurally cast into an ambiguous location between her husband and her father, both of whom are symbolically castrated males. Pedro, Soria's brother, indulges in the sensual life with no apparent intentions of pursuing marriage. The consummate politician in ascendance, Pedro struggles to make a name for himself and his family at all costs, cynically recognizing the rules of the game. His lack of interest in matrimony and reproduction may be seen as a measure of his commitment to the machinations of the corrupt political system; unlike his brother at the outset of the novel,

Pedro is not interested in guiding his actions through ideals, but in adapting to the corrupt milieu of national politics. In sum, the Soria children have been defeated: Rosa through her marriage to a sickly man, Pedro for his refusal to entertain serious relationships, and finally Alberto, who is seduced by Teresa. In a novel that underscores the importance of masculine virility for the national project, as in Emazábel's promotion of a messianic and patriarchal seeding of the nation, the failures of the Soria clan encode the failure of the national project as a crisis of masculine virility.

The intertwining of sexual and political themes, particularly in relation to masculinity, leads us back to monumentalism and the Plaza Bolívar. Soria's descent into sexual chaos is represented quite specifically in the novel as a wounding of the monument of Bolívar. In depicting Soria's affair with Teresa, Díaz Rodríguez restages previous descriptions of Caracas and of Teresa by describing the plaza as a disordered, diseased space that mirrors the illicit and morally injurious nature of their affair: "That afternoon, upon parting with Teresa, Alberto walked down to the Plaza Bolívar, like all afternoons at the same hour. The plaza's aspect had changed: it had grown little by little both in beauty and ugliness, without anyone daring to note if its ugliness was greater, or its beauty overlaid its ugliness like an opulent dress over an ulcer. . . . The acacias, all blooming, were like trees of fire. Above, on each branch, on each leaf, a cricket. And every cricket was a strident chirp, like the highest note of a crystal string vibrating in frenzy or jubilation until breaking. Below, staining the mosaic of the plaza, a mess of corrupt political players" (308–9). The image of the plaza as an ulcer in an opulent dress reiterates Soria's perception of Teresa throughout the novel as both base and beautiful, but takes it a step further: hiding beneath the folds of her seductive attire she is the very wound of sexual contagion, waiting to corrupt man. Moreover, the passage eroticizes the plaza as the very space in which Soria and Teresa experience each other sexually. The sounds of the vibrating crickets reproduce the sensory experience of Soria's pleasure upon his nerves, which are kept in a constant and deadening state of sensitivity by contact with Teresa (301). In conjunction with the din of crickets, Díaz Rodríguez's mention of "trees of fire" highlights the symbolic motif of the seductive flame of sunrise and sunset as a sign of both destruction and attraction. He goes on to populate the plaza with milling throngs of corrupt politicians, all of which add to the frenetic, carnival-like atmosphere of the city center (311, 316). Díaz Rodríguez's choice of the word *carnival* is particularly suggestive in light of the Bakhtinian connotations of the term; Teresa's unruly and disconnected body, corrupting boundaries and hierarchies, is carnival personified. Like the female sexuality that Soria fears so much, the plaza is an abyss in which excess corrupts sacral truths, breaking down limits between truth and falsity, patriotism and self-interest, beauty and ugliness. Most importantly however, is the fact that the monumental space of Bolívar is feminized and pathologized, as if Romero's despairing fantasy of the disappearance of the statue of Bolívar has ultimately come true. This space is no longer the space of genealogical foundation, of an august, nationalist patrilineality, but of a bodily corruption associated with woman.

Soon after this iconoclastic representation of the Plaza Bolívar, we come to the final scenes of the novel, when Soria discovers that hands and bayonets have mauled his sculptures in a simulacrum of rape. The Venezuelan Caesar has been overthrown and replaced by a new one when Soria and Romero arrive at the Palace of Fine Arts, which has been converted into a barracks for the revolutionary army. Soria discovers that his sculptures have been thrown down and assaulted: "The son of Leto, Apollo, descended from his pedestal, his arms and foot broken, defeated, not triumphant, was lying on the floor face down. In that same ignominious posture, very close to Apollo, was Antinoos of the divine forms. And both, as if murdered by betrayal, held in their backs, in the lowest part of the trunk, the mouth of a deep wound" (354).

Apollo the triumphant is now overthrown, placed in a position of submission, and penetrated in a simulacrum of homosexual violation. The passage underscores the corruption of art, but also of civilized political processes, which have been undermined once again by the perennial return to violence. More significantly, however, the integrity of the masculine form has been violated in a scene that echoes the fractured virility of Soria and the inconformes. Thus framed, it is not a stretch to suggest that the violation of Apollo and Antinoos references the violation of the most sacred of political sculptures in the novel: the bronze equestrian Bolívar. When Soria inscribes "FINIS PATRIA" on his heart, the failure is complete. Soria's hopes for becoming a respected artist in Caracas, for finding true love, and participating in Emazábel's modernizing, Bolivarian reforms, are all shattered. Soria, who had once aspired to fashion himself as a nationalist political subject with something to contribute to the nation, is immobilized and transformed into a monument to failure.

Monumental Ambivalence

Idolos rotos illustrates the desires and anxieties that aggregate around national monuments, strengthening or weakening their symbolic hold on the citizenry and nation-building intellectuals. Along with national historiography, republican catechisms, and the creation of a national literature, public monuments in nineteenth-century Latin America sought to envelop the citizen within the fold of the mythologies of the nation, not in the name of blind obedience, but rather personal devotion. Unlike print culture, however, monuments and their accompanying cultic spaces, such as plazas and parks, functioned quite literally as sites where the fiction of national unity could be fleetingly materialized through crowded public festivals and ceremonies. In this respect, monumental spaces functioned like the religious enclosure of a church or a cathedral, inviting their devotees to commune with higher realms in a site demarcated as sacred and separate.[9] And yet, monuments and monumental spaces are historically contingent and dependent on a constant process of renewal in order to remain alive as catalysts of national sentiment. Monuments that fall out of use, or which are decontextualized by changing urban landscapes, may fall into a forgetful sleep, and become cadavers of stone. Delmira Agustini described this ossification of the monument in her poem "La estatua":

> Move that body, give it a soul!
> See the greatness that in its form sleeps
>
> . . . .
>
> See it up there, miserable, inert.
> More miserable than a worm, always calm! (442)

The paradox is that monuments seek to inhabit material and ideal realms simultaneously, transcending their own materiality through their function as catalysts of historical memory and identity. Generally speaking, however, the paradox of the monument as both a titan of materiality and a titan of the spirit troubles the symbolic work of its fictions of identity by introducing the possibility of driving a wedge between the monument's physical presence and its transcendent purpose.

Díaz Rodríguez's novel is indeed iconoclastic, but only in the narrow sense of the destruction of representational idols. The spirit of Bolívar, which is mentioned fleetingly as the spirit overseeing the political designs of the *inconformes*, is not assailed in the novel, nor are the aesthetic values represented by Michelangelo's *Night* and the sculptures of Apollo and

Antinoos. Yet, it is significant that Díaz Rodríguez refuses to elaborate, in a programmatic way, on what shape these spiritual values should take in order to succeed in transforming Venezuelan society. If we take his analysis of *Night* as a cornerstone of the aesthetic and political themes of the novel, Díaz Rodríguez negates the very plausibility of sculpting the nation into an accurate simulacrum of ideal forms. With regard to Soria, we may assume that he will leave the homeland again. What began as a journey home, to the New World, is transformed into a flight to the Old World. Like Bolívar himself, during his final journey toward death, Soria discovers that all his plans have come to nothing, and that he has, in the famous words of the dying hero, "plowed the sea" (Masur 484).

3

The Promise of Bolivarian Paternity

For to teach morality is neither to preach nor to indoctrinate; it is
to explain. If we refuse the child all explanation of this sort, if we
do not try to help him understand the reasons for the rules he
should abide by, we would be condemning him to an incomplete
and inferior morality.
Emile Durkheim

To its heroes a nation erects statues of bronze; if the hero is a
great soldier he rides on a high pedestal above the public square.
But the nation wants to know also the psychology of its hero,
which of course no monument can represent. . . .
Emil Ludwig

In 1826 Simón Bolívar and his famous panegyrist, José Joaquín Olmedo,
were visiting their Guayaquileño friends Dr. Luis Fernando Vivero y To-
ledo and his wife, Francisca Garaicoa, when the couple's six-year-old son,
José María, also known as Pepito, rushed into the Liberator's arms. As
Bolívar held the boy on his lap, he was informed that Pepito was lazy and
had not yet learned to read. When Bolívar questioned the boy, Pepito complained of the poor quality of his alphabet primer. Bolívar inspected the
text and agreed with Pepito about its poor quality: "My little friend is
right: the primer is inadequate, and that is why Pepito does not learn
quickly. . . . Olmedo will be in charge of writing a satisfactory one, and I will
come and test the boy" (Olmedo 280). Olmedo delivered his primer a few
days later, and shortly afterward Bolívar listened as Pepito recited the alphabet, beginning with A for "Amor de patria" [Love of the Homeland]:

Love of the homeland encompasses
All that man must love:
His God, his laws, his home,
And the honor that defends them. (161)

Until Z for "zelo" (zeal):

Zeal in carrying out his duty
Under any condition,
Will be the only ambition
That a child should harbor. (163)

For his efforts, Pepito was rewarded by Bolívar with a bust and a package of candy (280). The image of Pepito on Bolívar's lap, playing with his medals, as the hero caresses the boy's head is memorable because the association of Bolívar with children is so unusual in official Bolivarian iconography and historiography. The myth of Bolívar is primarily martial and best illustrated by the institutionalized coldness of equestrian monuments in public plazas.

Despite the official silence surrounding the subject during his lifetime, Bolívar claimed that he had proof that he was not sterile.[1] Ever since there has been much speculation about the possible offspring of the hero. Most sensational of all, some scholars have suggested that Bolívar fathered Flora Tristan with Teresa Laisney in Paris in 1807 or 1808, which would make him Paul Gauguin's grandfather (Cacua Prada 146). Another noteworthy case is that of María Costas Quintana, from Potosí, who allegedly gave birth to a son by Bolívar in 1826.[2] Canonical biographies and histories, such as those by Masur (1948), Mijares (1964), and Liévano Aguirre (1956) do not mention any offspring at all, and neither does Ramón Darío Suárez's exhaustive 600-page study of Bolívar's genealogy (1970), which declares that the hero left no known offspring (55).

In canonical biographies, the story of Bolívar as a potential father is narratively truncated the moment his wife dies in 1801, ending his anonymous life as the mayor of San Mateo, where he and his wife lived for a short time. "'Had I not been widowed, my life would perhaps have been different' declared Bolívar. 'I would not have become General Bolívar or the Liberator of South America'" (Masur 45). Since the end of the nineteenth century, Bolivarian educators have sought to realize the promise of this interrupted domesticity by constructing a Bolivarian discourse appropriate for the education of children as citizens. In this canon of juvenile literature, Bolívar is constructed as an accessible parental figure who takes the time to sit around and chat amiably with children. For example, in Vinicio Romero Martínez's *Las aventuras de Simón Bolívar: Autobiografía del Libertador* (1976), a text authorized by the Venezuelan Ministry of Education for use in public schools, a little boy falls asleep on the doorstep of the house where Bolívar was born, and dreams that the hero of independence opens the door.[3] In his dream, Bolívar is a gregarious and warm presence. The boy catches himself speaking informally and asks permission to speak to the Liberator with the tú form:

> "First . . . let me tell you . . . may I speak to you in the tú form?"
> "Of course! That is what I most desire, that you treat me like your best friend, not like a God or Semigod; that all keep me in their hearts, like I keep all in mine. . . . Would you like to take my hand and travel with me, step by step, my whole life, my good and bad fortunes?"
> "I will follow you and I will listen to you, Simón Bolívar." (Romero Martínez 10–11)

Romero Martínez animates the hero of independence by situating him in a liminal dream state, in which expressions of filial tenderness, such as the use of the tú form and holding hands, are possible. Further, as illustrated in the passage, Romero Martínez has Bolívar declare that access to Bolivarian identity formation should be sentimental rather than hierarchical.

The didactic nature of Bolivarian children's literature makes it an invaluable site for the exploration of how Bolívar is used by nationalist intellectuals to create good citizens who will eventually contribute to the nation. The authors of these texts are faced with the daunting task of laying the very foundations of Bolivarian identity in readers who are just beginning to learn about themselves and their place in the world. For example, in *Bolívar, un hombre diáfano* (1981), José Salcedo-Bastardo begins with the most straightforward and elementary question of all: Why should the lives of great men matter? "Great personages, the saints and the heroes, teach us a lot with their lives," he writes. "When we read and comment and learn about what Bolívar was like, it is to imitate him and to try to approximate his virtues" (29). Bolivarian children's literature thus provides us with a blueprint for the nationalist project at its most self-conscious. Yet, this literature is charged with the difficult task of making a connection between a child and a mythological republican deity. Monumentalist heroes are cast in the glory of battle; they are leaders celebrated for their martial feats, their acts of justice, and public role as founders of the nation. In this respect, the monumentalist hero encodes a masculinity that is circumscribed by nationalist mythologies and institutions. This masculinity, so useful for some narratives, is less adequate for others, such as children's literature. By constructing Bolívar as an accessible teacher and interlocutor of children, Bolivarian educators recover paternity for the national project by fashioning a different kind of masculinity, one that is less dependent on the authoritarian contours of monumentalism. If monumentalism commands its subjects to recognize the absolute power that springs from its mythic nature, and to obey, didactic children's literature seeks to create consent through sentiment. Although patrilineal in its preservation of Bolivarian authority, this new version of the foundational father challenges the impermeable contours of monumentalism.

This chapter explores paternity in relation to gender and modernity in nineteenth- and twentieth-century literature for and about children. I suggest that Bolivarian narratives of paternity discard the contours of the distant, monumental Bolívar and substitute a more accessible, filial figure. Yet, if the task of tailoring the iconic Bolívar to speak to children is difficult, the notion of having Bolívar speak to the experience of girls is particularly problematic. The writings of Teresa de la Parra offer us some important insights into the complex gendering of Bolívar by nationalist educators, and into Bolívar's failure in connecting with girls. In *Las memorias de la Mamá Blanca* (1929), her novel about childhood in nineteenth-century Venezuela, Parra suggests that the hero of independence is distant and irrelevant to childhood, its pleasures, and sensibilities. Parra's protagonists, four sisters who grow up on a sugar plantation, are as separated from Bolívar as they are from their father, who had wished for a male heir. However, Parra returned to Bolívar, and came to reconsider her view of the monumental hero. In subsequent essays and letters, Parra explored the possibility of integrating Bolívar into a premodern domestic realm dominated by the presence of women, their affective world, and oral traditions. Like sincere Bolivarians past and present, Parra believed that Bolívar could be a principle of renewal and national reconstruction in Venezuela. Paradoxically, Parra's formulations are both more radical and more conservative than those of other Bolivarian educators. On the one hand, Parra's emphasis on locating Bolívar in women's affective world may be read as an important feminist statement. On the other hand, Parra also frames Bolívar in a cultural world that predates independence, effectively rejecting Bolívar as a principle of modernity. Her rediscovery of Bolívar is predicated on a nostalgic flight into the past. In the pages to follow, I frame my discussion of Parra with a brief overview of attempts to modulate Bolivarian ideology for the purposes of education in the nineteenth and twentieth centuries. I suggest that these pedagogical narratives struggle to stir the monumental Bolívar into life by breaking with the catechism form, and reifying the filial possibilities of casting the Liberator as a domestic educator.

From Catechisms to Historical Episodes: The Emergence of Bolivarian Children's Literature in Latin America

Apart from scripted question and answer catechisms used for the education of children, there was no Bolivarian children's literature prior to 1881. While the catechism was clearly a disciplinary narrative intended to fashion subjectivity, its dry and declarative presentation of questions and answers did not allow for the development of political subjectivity, of an independent moral imperative to serve the republic to which the child was ostensibly connected. Three texts, however, broke with the catechism form and began to plot Bolívar's life in ways that are informed by an awareness that a certain measure of sensitivity and imagination are required to reach children as readers: Eduardo Blanco's *Venezuela heroica* (1881), José Martí's "Tres héroes" from *La edad de oro* (1884), and Manuel J. Calle's *Leyendas del tiempo heroico* (1905). Unlike the catechism, these texts renewed forms of historical instruction by attempting to create an emotional connection to the heroism of the past through lyricism, adventure, and the grotesque. The new Bolivarian children's literature would no longer be about the unquestioned authority of the written word, but about nurturing of social attachment and personal subjectivity through the written word.

One of the common features of didactic, moralizing children's literature since the eighteenth century is its investment in the concept of dialogue. In French culture, two notable examples come to mind: *Le magasin des enfants* (1757) by Madame Le Prince de Beaumont (1711–1780), translated and disseminated in Spain as *Conversaciones familiares*, and the works of Armand Berquin (1747–1791), whose preferred form in numerous children's books was also the dialogue (Bravo-Villasante 623, 630). In eighteenth-century Spain and its colonies, apart from Beaumont's text, catechisms were utilized to educate children as religious subjects. Derived from the Greek *katekhein* (to instruct by word of mouth), the catechism hearkens back to oral instruction; its straightforward, disciplinary narrative model of scripted questions and answers associated it with the education of the uncultivated and innocent, such as Indians and children (Sagredo Baeza 275). In 1784, *Instrucción o catecismo real* by José Antonio de

San Alberto, the bishop of Tucumán, inaugurated the trend of using the genre to shape children as loyal political subjects of the Spanish monarchy (Sagredo Baeza 275). The crisis of the Napoleonic invasion of Spain undoubtedly spurred the proliferation of royalist catechisms in the first quarter of the nineteenth century, attesting to their perceived importance as a method of disseminating and maintaining the influence of the Spanish Crown (278).

In the postindependence era, catechisms were the centerpiece of republican instruction for children. Although education was frequently invoked as a crucial element for national progress throughout the nineteenth century, schools were primarily under municipal rather than state control until the twentieth century, and were plagued by a scarcity of trained teachers and adequate resources.[4] Under these circumstances, the catechism was convenient because it did not require any special skill from the teacher, and because its dependence on oral drills and written transcription compensated for the limited number of copies that might be available for use in the classroom (Harwich Valenilla 358). As of the middle of the century, properly nationalist catechisms began to emerge and to be used in the classroom to teach national history and civic virtue. The lives of the founders were articulated as exemplars for children to follow as they entered public life as citizens. In the words of the nineteenth-century Mexican educator Aurelio Oviedo y Romero: "Child, as you step forward to live your life, child, you who will perhaps defend the integrity and honor of the homeland with your word or your arm; as you travel the pages of this book, try to do so with the conviction of imitating the noble examples of heroism, love of the homeland, and honesty that are offered by Cuahtemoc, Hidalgo, and Juárez" (Vásquez de Knauth 73). Such was the case of Bolívar in Venezuelan catechisms, which drew on the genre's religious roots to instill in children the absolute primacy of Bolívar as a republican deity. In his *Manual de historia de Venezuela para el uso de las escuelas y colegios* (1875), Felipe Tejera recurs to the image of flaming meteors to describe the historical impact of Bolívar: "with the passing of the centuries, there appear men who shine like suns, immense aerolites that pass through the night of history, archangel voyagers who, as they cross the earth, drop tongues of luminous flames from their wings" (Harwich Valenilla 382). Germán Carrera Damas observes that these texts were transparently propagandistic, extinguishing the critical impulse and constructing an artificial and authoritarian cult of Bolívar that did not admit dissent or variation (226). In part, this was due to the fact that Venezuelan catechisms all sprang from the same source, Rafael María Baralt's *Resumen de la historia de Venezuela* (1840), which homogenized their content, structure, and tone. Although the catechism began to fall out of favor in the twentieth century, the fact that Antonia Esteller's *Catecismo de historia de Venezuela* (1885) and Felipe Tejera's text remained in use in Venezuelan schools until the 1950s underlines the powerful influence of the catechism on the modern cult of Bolívar in Venezuela (Harwich Valenilla 385).

In Venezuela, Eduardo Blanco's *Venezuela heroica* (1881) broke with the catechism tradition in form, tone, and style, and suggested that the instruction of national history was to take place in the intimacy of the home, where the heroic stories of the past are passed on from generation to generation. In place of the rigid, declarative script of the catechism, impersonally organized around the classroom characters of the teacher and pupil, Blanco's exciting historical episodes were clearly intended to entertain, instruct, and move the reading public at home. Blanco's narrative takes the idealistic themes of previous celebrations of Bolívar to grotesque extremes, focusing particularly on the body in relation to specific historical episodes and battles. For Blanco, the battle sites where the Wars of Independence were fought and won are the sacred spaces that have become imprinted on the memory of the Venezuelan collectivity. Those holy plains, fields, and mountains, marked by blood, are places where each Venezuelan can experience historical memory in a personally intimate manner.[5] Blanco's task is to evoke these glorious sites in ways that foster a sense of national belonging in space and in time.

Blanco situates the responsibility for the creation, transmission, and maintenance of this sense of national identity in the home, and frames his text as a conduit for a domestic transaction between parents and their children. In the introduction, colonial Venezuela is described as a kind of cultural orphan and infant, deprived of the memories that bind generation to generation in a continuous narrative of the self: "The captive of Spain, abandoned to her destiny, suffered the heavy lethargy of slavery in silence. Nothing reminded her of a better time; nothing spoke to her in flattering tones about her own brilliant prowess, through which peoples in their infancy learn how to venerate the soil where they are born and to love the sun that makes it fecund . . . our own history was barely a blank book and no one could have foreseen that soon its pages would be filled with epic" (Blanco, *Venezuela heroica* 19). When Blanco returns to the image of the book in his description of the Battle of Carabobo (1821), Bolívar is presented as a paternal figure that fulfills the potential of a nationalist dissemination of collective memory. Bolívar reads to his soldiers from the "book" of Venezuela's glories and tragedies up until 1821, an "arsenal" through which the "prestige of the past" musters up the "sparks of fire" that the soldiers need to triumph in the battle (439). Carabobo is not a single battle past, but a metaphor for the continuing triumph of Venezuela, for the maintenance of her glory and health, which operates out of the example of the textuality of national history. Blanco's readers were poised to draw inspiration from the fact that they too, sitting in their homes, could participate in Bolívar's epic by holding *Venezuela heroica* before them, and transmitting its stories from one generation to the next.

The celebrated Cuban writer and patriot José Martí, who lived in Venezuela in 1881, writing articles for *La opinión nacional*, and working in a house a few blocks from the Plaza Bolívar, provides us with another example of a reimagining of the catechism form with his short-lived children's magazine *La edad de oro* (1889). Martí's purpose was to present children with an attractive and well-illustrated series of gently didactic articles, stories, poems, and translations. Like the catechism, Martí conceives his education as predicated on dialogue, but instead of an inflexible and impersonal monologue, he constructs his role as an educator through respect for the creativity and needs of children, and by highlighting that the relationship between child and magazine will be defined through sentiment and friendship: "We work for the children, because the children are those who know how to love, because children are the hope of the world. . . . And we want them to love us, and to see us as a thing of their heart" (30). Martí makes a call for boys and girls to send letters and their own articles to the magazine, emphasizing that they too have talent and knowledge to share with the world. Inspired by Eduard Magnus's painting *The Golden Age*, which Martí reproduces in the first issue of the magazine, Martí imagines young readers as idealized innocents whose voice needs to be preserved and harnessed for a greater social good. The inhabitants of the "golden age" of childhood are charged with reinventing society after their own image, creating a better future. For this task, Martí avoids the disciplinary diction of the catechism and modulates his voice to speak gently and lovingly.

Martí's softening of the catechism is illustrated by a brief article on Bolívar, Miguel Hidalgo, and José de San Martín. The purpose of this article is straightforward: the lives and sacrifices of these heroes provide children with models of honor and courage to follow in their own lives. Specifically, Martí's representation of Bolívar presents us with an effective metaphor for the challenges facing Bolivarian nationalists intent on effectively teaching children about Bolívar: "They say that a traveler arrived one day in Caracas at nightfall, and without shaking off the dust of the road, did not ask where there was food or lodging, but rather how to get to the statue of Bolívar. And they say that the traveler, alone with the tall and aromatic trees of the plaza, cried before the statue, which seemed to move, like a father when a son approaches. The traveler did well, because all Americans should love Bolívar like a father" (32). Martí suggests that the bronze Bolívar is stirred into life by the proximity and sentiment of the traveler. As long as we approach the monument with humility and sincere love, Martí argues, the bronze Bolívar awakens and becomes tender, like a loving father. Martí's brief description of the Plaza Bolívar serves as a reminder of the two worlds he seeks to bridge as an educator of children: on the one hand, the world of national and martial foundations, and on the other, the world of sentiment and filial connection. Across the distance that a body of bronze communicates to those standing at its pedestal, Martí inscribes the love of the father, and creates the possibility of contact.

A different approach to the problem of educating the young through the example of Bolívar can be found in a book of historical episodes modeled on Eduardo Blanco's *Venezuela heroica. Leyendas del tiempo heroico* (1901) by the Ecuadorian journalist Manuel J. Calle, was specifically written to replace historical catechisms. His version of Bolívar was also invested in stirring the bronze into life and accessibility, but was considerably more pessimistic in its urgency about the failures of the present. Calle came of age as a liberal journalist in the chaotic period of civil war between conservatives and liberals that ensued after the assassination of the conservative autocrat Gabriel García Moreno in 1875. Calle's most enduring work, *Leyendas del tiempo heroico*, did not focus exclusively on famous battles like *Venezuela heroica*, although it did include them. Calle's book is an album containing didactic and dramatic vignettes about political intrigues, massacres, and the primary actors of the Wars of Independence.

In his preface, Calle signals the purpose of his text vis-à-vis a rejection of instructional catechisms and particularly the *Manual de urbanidad y buenas maneras* (1854), an influential and widely disseminated conduct manual by the Venezuelan Manuel Antonio Carreño. In his critique of catechisms, Calle rejects their "arid" system of questions and answers for fostering confusion and dissipating inspiration (8). Carreño's conduct manual, while useful for instructing children about social mores and re-sponsibilities, fails to instill a love of nation and the values of sacrifice upon which modern societies rest. Thus, Calle's *Leyendas* exemplifies a new kind of instructional literature, one predicated on the imagination and on sentiment. At one point, Calle frames his description of a battle by invok-ing the romance of jousting knights, medieval honor, and embroidered lace, suggesting that the epic of independence should be read as myth and fairy-tale, and not simply military history (208). To this end, Calle adds dialogues and characterizations, making the narrative strategies of fiction available to his didactic project. By far the most dramatic example of this fictional reconstruction of the past comes in a monologue by Bolívar him-self, which is composed primarily out of a collage of known quotes by the hero, with Calle's own changes and additions, which he terms "absolutely insignificant" in a footnote (243). Calle's recognition that imaginative lit-erature can be a particularly useful tool for creating inspiration in its youngest readers results in a collection of historical miscellany full of ro-mantic energy and power.

One of the striking aspects of *Leyendas del tiempo heroico* is Calle's insistence on narrating the destruction of the bodies of young patriots such as Atanasio Girardot (1791–1813), Antonio Ricaurte (1786–1814), and Abdón Calderón (1804–1822). The purpose is to politicize the young to surrender their lives to the ideal of liberty. In the cases of Girardot and Ricaurte, Calle cites the lyrical words of his contemporary Juan Montalvo, from his *Siete tratados* (1882), who describes the beauty of shattered bod-ies offered upon the altar of independence. For example, Montalvo con-templates the "beautiful, youthful face" of Girardot, his forehead perfo-rated by a gunshot wound and his brains slowly moving down to his cheeks (Calle 48). Similarly, regarding Ricaurte's destruction in an explo-sion, Montalvo muses: "Where have your limbs been dispersed, generous youth? . . . Burnt, blackened, without eyes in your face or hairs on your head, you would still seem beautiful to me . . ." (Calle 65). Calle vividly rewrites this narrative of the beauty of adolescents who sacrifice their bod-ies to the cause of independence. In his dramatic telling of the death of eighteen-year-old Abdón Calderón at the Battle of Pinchincha (1822), Calle describes the youth being torn limb from limb by bullets and can-nonball. The expiring torso of Calderón dies like a white lily folding into a pool of blood, offering one last hurrah for independence with his dying breath.

"Forward, my friends! Advance comrades!" He exclaims deliriously to his men, and he enters where danger rages and where death hovers, with his burning gaze and unsheathed sword in his right hand. . . . A bullet whistles and breaks his right arm. Calderón transfers his sword to his left hand and continues in the battle, to the cry of "Long live the Homeland!" . . . Another bullet whistles and breaks his left arm. "Long live the Republic!" the heroic adolescent cries out, and still on his feet, still serene, he encourages his men, running ahead of them with his sword between his teeth. "Advance! Take them!" Another bullet whistles and penetrates his thigh. "Homeland! Homeland! Liberty! Liberty! And forward!" He shouts as best he can, letting the useless sword drop. A cannonball takes his legs. "Long live Independence!" And he falls upon his sword. And there, on the ground, without arms, without legs, destroyed, the smallest part of himself, he still breathes the air of his gigantic valor and before the last gasp of death, he hurls the last hurrah for the Republic. And later, like a pale bent flower, white like a lily that shrivels in a lake of blood, he surrenders his great soul. He was eighteen years old. (189)

These tales of the literal destruction of bodies illustrate Calle's passionate commitment to promoting national subjectivity by promoting the sacrifice of the body and affirming transcendental heroism and memory. Further, these passages underscore how Calle constructs the present as an arena of combat and struggle analogous to the heroic scenes he describes. At the close of his book, Calle declares that bloodletting and martyrdom are facts of political life, defined by humanity's propensity for error and tyranny. In his political imaginary, liberty is religion and civilization is a constant state of struggle and combat (304). Calle suggests that his young readers, like Abdón Calderón, are struggling forward against terrible odds and terrible blows. The triumph lies in the ultimate sacrifice through which they will find communion with the overseeing spirit of Bolívar.

Calle's episodes, like *Venezuela heroica* and *La edad de oro*, reimagine the form and the task of didactic literature by doing away with the inflexible dictums of the catechism and promoting an intimate engagement with epic. Calle's stated purpose is to shape national subjects through the example of Bolívar, but his grim assessment of the past results in a fatalistic view of the present. Bolívar becomes distant and abstract, reminding his devotees of the inadequacies of the present. Instead of inhabiting an institutionalized discourse of identity, Bolívar exists on the margins of the national experience, as a call to arms. This wedding of Bolívar to failure has continued to be a feature of Bolivarian didacticism, suggesting that Bolivarian fervor is more often than not fueled by a sense of disillusion- ment.

An interesting case in point is Santiago Key Ayala's *Vida ejemplar de Simón Bolívar* (1942), which self-consciously articulates Bolívar as a filial figure framed by the crisis of the present. Santiago Key Ayala (1874–1959) belonged to the generation of positivist intellectuals that supported the dictatorship of Juan Vicente Gómez in Venezuela between 1908 and 1935. In addition to being a prolific essayist, literary critic, and bibliographer, Key Ayala held high-profile posts in the Ministry of Foreign Relations and the diplomatic corps until 1940. The *Vida ejemplar de Simón Bolívar*, which won the Municipal Prize for Literature in 1942, resulted from Key Ayala's experiences in Italy as minister plenipotentiary in 1936, where he discovered the writings of Niccolò Machiavelli. In *The Prince*, Key Ayala saw a pedagogical model for training individuals to obey a coherent set of principles embodied by a single leader. Exemplarity, the notion of a person's life as a logos of public and private conduct, afforded Key Ayala a structure for imagining Bolívar as script for republican conduct.

Bolivarian paternity, its failure and its promise, is at the center of Key Ayala's social project. Key Ayala concedes that "the satisfactions of filial tenderness" were mostly unknown to the hero, whose life was defined by war, politics, and by the disappointments and disenchantments that char- acterize a public life (64). If Bolívar had fathered children, Key Ayala ex- ults, the very source of him would have been uncovered for all posterity to know and to build upon: "If Bolívar had had children! History would know them. The tenderness of the father would have brimmed over in lovely documents and they would have conferred upon us the most intimate se- crets of his soul. We have lost the pathways that would have revealed the origin of the river, the great river, running over masses of granite and iron, carrying gold sand" (173). This passage exposes an underlying anxiety about Bolívar and paternity; Bolívar's lack of biological offspring troubles the ability of Bolivarians to better understand their hero through geneal- ogy. In other words, the source is hidden, and Bolívar's symbolic offspring have been deprived of the intimate knowledge of their father's soul. In passages evocative of a passage in Gabriel García Márquez's *The Autumn of the Patriarch* (1976), in which nameless narrators describe their anomie before fictional images of the dead patriarch, Key Ayala argues that the image of the national icon has become all surface, an image without an original model: "It is frequent, however, that the decorations of our national life be painted paper. . . . Behind there is coarse cloth and rough wood" (173). The originary father has become divorced from his own image, becoming a principle of absence rather than presence.[6] In this absence, Key Ayala's task is to provide an exegesis of the hero's actions and written words that will demonstrate that Bolívar was a wise and effective educator, a symbolic father. Bolívar's acts with his friends and the men in his command provide evidence of his good humor, morality, and ability to teach gently. "Despite being a great man among great men," writes Key Ayala, "he did not divorce himself from tenderness" (65).

The theme of crisis and disjunction that I have outlined in Bolivarian didacticism endures into the present. In Helena Naranjo's *Un niño de nombre Simón* (1992), the author declares that Venezuelans have let Bolívar down by not working as selflessly and passionately for the homeland as he would have wished (16). A more striking example is *Entrevista al Libertador en el bicentenario de su nacimiento* (1984) by J. J. Cordero Ceballos, in which Bolívar is interviewed through a collage of quotes to match the author's questions. In his preface to the text, Armando Rojas puts it bluntly: Latin Americans need to go on a crusade to recover the moral and spiritual values that have been lost in the 1970s (8). The dedication of the text is marked by an urgency and anger that represents the national experience of the present as an utter failure: "TO THE: the youth of Latin America, so that they never allow themselves to be perverted by figureheads, amoral individuals, demagogues, racists, defaulting taxpayers, traffickers of influence, tyrants, adulators, homeland betrayers, false democrats, imperialists, lackeys, negligents and laggards, abominable personages that are not satisfied with their evil deeds and try to drag the new generations with them" (11). Ceballos places the youth of his continent, with Bolívar at its head, in the midst of the wars of the present. His call to the young is a combative one, predicated on the concept of struggle. Like Calle and Key Ayala before him, Ceballos's text operates in the intersection between the sought after utopia of Bolivarian progress and the dystopia of contemporary decay and danger. In these texts, modernity is a competitive arena in which the idol of Bolívar must be seized and protected in the name of remaking the nation after its image.

Teresa de la Parra's Bolivarian Reconciliation

> We have very beautiful things in these countries, but we don't see them because they are covered up by exported literatures that deform them. It is my wish to discover Bolívar behind that Great Wall of adjectives. . . .
> **Teresa de la Parra**

A variation on the filial narratives of Martí, Blanco, and Key Ayala can be found in the fiction, lectures, and letters of the Venezuelan novelist Teresa de la Parra (1890–1936). Born in Paris to Venezuelan parents, Parra spent her childhood in Tazón, a sugarcane hacienda on the outskirts of Caracas, where she came to appreciate the Venezuelan landscape and its rural traditions. After spending her adolescence in Spain, Parra returned to Venezuela and was a part of Caracas's high society until 1923, when she moved to Paris. Her first novel *Ifigenia (diario de una señorita que escribió porque se fastidiaba)* (1923), which won the Grand Prix du Roman Américain au Concours in France, explored the conflicts between women and the conventions of high society, and was an immediate success in Latin America. The popularity of *Ifigenia* brought much fame to Parra, who traveled to Panamá, Cuba, and Colombia to deliver lectures about women and Latin American identity. Her second novel, *Las memorias de la Mamá Blanca* (1929), largely based on her childhood experiences in Tazón, received little attention during her lifetime. Between 1930 and 1936, as her health began to fail, Parra embarked on an ambitious and often all-consuming research project: the writing of a biography of Simón Bolívar that would highlight the affective and the sentimental. All that remains of this project is a wealth of enthusiastic letters to a few friends, particularly her mentor, the Bolivarian scholar Vicente Lecuna.

A careful reading of *Mama Blanca's Memoirs*, Parra's three lectures titled "Influencia de las mujeres en la formación del alma americana," and her correspondence reveals the evolution of a consistent and well-defined project to reinscribe Bolívar within a feminine genealogy and a colonial context. Although Parra's project continues to be invested in Bolívar as a national force, she breaks with a long-standing tradition of linking Bolívar with modernity. Her Bolívar is not only redefined as a more feminine character, but as a link to a lost, colonial Eden. In *Mama Blanca's Memoirs*, a novel in the form of one woman's memoir of her childhood, Parra rejects the martial narrative of Bolívar and paves the way for an alternate model of the hero as a sentimental being, one that is further developed in her lectures and correspondence. Instead of Bolívar-the-soldier, Parra gravitates toward Bolívar-the-boy, Bolívar-the-confused-adolescent, and Bolívar-the-sentimental-lover. These versions of Bolívar belong to an epistemology that Parra associates with orality and women's experience. In her lectures on women and Latin American identity, Parra suggests that women's experience and stories constitute an oral culture that has been marginalized by official historiography and modernity. In embedding Bolívar in this premodern culture, Parra responds critically to martial historiography and rejects the positivist notion of liberal progress. Her Bolívar is still very much a principle of renewal and national regeneration, but it is a version that results from a critique of monumentalism.

Parra's journey to Bolívar began with *Mama Blanca's Memoirs*, in which the cult of Bolívar is presented as an alienating narrative of identity associated with a distant father figure unable to forgive his daughters for their sex. The novel is framed by a preface that is narrated by an unnamed woman who receives a manuscript from her elderly friend Mama Blanca. The narrator presents the narrative to follow as an edited portion of Mama Blanca's memoirs, celebrating its romantic style as a viable alternative to a more European, avant-garde aesthetic. The first person narrative that follows tells the story of Mama Blanca's idyllic childhood spent in a sugarcane plantation called Piedra Azul. Piedra Azul is presented as an edenic, preindustrial space inhabited by Mama, Papa, their six daughters (including Blanca Nieves, Mama Blanca's childhood self), maid-servants, and plantation workers, most notably the *zambo* (half Indian, half black) peon Vicente Aguilar and the plainsman cowherd Daniel. Elizabeth Garrels's subtle analysis of the novel establishes that some characters are associated with orality, nature, preindustrial forms of economic production, nativism, and romanticism, while others are identified with the ideology of positivism and progress, industrialized society, a monetarized economy, and hermetic modes of representation (22–23). Within this schema of symbolic oppositions, which is loosely conceptualized around the opposition of the characters of Mama and Papa, Parra may be read as gendering her characters as either masculine or feminine; the protagonist's older sister Violeta, who defends the concept of private property and who is willing to wield violence to defend it, is described as containing the soul of a boy, whereas Vicente Aguilar and Daniel the cowherd, both of whom are linked to nature's fecundity and openness, as well as a crazy and "delightfully incoherent" relative named Juancho, share the regenerative and harmonizing oral skills associated with the protagonist and her mother, Mama.

Since the appearance of a revised English translation of the novel, and a critical edition edited by Velia Bosch, Parra's text has been recontextualized in Latin American literary history as a narrative in which the nexus of power, gender, and representation is not easily adjudicated. Indeed, Teresa de la Parra's childhood memoir can be read on several different registers: as children's literature, as a critique of avant-garde modes of representation, as a feminist text, and as an indictment of the positivism that defined notions of Latin American (and specifically Venezuelan) progress in the last quarter of the nineteenth century and the beginning of the twentieth. The challenge in ongoing conversations about this novel is how to reconcile these dimensions constructively. The feminist rescue of the text might leave some readers concerned about the more reactionary dimensions of the novel, whereas simplistic, materialistic readings of the novel that present it as ideologically conservative run the risk of glossing over the text's very real contestatory voice in terms of gender and language.

Nonfeminist approaches to the novel, such as those of Ramón Díaz Sánchez and José Carlos González Boixó, emphasize the ideological conservatism of pining away for a lost colonial arcadia and are predicated to a great degree on indications of Parra's sympathy toward the dictatorial regimes of Machado in Cuba and Gómez in Venezuela. In 1928, for example, when the Gómez regime massacred protesting students in Caracas, Parra sent a supportive letter to the dictator, enclosing a published interview in which she had praised the reign of progress in Venezuela.[7] As read through that biographical register, the contestatory voice of the novel is attenuated if not negated completely. González Boixó goes as far as to suggest that this ideological conservatism is reproduced through the reinscription of traditional gender norms (234). The problem with these readings is that they pay short shrift to the ways in which Parra subtly subverts traditional modes of representation and power relations.[8] Notwithstanding Parra's sympathetic view of the dictatorship of Gómez, her rewriting of Bolívar challenges the positivist ideology that underpinned the patriarchal, Bolivarian nationalism of the Gómez regime (Garrels 81–82).

Elizabeth Garrels and Doris Sommer have negotiated the divide between gender and the novel's nostalgia for colonial relations in ways that are more sensitive to the nuances of Parra's artistry. Garrels underlines Parra's attachment to socially conservative definitions of Venezuelan rural life and race relations while suggesting that the novel explores the failed promise of a horizontal relationship between women, children, and the masses, an alliance impeded by the domination of Papa, father, husband, and *patrón* (37). Sommer argues that Parra creates a feminist space of narrative and linguistic alterity that challenges the masculinist foundational fictions wielded by the father of the state and the father of letters. "If women, more consistently than men, are exiled from the athletic paradise where signifiers reach what they signify," Sommer writes, "it is possible that their conscious frustration may become an impetus to play with possible miscombinations" ("It's Wrong to Be Right" xx). Sommer's comparative reading of Rómulo Gallego's *Doña Bárbara*, also published in 1929, alongside *Mama Blanca's Memoirs*, underlines how Gallegos posits his project of national regeneration on the patriarchal authority of the sign itself, whereas Parra's approach to both diversity and language itself configures a kind of feminist and social polyphony ("Mirror, Mirror, in Mother's Room" 180). Both Garrels and Sommer see a necessary synthesis between the question of gender and the question of power; since power has been and continues to be symbolically figured as masculine, the critique of masculinity challenges power relations writ large, and not only traditional gender norms.

With regard to Bolívar, Garrels is the only critic to note the significance of his presence in the novel, as an axis for the representation of gender (65). In the first chapter of the novel, Mama Blanca recalls the alienating effect of her father on her and her sisters. Distant in his quiet disappointment at not having fathered a male heir, Papa's coldness is in actuality a silent reproach that creates a gulf between him and his daughters. Mama Blanca describes the girls' perception of Papa in relation to the iconic Bolívar: "That resignation of yours was like a huge tree that you had felled across the pathway to our hearts. So you shouldn't complain if, as you rode off in the morning until you disappeared from sight in the green cane fields, your remote silhouette seen from the railing—rising and falling with Caramelo's gallop and crowned by your broad Panama hat—meant no more to us than the Bolívar in battle dress with drawn sword, who, galloping on horseback like you, hung above the closed door of your study and from his mahogany frame all day long majestically directed the glorious battle of Carabobo" (Parra, *Mama Blanca's Memoirs* 21). Parra clearly articulates a critique of Bolivarian patrilineality in this rich passage, which separates Papa/Bolívar from the realm of experience of the little girls. As daughters and not sons, the girls are unable to recognize themselves in the heroic public narratives of the masculine, and are thus relegated to the margins of the public sphere (Garrels 106). The closed doors of the study

represent the power of the law, inimical to the openness of the rest of Piedra Azul, and Bolívar's martial image suggests that the glorious, public
business of the state is closed off from the world of the girls, their mother,
and the workers of Piedra Azul.

The other ruling deity of Piedra Azul, Mama, offers an alternative to
this patrilineal, exclusionary narrative. Mama is described as the initiator
of romanticism because of her ability to fuse opposites harmoniously
without violating their difference. Mama has the soul of a poet and is able
to reject reality and subject it "to a code of pleasant and arbitrary laws
dictated by her imagination" (17). Instead of the language of law, of conquest, hers is the language of reconciliation and harmony. In this respect,
to paraphrase the narrative voice that explains the origin of the name of
Mama Blanca in the foreword, Mama is like a child or the common folk,
who shun abstraction and effectively join words to the objects they represent (5). The concept of Mama as agent of textual reconciliations is further
developed by characterizing her as the fount of romanticism. Mama
Blanca states that romanticism is a tropical fruit native to the Americas
that was carried to Europe by one of Napoleon's lovers, Josephine Tascher,
and spread militarily by the famous Corsican and René de Chateaubriand's
René. The comparison of Mama to Napoleon, a military figure analogous
to Bolívar, effectively establishes a gendered distinction between the act of
conquest, associated with martial communities of men, and the act of creation, which belongs to mothers and daughters: "They can laugh at me as
much as they like, but I firmly believe that Mama and Napoleon were very
much alike. What could be more like that boundless determination of
Napoleon's to seat his brothers one by one on the proudest thrones of
Europe than that determination of Mama's, boundless too, to seat her little
daughters on the thrones of Creation? To be Estrella, Aurora, Blanca
Nieves—isn't that exactly the same thing, from a certain point of view, as
being king of Spain, of Naples, or of Holland? Only Mama, bless her heart,
set out on her conquest of thrones without military fanfare or human sacrifice" (22–23). Napoleon's power is the power of patrilineality and martial
brotherhood, and is marked by violence, whereas Mama's power is characterized by motherhood and harmony. The novel as a whole affirms the
feminine realm exemplified by Mama and dismisses the possibility of a
heroic reading of Papa. Papa does have brothers, and yet the promise of a
functional and successful martial brotherhood is rejected, because unlike
Napoleon, whose geopolitical power grew outward, Papa's power is in de-

cline, and shrinks to the point that he must sell Piedra Azul and move the family to the city.

The passage in which Mama Blanca dismisses Papa by comparing him to an image of Bolívar directing the battle of Carabobo may also be read in relation to the friction between official historiography, characterized by the conventions of heroism and martial brotherhood, and orality, which is defined as a dialogic and hybrid form of expression associated with Mama the romantic. The print above Papa's door is revealingly similar to the widely known painting *Batalla de Carabobo* by Martín Tovar y Tovar, which was painted between 1884 and 1888 and placed in the National Capitol of Caracas. Tovar y Tovar's famous painting depicts Bolívar in Napoleonic garb and on a white horse, directing the famous battle from a hilltop with his outstretched arm, as four of his lieutenants, also in full military uniform and on horses, gather around him. This image, presented as a point of comparison to describe the irrelevance of Papa's affective influence over his daughters, presents a martial story of epic Bolivarian leadership that the girls cannot appreciate or connect with.

In contrast to this alienating story of Bolívar, which is Papa's emblem, Parra offers us an alternative narrative, channeled through the regenerative stories that Mama passes on to Blanca Nieves. Mama's emblem will not be the authority of the text, but rather a collaboration with her daughter that results in a fusion of existing narratives and the seamless wedding of these narratives to the local landscape of Piedra Azul. To help Blanca Nieves pass the time while she curls her straight hair, Mama accommodates her daughter's request that she fuse disparate characters and plots into stories.

The personages and events of these stories were never original, I must admit. One after another there came from Mama's lips fairy stories, tales of mythology, fables by Samaniego and La Fontaine, ballads by Zorilla, scraps of Bible history, novels by Dumas pere, and that sweet poem by Bernardin de Sainte-Pierre, "Paul and Virginia." Poor Mama, who for all her isolated, rustic life was well read, as they say, laid hold of everything her memory could turn up. Then it became my task to give unity to the whole. In my hours of dreaming, as I recalled the more thrilling incidents, I invited those personages I thought most noble or interesting to take part in my spiritual jousts. As nobody ever refused, Moses for example might be defeated by d'Artagnan, or sweet Virginia sadly shipwrecked in Noah's ark, then rescued just in the nick of time by the heroic efforts of Beauty and the Beast.... Through Mama's art, fiction and reality were harmoniously mingled ... cross fertilizing each other with a wealth of fact and fancy in nice balance. In this way my imagination could travel paths of fancy dotted with familiar landmarks to give them verisimilitude. (31–32)

The colorful canvas evoked by Mama's intertextual narrative clearly speaks to the sensibility and imagination of a child, and serves as a bond between mother and daughter. Moreover, the stories Mama tells to Blanca Nieves privilege orality over print forms of expression, redefining representational power in substantial ways (Garrels 111–12). Authorship is plural insofar as it includes Blanca Nieves' participation in the story-telling process. Further, these stories are an instance of narrative transculturation between the Old and the New World; foreign, European stories are implanted into familiar, local landscapes. Blanca Nieves's world of Piedra Azul is not a peripheral space to be "civilized" through an eclipse by European narratives. Rather, Piedra Azul becomes the site of new and harmonious narrative combinations that do not negate the local in favor of European, metropolitan discourses. Mama's narrative clearly challenges the conventions of the kind of monumentalist representation symbolized by Tovar y Tovar and nationalist iconography in general, which posit official narratives of identity as fully formed monological scripts meant to promote authoritatively the ideology of progress. The rejection of such iconography in *Mama Blanca's Memoirs* and the exalted embrace of Mama's representational techniques demonstrate a critical awareness of the ineffectual artifice of disciplinary narratives of identity as opposed to the more subjective and affective model of identity formation invoked by Mama.

The critique of Bolívar that was begun in *Mama Blanca's Memoirs* was clearly the beginning of a new direction in Parra's intellectual production, one that unfortunately could not be brought to complete fruition because of her premature death in 1936. Shortly after completing the novel, Parra traveled to Colombia and delivered her three lectures, "Influencia de la mujer en la formación del alma americana" to enthusiastic crowds in Bogotá. The lectures highlight Parra's familiarity with centuries of Latin American history, culture, and letters, and outline an ambitious new form of historiography in which the uncovering of women's genealogies is defined through the language of memory, and with orality itself. Parra argues that the historical role of women is to soften the blows of history and refashion them into tradition and identity. Although more often than not anonymous, Latin American women have provided, through the home, the very base upon which cities were founded and traditions were transmitted from one generation to the next (690). This work of cultural transmission is identified with orality and dialogism, and with the undisciplined and mystical subjectivity of social agents on the margins of official, scriptural narratives (Garrels 63, 107). In addition to writing about some of the women in her own family, Parra singles out figures such as la Malinche, Sor Juana Inés de la Cruz, and Manuela Sáenz, among others. These women embody tradition and the mysterious rhythms of nature, harmonizing the disparate in the same manner that Mama Blanca's mother fused separate stories and fragments into a cordial whole in *Mama Blanca's Memoirs*. In particular, Parra privileges the colonial period of Latin American history, casting it as a naïve and happy time best symbolized by a disembodied woman's voice, whispering through the blinds of the protective, enclosed spaces of the home, the church, or the convent (711–12). These feminine spaces have been victimized by postindependence liberalism, which has fragmented and exiled these spaces where women's expression has decisively shaped customs and nurtured tradition. Parra is thinking here in particular of nineteenth-century liberal measures against the religious institutions of the colonial ancien régime, which resulted in the disruption of church authority and property. The recuperation of the colonial era and its distinctly feminine voice, like the preservation of tradition, is thus irrevocably intertwined with an awareness of loss and extinction, and with the oral traditions of women, who keep alive the memory of that vanished era.

In her third and final lecture, Parra returns to Bolívar and recovers him for her feminist genealogy, privileging romanticism and the affective world of woman for an understanding of the hero's greatness. Parra argues that common women were central to the success of the patriot cause during the Wars of Independence. When patriot men were forced to go underground to flee persecution, the home became a site of political meetings and debate in which women could intervene. Women thus provided the hidden essence of independence, and Bolívar serves as a case in point. Bolívar is presented enveloped in the mantle of orality and sentimentality that is central to women's experience and discourse. First, in childhood, his servant la Negra Matea introduced him to the wonders and nobility of his homeland through her fantastic narratives. Bolívar's lovers, such as his wife, María Teresa del Toro, or his lover Fanny du Villars, added melancholy, sentiment, and refinement to his character, opening up new vistas and possibilities to his education. As in the case of Cousin Juancho in *Mama Blanca's Memoirs*, this nurturing feminine zone is not defined by sex, but by a symbolic transaction that renders agents identified with nature and orality as feminine. Simón Rodríguez, Bolívar's teacher, is thus presented as a kind of cross between Cousin Juancho and Blanca Nieves's Mama; for Bolívar, the friendship of Rodríguez operates analogously to a woman's love, forming a kind of zone of domesticity where Bolívar can come to rest to plot his mythic triumphs ("Influencia de las mujeres" 751). As in *Mama Blanca's Memoirs*, Parra rejects the martial hero of official discourse in favor of a romantic and tropical man of sentiment, capable of connecting piously and tenderly to his lovers, friends, and family. In the wake of her indictment of Papa, the authoritarian and distant deity that oversees the childhood of the girls of Piedra Azul, Parra rewrites the image of the patriarch so that he might touch Mama Blanca the child, and hold her in his arms.

Upon completing her lectures, Parra was drawn to the project of writing a kind of sentimental biography of Bolívar, one that would underscore the amorous dimensions of his heroic life, and the feminine colonial era that framed his childhood and adolescence. In a rich correspondence with the Bolivarian scholar Vicente Lecuna from 1930 to 1931, Parra outlines the stops and starts of her research for this biography. Throughout, however, she remains focused on evoking the mysticism of the Latin American landscape and the harmonious, sentimental world of the colony. As in her previous texts, Parra is suspicious of writing itself, and seeks to experience the natural and cultural landscape of Bolívar's life in order to overcome the alienating image of the official Bolívar. In a letter to Lecuna dated November 29, 1930, Parra declares that such an encounter with Bolívar would recover him for the moral progress of Venezuela: "A history of Bolívar in which his feats and extraordinary triumphs are reported would be absurd. . . . In order to make him more cordial than admirable, what needs to be insisted upon is the humble facts of day to day life, the suffering, the loves, the injustices, the disappointments, mixing in the charm of the landscape and of the atmosphere" (*Obras completas* 796–97). Hers was a Bolívar that could not be separated from the intimacy of family and the intimacy of place, a gentle giant who would speak to the experience of women. Sadly, despite her two years of research, guided by Lecuna's bibliographical and archival materials and by her own passion for travel to those places that she felt were close to Bolívar's colonial realm, Parra's failing health put an end to the project before she could begin. Perhaps it is fitting that this should have been the case considering Parra's continual wariness of scriptural narratives and the printing press; in the end, the Bolívar she produced lived between the lines of her fiction, and in the personal letters between her and a few friends.

Despite its originality and feminist overtones, Parra's version of Bolívar illustrates two broad trends within Bolivarian nationalism that I have explored in this chapter. First is the construction and promotion of a sentimental masculinity that is not equivalent to a monumentalist definition of the hero. Although we may choose to call this redefinition a feminization of Bolívar, and celebrate its contestatory nature, the logic of Parra's own complex formulations conspires against this essentialist characterization of her Bolivarian vision. While Bolívar is resituated among women and their affective realm in her writing, he remains a foundational figure around which the renewal of the present may be carried out. In other words, residues of Bolívar's association with power and the nation remain, indicating that this version of the hero is not as iconoclastic as it might appear at first glance. Second, her Bolívar appears in the fissures of a present that is represented as a failure. Unlike other promoters of Bolívar, Parra sees the crisis of the present not as an invitation to reiterate Bolívar's role as an agent of republican progress, but rather to look back and pine away for a lost colony. Both of these problems, the definition of Bolivarian masculinity and its complex relationship to the present, illustrate the challenges of writing national narratives capable of transforming citizens into committed, national subjects. I have demonstrated how these questions are accentuated and made particularly transparent in relation to narratives for children, which reconstruct Bolivarian masculinity against martial definitions of the hero. In a sense, the relationship between children's literature and nationalist conduct goes to the heart of nationalism's sentimental nature in general. If people cannot experience the nation in a personally transformative way, they cannot feel connected to the homeland and their fellow citizens. Therefore, in order to be an operative national symbol, Bolívar needs to be approachable. The filial narrative of Bolívar, with its softening of the martial Bolívar, ultimately demonstrates that Bolivarian nationalism and modernization are not predicated on a single definition of masculinity.

Postscript: Bolivarian Paternity and
the Presidency of Hugo Chávez Frías

Since the construction of Bolívar as father continues to be the centerpiece
of Bolivarian instructional literature for children, I close this chapter with
a brief discussion of the question of Bolivarian paternity and Venezuelan
nationalism at the beginning of the presidency of Hugo Chávez Frías, the
controversial Bolivarian president of Venezuela. In February 1992, the
then Commander Chávez led a failed coup attempt and was imprisoned.
After a presidential pardon in 1994, the immensely popular Chávez became a politician and swept into the presidency in 1999 on a neo-
Bolivarian, populist program that promised, and ultimately delivered, a
restructuring of the Constitution. The Chávez program, with its emphasis
on strengthening the executive branch, renaming the nation the Bolivarian Republic of Venezuela, and its distrust of civil society, struck many as
a return to the culture of paternalistic dictatorship. President Chávez's
newspaper, *El correo del presidente* (an echo of Bolívar's own *Correo del
Orinoco*), published weekly in the months before the referendum on his
new constitution in 1999, confirms how Chávez refigured himself as a
Bolivarian father of the nation. The paper contains a "Letters to the President" page in which individual citizens decry specific run-ins with political
corruption and request the president's help. The dynamic between citizen
and president is thus presented in a deeply personal manner through the
illusion of personal access to the president. In short, Chávez reinvented
himself as a *taita*, a nickname meaning father.

Chávez's commitment to reshaping Venezuelan society had an ambitious educational component that reflected his paternalistic vision of authority and Bolivarian identity. The Escuelas Bolivarianas project sought
to disseminate Chávez's brand of Bolivarian ideology, modernize the infrastructures of Venezuelan education, and transform the schoolhouse
into a shelter for the poor and undernourished. In Chávez's government
program, the mission of these schools is described as follows: "All schools
at the level of Basic Education I and II should be transformed into
Bolivarian Schools, the mission of which is: A school for social transformation and national sovereignty; a school of community building, center and
base of participation, autonomy and democracy; a school where the dialogue of knowledge and cultural production, in search of universal and
popular knowledge, generates an equilibrium of the tensions between glo-
balization and national identity; a model of integrated attention with social

justice and an example of permanent pedagogical renewal and a space that integrates science, art, work, and learning" ("Programa de gobierno"). Childhood, once again, is an arena of tension, between global and national interests and between universal and populist values. The schools enshrine Chávez's mix of nationalist fervor, deep admiration for Bolívar, and revolutionary ideology. For example, the Ministry of Education sponsored an essay contest titled "Che Guevara, Example for Youth," and called the famous socialist revolutionary "a figure of dignity and global stature" (Rohter A4). Further, the education of children at these schools was to be overseen by "Bolivarian supervisors," often soldiers, provoking fears that the Bolivarian school model institutionalizes the ideological indoctrination of children.

Chávez's Bolivarian Schools were a part of a broader project of urban and social renewal that seeks to restore the lives of homeless and poor children. In the urban exploitation movie *Huelepega* (1999), which focused on the lives of glue-sniffing, indigent street children, the teenage protagonist has a knife duel with an adversary in front of the large monument of Bolívar in the Plaza Caracas, as the electric lights of the nightscape shimmer around them. The pessimism of this vision of the city of Bolívar has been replaced by initiatives to rescue these children, whom Chávez termed "hijos de la patria" (sons of the homeland). Chávez's supporters hoped that the Bolivarian School system would provide protection to the urban poor by providing food and a wealth of social services to children from within the school. On another, related front, the Instituto Nacional del Menor (INAM) spearheaded a program called "Los hijos de Bolívar" [The Sons of Bolívar], to rescue street children through outreach and education.

I return to *El correo del presidente*, however, to consider a text that synthesizes the question of Bolivarian paternity in relation to President Chávez. The paper contains a children's section with games and activities, as well as a section of readings for children titled "Mi paginita" [My Little Page]. In an article titled "Madrecita del Alma" by Angel V. Rivas, young readers are drawn into the narrative of Isabel de los Angeles, a young Venezuelan woman whose son David Nazareth was born with a disability that does not allow him to walk. The authorial voice presents the story in a first-person narrative, describing how he has met Isabel and her son David on one of the *microbuses* of Caracas. Isabel has given up working to care for her son, who needs to be carried up and down stairs and moved in and out of the school yard while he is at school. Isabel cannot afford a wheelchair for her son, and no one has offered to help. One day, she sees people milling at the stadium and learns that President Chávez will be there to address the multitudes. Filled with hope, she brings David to the stadium and is able to make her personal request of the president: "It was the opportunity to speak with the president. Isabel de los Angeles was rushing so much that one of David Nazareth's shoes fell from his foot and she did not even realize it. She got an appointment for a place on Andrés Bello Avenue. Now, on the bus, Isabel de los Angeles and her little son David Nazareth have hope. They hope to find the fruition of their desires. They wait for the promised help so that her little David Nazareth will have the wheelchair for moving about in. Oh! Upon finishing the event in the stadium, David Nazareth's little shoe appeared, hanging on the metal fence that divides the field" (Rivas 4). The Christian surnames reimagine the Virgin Mary, Jesus, and God within the ideology of Chavismo. "The president" is not named directly in the story, and direct observation of his act of charity and salvation is elided in the text as if it were a miracle. The populist theme of the story suggests that David symbolizes the plight of the urban poor, orphaned, and crippled, who need the intervention of a patriarchal presence to help them fulfil their promise. The abandoned shoe hung on the fence symbolizes the trespass of the traditional separation of the state from the concerns of these wounded masses, and monumentalizes the site of the miracle of Isabel and David's fateful contact with the state. Dependence on the state, and the embodiment of the state in one person, the president, whose powers and agency belong to the celestial realm, are the most important lessons that children might draw from this tale. Yet, a negative lesson is embedded in this Christmas story as well. Alongside the affirmation of rebirth under the tutelage of Chávez, the disability of David of Nazareth and his mother's financial limitations paint a rather desperate picture of a nation paralyzed by poverty and an unresponsive bureaucracy. Once again, the inspiration of children is plotted at the intersection between the promise of the future and the failures of the present. But most important of all, young readers might discover in this story a lesson that I have underlined throughout this chapter in relation to Bolívar: in spite of the president's awesome stature and power, he is good and he is accessible. He is the Father.

The story of David of Nazareth illustrates how Chávez's cultivation of parallels between himself and Bolívar sought to capitalize on the image of Bolívar as symbolic father of the nation at the very same time that the nation was constructed as a space of crisis and rupture. The works of

Manuel Calles, Santiago Key Ayala, and Teresa de la Parra echo this phenomenon; the definition of Bolívar as father is accompanied by a sense of loss, and by nostalgia. The heroism of the father lies in the past, and his resurrection in the present hinges on a sense that the nation is failing or has failed. The contradictory nature of this version of Bolivarian paternity also reminds us of a self-evident truism: Bolivarian nationalism is a patriarchal ideology that negates the feminine in favor of a defense of the patrilineal transmission of values. Bolívar has nothing to say to girls, it appears, unless his masculine nature is radically reimagined, as in the case of Teresa de la Parra's work. Her feminist reconstruction of Bolívar redefines the titan of bronze, softening the lines of his body, giving him the grace, sensitivity, and compassion she associates with women's experiences and character. Her Bolívar, however, like that of Key Ayala and other promoters of Bolivarian masculinity, is the product of a self-conscious act of renewal and invention, as well as a sense of disillusionment. It would seem that the power of the father looms large when the nation itself is imagined as incapacitated, like little David Nazareth.

"A Whore in the Palace"

The Poetics of Pornodetraction

Of the book, I've only read the chapter that *El país* of Madrid reproduced, and which friendly hands put in mine. But it is enough.
Didn't Unamuno say that it is not necessary to eat a whole egg to
know that it is rotten? Not even the magnitude of the disgust that
my reading of this text produced in me will allow me to transcribe
some phrases, such are their state of abjection; nor would the
newspaper dare to print them. But the reader needs to know the
slightest of all expressions attributed to Manuela: "Whore, I was
born a whore, I am a whore.". . . The reader must believe me: until
today there have never existed pages so loaded with ignominy, im-
posture, of great falsehood. . . .
Jorge Rivas Rivas

The publication in 1988 of *La esposa del doctor Thorne*, Denzil Romero's
historical novel about Simón Bolívar's mistress, Manuela Sáenz, generated
enormous public outrage. Arguably the most controversial historical novel
written to date about Bolívar, it narrates the sexual adventures of a cross-
dressing woman whose pursuit of pleasure includes bisexual encounters,
incest, and sex with multiple partners. To add insult to injury, Manuela
declares that she's Bolívar's "whore." Romero's novel won the 10th An-
nual Sonrisa Vertical literary prize in erotic literature sponsored by the
Tusquets publishing house in Spain, which published the title in its
Sonrisa Vertical series (the "Vertical Smile" is a visual pun on the image of
a small girl's mouth, which is framed in the series' pink book jacket in such
a manner as to suggest genitals). The secretary general of the Bolivarian
Society of Ecuador, Manuela's birthplace, called for legal action by the
Venezuelan government against Romero (Valero Martínez and Calderón
Chico 180). Ecuadorian lawmakers lodged a formal complaint against
Romero, and lobbied Venezuela's National Academy of History to insti-

tute standards that would regulate discourse on national heroes and heroines (16). And in perhaps the most memorable incident in the controversy, Romero was challenged to a duel by a "a Bolivarian gentleman" (16). Since the initial controversy, Romero has been the object of passionate critiques intended to refute his frankly sexual version of the relationship between Manuela and Bolívar. His critics have accused him of moral corruption, ignorance, greed, and literary and linguistic incompetence. The cover of Jorge Rivas Rivas's *Carta de Manuela Sáenz a su pornodetractor* [Manuela Sáenz's Letter to Her Pornodetractor] sums up the prevailing view of Romero among defenders of the honor of Bolívar and Manuela by depicting him as Pinocchio with an elongated nose in the shape of a scalpel-like, metal quill. Despite the controversy, or perhaps because of it, the novel has sold well, going through four printings between 1988 and 1990 alone.

La esposa del doctor Thorne begins with Simón Bolívar's Organic Decree of 1828, by which the Colombian Constitution was abrogated in favor of a temporary dictatorship. Disgusted with his necessary participation in this turn of events, and frustrated by frequent comparisons to Napoleon, Bolívar fantasizes about making love to Manuela Sáenz. After the establishment of this narrative frame, the novel recounts the story of Manuela's life up until 1828, emphasizing her nymphomania. The illegitimately conceived Manuela is raised in colonial Quito, where moral depravity is the norm. Her life in the convent of Santa Catalina does not protect her from the excesses of lusty and slothful priests and friars who regularly plunder convents for sexual pleasure, while the nuns inside hold each other in lesbian bondage (31). In the convent, Manuela is sexually initiated by her mother's cousin before being taken as a concubine by the lustiest and "most well endowed" friar of Quito, who shares her with his Dominican brothers. Her next lover is Captain Fausto D'Elhuyar, a royalist soldier with whom she elopes to the port city of Guayaquil for a short affair. When Manuela returns to Quito, she enters into a marriage of convenience with an Englishman much older than herself, Dr. James Thorne. Thorne moves to Lima where his wife quickly becomes the most beautiful, notorious, and trend-setting woman of the city. During her stay in Lima, Manuela seduces her husband's adolescent page and enters into a sexual relationship with her friend Rosita Campuzano, in which she takes on the dominant masculine role. After a ménage à trois with her half brother and Rosita, Manuela meets and falls in love with Bolívar, who proves to be a true match for her imaginative, sexual prowess. In the end, the novel returns to the framing device of 1828, when Bolívar arrives at his mansion and informs Manuela that he wants her to move into the palace. "A whore in the palace? How can you think of such a thing?" but Bolívar is insistent, and his mistress begins to gather her things.

By presenting Bolívar's lover as independent and sexually insatiable, Romero's novel criticizes dominant representations of Bolívar's sentimental and sexual life. At the symbolic level, the cult of Bolívar is constructed out of several interlocking stories, all of which contribute to the construction of Bolívar as a powerful and great man. For example, it is de rigueur in many biographies that the story of Bolívar's life begin with that of his patrilineal ancestry, constructing Bolívar's heroism as a function of genealogical greatness. The story of an exemplary education is also central to telling the story of Bolívar, for it situates the heroic subject into a network of great men, such as Bolívar's childhood tutors and mentors Andrés Bello and Simón Rodríguez, who are well known in their own right as influential men of letters. More importantly, however, is the story of a martial brotherhood, which focuses and amplifies the hero's superior military and tactical skills by embedding him into a masculine collectivity of great warriors. Finally, in the telling of the life of Bolívar there are stories of love and/or seduction, which restage the hero's prowess among men through the cliché of sexual conquest. The cult of Bolívar delights in the tale of the death of Bolívar's young wife, which propels him into a life of politics and military epic, throughout which he seduced many memorably beautiful and dedicated young women, the most famous being Manuela Sáenz.[1] Romero's novel critiques this patrilineal narrative by displacing the freedom and power to be promiscuous onto Manuela Sáenz, who rather than being a conquest is a powerful seductress of men and women.

Romero's focus on the body and his commitment to wordplay results in a narrative that celebrates performative and provisional meanings over absolute and essentialist ones. His focus on bodies and pleasure results in passages that not only challenge conventional gendered categories, but also conceptual absolutes in general. In the pages to follow, I argue that *La esposa del doctor Thorne* both contests and reinforces the cult of Bolívar through this emphasis on sexual and linguistic excess. On the one hand, the novel unflinchingly underlines Bolívar's failures at the end of his political career, which saw a return to the policies and attitudes of the ancien régime against which he had fought. On the other hand, Romero reinforces and preserves Bolívar's phallic power, which is measured by his ability to dominate the formidable Manuela. Moreover, while the novel seems to trouble Bolívar's virility by representing him as a naïve dreamer who submits to Manuela's pleasure, Romero also scripts the failure of Latin American independence upon the body of Manuela without symbolically castrating Bolívar himself. This plundering of Manuela's body for the purpose of political critique stages the allegorical narrative of woman as an unruly landscape that is defeated, possessed, and contained by a phallic man. Although we may be tempted to celebrate *La esposa del doctor Thorne* for its indictment of official Bolivarian ideology, and praise it as a democratic novel, I demonstrate that Romero's insistence on preserving Bolívar's virility, and quite literally his phallic power, leads the novel back into the fold of the monumentalist definition of Bolivarian masculinity.

Dilemmas of Incorporation: Manuelita Sáenz between Epic and Romance

> The impudent woman, who has always followed in the footsteps of General Bolívar, presents herself every day in attire that does not correspond to her sex, and directs her servants to go forth insulting decorum and displaying their disdain for the laws and for morality. . . . That woman, whose mere presence sums up Bolívar's own conduct, has extended her insolence and shamelessness to the extreme of going out on the 9th of the present month to vex the very government and the people of Bogotá. In a man's attire she arrived in the public plaza with two or three soldiers (they were the two negro women . . .), whom she keeps in her home and whose service is paid by the State, and charged the guards that guarded the castle destined for the firework celebration of Corpus; and waving a pistol she was carrying with her, she railed against the government, against liberty, and against the people.
> **Editorial of *La aurora*, Bogotá, 1830**

In their passionate defense of the honor of Manuela Sáenz, most of Denzil Romero's critics glossed over Manuela's ambivalent position in Latin American history. From the outset of her public career as Bolívar's "favorite" confidante and secretary, Manuela elicited violent opposition from Bolívar's enemies. In the final years of Bolívar's life, rumors swirled in Bogotá about her unfaithfulness to Bolívar, and about her bisexuality, as evidenced by the memoirs of one of her acquaintances, Jean Baptiste Boussingault.[2] After Bolívar's death, when the Liberator's name became synonymous with despotism and militarism in Colombian circles, Manuela's commitment to Bolivarian agitation resulted in her expulsion from Colombia and, later on, Ecuador. Enemies and friends alike paint a portrait

of her as a forceful and politically engaged personality that did not conform to socially sanctioned norms of feminine behavior. As such, she has
proven to be a conceptual challenge to historians and mythmakers. How to
write this woman warrior and political agent into a coherent tale of
Bolívar? María Teresa del Toro, Bolívar's young bride, who died shortly
after marrying him, is an interesting point of contrast; María's youth and
fragility lend themselves to the stereotype of the pure, tubercular virgin.
The often cited claim, by Bolívar himself, that her death opened up the
doors of his military and political career adds to the aura of feminine domesticity surrounding María, and points to an alternate version of Latin
American history, in which the Liberator might have lived out his life in
relative anonymity. The independent and politically active Manuela does
not conform to the notion of fragile femininity represented by María,
forcing her biographers to question the standard dyad of male/female to
define her identity. In short, Manuela's iconic stature as Bolívar's lover has
made her eccentricity the site of some surprisingly serious, if uninten-
tional, explorations of gender.

In light of this chapter's stake in the study of representations of Manuela and Bolívar, it is not my purpose to present an objective introduction
to the life of Manuela Sáenz against which others should be judged. It will
suffice to list the most commonly accepted elements of her life story before considering the question of Manuela's representation as a heroine.
Manuela Sáenz was born in 1795 or 1797[3] in Quito, the illegitimate prog-
eny of Simón Sáenz de Vergara and Joaquina Aizpuru. After the death of
her mother, Manuela was raised in the Convent of Santa Catalina, and
traded back and forth between her maternal grandparents and her father,
who was married and had other children. She was cared for by two young
black servants, Jonatás and Nathan, who would accompany her throughout
her life and acquire notoriety as fellow provocateurs and subversives. During her adolescence Manuela eloped with a royalist soldier named Fausto
D'Elhuyar, provoking much scandal, but the relationship was short-lived
and soon she was back in Quito. In 1812 she married an English doctor,
James Thorne, who moved his new bride to Lima, where Manuela befriended another heroine of the Wars of Independence, Rosa Campuzano,
who was to become one of José de San Martín's lovers. Both women were
sufficiently involved in Lima's pro-independence circles to receive the
award *La caballeresa del Sol* from San Martín when he marched into the
city in 1821. A year later, Manuela met Bolívar in Quito, and became his
lover. At the time, Bolívar was in the process of securing Andean indepen-

dence and consolidating Colombian control over the Audiencia of Quito and the Viceroyalty of Perú after the liberation of Venezuela and Colombia. Manuela's status was evidently more than that of any other of his lovers, since she was charged with caring for the archive of his personal correspondence.

In September of 1828, Manuela entered into myth as more than simply a lover when she played a key role in saving Bolívar from a party of would-be assassins. Manuela convinced him to escape from their balcony while she stalled his enemies in their bedroom, receiving a beating in the process. Later, when most of the conspirators had been brought to justice, Bolívar conferred upon her the title of La Libertadora del Libertador (The Liberatrix of the Liberator). In 1829 she wrote memorable lines to her husband, who continued to pine for her in spite of her continued association with the most powerful and feared man on the continent: "Leave me alone my dear Englishman. Let's do something different: in heaven we will marry again, but on earth no" (Rumazo González 256). Although Bolívar was not at all times faithful, Manuela remained intimate with him until his departure from Bogotá to the Colombian coast in 1830, where he died several months later.

During Bolívar's final months and following his death, Manuela became the focus of anti-Bolivarian sentiment in Bogotá. Upon learning that effigies of herself (representing tyranny) and Bolívar (representing despotism) were to be burned at a local garrison, Manuela, Jonatás, and Nathan attacked the garrison and destroyed the effigies, riding as men and attired as soldiers. Not surprisingly, President Francisco Paula de Santander exiled Manuela from Colombia, and she traveled to Jamaica before returning to Quito, where she was expelled once again, this time by President Rocafuerte of Ecuador, who viewed her as a dangerous subversive. Manuela finally settled down in the Peruvian village of Paita, where she conducted an extended personal and political correspondence with her friend General Flores, one of Bolívar's loyal caudillos who later became president of Ecuador. Manuela remained in Paita, however, where she entertained distinguished visitors such as Simón Rodríguez, Bolívar's childhood tutor, the Peruvian writer Ricardo Palma, Giuseppe Garibaldi, Italy's own "Liberator," and the American novelist Herman Melville. In the late 1850s, the wheelchair-bound Manuela succumbed to an epidemic of typhoid, and was buried in a common grave. Her house, containing trunks of papers relating to Bolívar's life, was burned to the ground to prevent further propagation of the disease.

Pamela Murray's diachronic study of the representation of Manuela Sáenz in Latin American historiography identifies four schools of thought regarding Bolívar's confidante: (1) the bad girl thesis, which views her as a deviant being; (2) her idolization in the Bolivarian-heroic school; (3) the twentieth-century nationalist appropriation, which makes her a symbol of Ecuadorian contributions to Latin American independence; and (4) an emergent feminist version of the heroine "meant to inspire those committed to reforming Latin American societies in accordance with feminist and social democratic ideals" (Murray 307). In the analysis that follows, I elaborate on the issues of deviance and proper feminine conduct that Murray highlights in her periodization by suggesting that representations of Manuela Sáenz oscillate between the demands of epic, according to which her violation of feminine norms is singularly heroic, and those of romance, in which her actions are framed as conventionally feminine. Neither model is capable of providing closure: the epic Manuela is androgynous and ultimately threatening to the cult of Bolívar, while the romantic Manuela is destabilized by the impossibility of deploying marriage and reproduction as viable conditions of identity. These ambiguities demonstrate how much Bolivarian monumentalism is predicated on the naturalization of gender. Because monumentalist ideology posits the body of the hero as a model of unassailable masculine power, and structures meaning as univocal, the cult of Bolívar is threatened by narratives in which women do not behave like "women," and men do not behave like "men." In the pages to follow, I explore how a sampling of biographers and commentators either deny Manuela her difference or develop a new vocabulary to talk about her gender.

I begin with the epic characterization of Manuela in the nineteenth century, which genders her as a "manly woman." Ricardo Palma, the celebrated author of *Peruvian Traditions*, visited Manuela in Paita repeatedly and wrote revealingly of the differences between Manuela and her friend, Rosa Campuzano: "Rosa Campuzano was decidedly a woman through and through, and without scruples; had I been young in her days of graciousness and elegance, I would have enrolled in the list of her . . . platonic lovers. Doña Manuela, even in the days when she was a beauty, would have inspired in me only the respectful feeling of friendship that I professed for her in her old age. Doña Rosa was a womanly woman. Doña Manuela was a manly woman."[4] Arístides Rojas, a Venezuelan chronicler of customs and traditions, viewed Manuela in similar terms in his *Leyendas históricas de Venezuela* (1890–1891). He argues that Manuela can be read in one of two ways, as a woman or as a heroine of the homeland. The categories already suggest a gendered division in which what is feminine is precluded from the public arena of heroic, national foundations. However, the overlay of gender onto the dyad of public versus private is still inadequate to describe Manuela. Rojas takes it one step further, and subdivides the category of heroine into two types: the martyr that dies like a traditional, self-sacrificing woman, and the Amazon or *mujer varonil* (manly woman), which best suits Manuela (79). The manly woman model has endured into the twentieth century, appearing in important works such as Emil Ludwig's *Bolívar: The Life of an Idealist* (1938), a biography that was commissioned by the Venezuelan government. Ludwig mentions Manuela's skills as a rider, the pants she wears, and her accuracy as a rifle shot. Yet, he closes the description with an interesting aside that draws attention to her ambiguous gender. "Such was Manuela Sáenz," he writes, "whom he used to later call Manuelita, as if the tenderness of the diminutive could recall her to her role as a woman" (215). Ludwig goes on to say that this is a woman of the "Amazon type who combines womanly pliancy with masculine pride" (219). Yet, Ludwig, like most biographers of Bolívar, does not dwell on Manuela. The most articulate and detailed analysis of Manuela as manly woman may be found in Alfonso Rumazo González's seminal *Manuela Sáenz: La Libertadora del Libertador* (1945), a biography that is clearly the basis for the structure and several of the episodes of Romero's novel.

Rumazo González's biography of Manuela's life was not welcomed in Ecuador until twenty-six years after its initial publication date, amply demonstrating official discomfort with the subject matter (Mogollon Cobo and Narváez Yar 101). Rumazo González embraced the sensational aspects of Manuela's life, and constructed his protagonist as a swashbuckling heroine of independence. In his text, her native Quito is a decadent society where free love and sexual excess run rampant. The libidinous and beautiful Manuela, who combines the strength of character of her cruel royalist father and the freethinking ways of her mother, absorbs the injustices and excesses of colonial rule into her character and becomes a revolutionary subject (Rumazo González 69). The ideological gulf separating her from her father creates an emptiness in her that fuels a desire that will be fulfilled by Bolívar: "For every girl the first love of man is that of her father. The emptiness will turn into desire, into restlessness, into thirst that will be satisfied abundantly, tumultuously" (46). Besides signaling this desire for a man, Rumazo González does little to feminize Manuela, and further develops Palma's manly woman argument. He places her at Ayacucho, the last and greatest battle of independence, and dramatically highlights one memoirist's claim that she tore a moustache off a fallen Spanish foe to wear on her own face (90, 186–87). In a passage that Romero will riff on to great effect in his novel, Rumazo González makes her defining characteristic the ability to laugh, which marks her as a manly woman: "Laughter is man's prerogative; knowing how to laugh is more difficult than knowing how to think. . . . No one ever could escape Manuela's laughter, not even Bolívar" (90). This laughing woman, dressed as a man to the moustache, killing Royalists with a heavy spear at Ayacucho, is a subversive figure that flies in the face of liberal and conservative codes of acceptable gender roles. In the end, Rumazo González's self-conscious celebration of the epic of independence tempers the allusions to Manuela's infertility, sexual escapades, and cross-dressing. The critical edge of Denzil Romero's novel lies in the fact that it foregoes Rumazo González's epic narrative of independence in favor of a focus on the issues of androgyny and illicit sexuality.

The more conventional womanly woman model for reading Manuela Sáenz also has roots in the nineteenth century. Manuela died just as the era of President García Moreno (1860–1895) was beginning in Ecuador; the regime privileged Catholicism in its public policies and was quite conservative in its views of the kinds of education and roles women were to have in society. Historians such as Fermín Cevallos (*Resumen de la historia del Ecuador desde su orijen hasta 1845*, 1870) and Pedro Moncayo (*El Ecuador de 1825 a 1875*, 1886) were conspicuous in their downplaying of Manuela's role in Bolívar's life. In his treatment of the assassination attempt, for example, Cevallos underlines the inappropriate circumstances of the lovers' cohabitation and foregrounds Bolívar's heroism in the incident. Moncayo, one of Manuela's political enemies, does not mention Manuela or the assassination attempt at all in his history (Mogollon Cobo and Narváez Yar 72–74). The first Ecuadorian text to celebrate Manuela was Manuel Calle's *Leyendas del tiempo heroico* (1901), a book of historical episodes that presented Manuela as a fragile and self-sacrificing heroine. Moreover, Calle rewrites all documentary accounts of the 1828 assassination attempt and presents Bolívar alone in his chamber. When he hears the din of assassins overcoming the palace's sentries, he arms himself, at which time a hysterical Manuela appears, kneeling and imploring Bolívar to escape through the window. She is able to compose herself to stall the assassins, but slips back into tears as she sees Bolívar's trusted Ibarra in a pool of blood: "Upon seeing him, the Sáenz woman can no longer contain herself and, woman at last, breaks into desperate sobs" (92). Here is a woman capable of heroics, but only through the function of fragility, sentiment, and dependence. Simply put, she is a womanly woman.

Demetrio Aguilera Malta's *La caballeresa del sol* (1964) is a thinly fictionalized account of Manuela and Bolívar's life together that illustrates the representational instabilities that the model of the womanly woman entails. In the novel, Bolívar's virility is underlined early on through exalted descriptions of his ability to seduce and make love to Manuela, whose body and self disintegrate during the sex act.[5] In spite of this gendering of the lovers (he as phallic male, she as passive receptacle), Aguilera Malta's determination to explain and exalt the Bolívar-Manuela love relationship leads him to infantilize the Liberator and cast Manuela in the role of a mother figure. In the absence of marriage and procreation, the maternal frame enables Aguilera Malta to validate their relationship and idolize Manuela as a mentor of Bolívar. This maternal theme is presented by imposing the dyad of dreamer/realist on Bolívar/Manuela; Bolívar thinks himself into distraction, dreaming up grandiose and unrealistic geopolitical schemes, while Manuela's talent lies in her ability to perceive her lover's limitations and the difficult political realities that surround them. Her voice, like that of a learned Bolivarian scholar who annotates the Liberator's enthusiastic exclamations, foreshadows the failures to come and the oversights that would cost Bolívar so dearly (58, 251–52). As Bolívar's health fails, Manuela the maternal realist takes on an increasingly important role in caring for her lover. Bolívar's triumph in his Andean campaign, for example, provokes an exchange that clearly casts the hero in an infantilized role:

And Bolívar was like a child with a new toy. He had accepted Lima just as the City of Viceroys accepted him. Sometimes he would get excited and tell her a lot of things she already knew. But she never interrupted. Once he was especially happy:

"Did you hear? Congress has given me a sword with the handle adorned with diamonds and emeralds. And a uniform with so much gold decoration that I'm sure I'll never use it. And José Joaquín de Olmedo, an Ecuadorian poet and politician, wrote a hymn to the victory of Junín that is one of the finest epic poems in Spanish. Though it is too eulogistic about me."

She looked at him entranced.

"For Simón Bolívar, regardless of where it comes from, no praise is excessive." (232)

Bolívar comes across as an immature child who craves the approval of Manuela, whose proud disposition mirrors the attitude of an adoring mother. Further, in an even more dramatic passage, Manuela swings Bolívar in his hammock as he makes his grandiose plans, studying him intently for signs of distress of any kind, evoking the protective image of a mother with a child in a cradle (152). The characterization of Manuela as mother legitimates their bond in a context in which the socially sanctioned role of wife is not available. By making the maternal the source of Manuela's privileged status in relation to Bolívar, Aguilera Malta effectively subordinates the hero to Manuela, negating his virility and claim to the title of founding father. Moreover, the patronizing tone of Manuela's warnings to Bolívar disempowers the hero of independence on another level: Manuela embodies a kind of contemporary hindsight that diminishes Bolívar's choices and political strategies. In contrast to wise Manuela, Aguilera Malta's Bolívar is a foolish character.

Manuela's experiences as a combatant of independence, her public role as defender of Bolivarian ideology, and her status as a lover of Bolívar have placed her in an ambiguously gendered position. The narration of epic cannot help but reinforce the image of the androgynous, mustachioed, manly woman and challenge Bolívar's status as a virile and masculine subject. The discourse of feminine submission, which invokes Manuela as a kind of domestic angel, fails in the absence of the legitimating contract of marriage and procreation. These contrasting trends in the representation of Manuela highlight the artifice and relational quality of conventional gender identity. As a supplement to Bolívar, Manuela is either his woman or his martial partner in war, with each role coding a different gender identity. The womanly woman model is the more artificial and reactionary of the two because it self-consciously disregards the wealth of reports in the historical record about Manuela's public and controversial role in Bolívar's life. This model, exemplified by Calle's insistence on showing Manuela as an emotional being rather than a heroic one, and Aguilera Malta's effort to make her a maternal character, attempts to recover a narrow and conservative definition of femininity for Manuela. The proponents of the manly woman model embrace to differing degrees the possibility of reading Manuela as an example of a third gender: not woman, nor man, but something in between that combines elements from both. Their versions of Manuela, as exemplified by Palma and Ludwig, explore the possibility of redefining or problematizing the simplistic model of feminine/masculine in response to Manuela's character and conduct. In essence, their struggle to categorize Manuela suggests that there may be ways of being a woman that are both feminine and masculine. Seen in this light, Manuela's challenge to posterity is extraordinary: if she could avail herself of masculinity for the performance of her own identity as a woman, then should we accept the masculinity of Bolívar as something biological or providential? Or did he too have "feminine" qualities? The manly woman biographers did not follow these questions to their logical conclusion. However, Denzil Romero did recognize the dramatic possibilities of the enigma of Manuela's identity and took it further than anyone before had ever done. Despite the clamor of critics intent on vilifying him, Romero belongs within a well-delineated and accepted corpus of historical interpretations of Manuela Sáenz. His novel may be the most sensational statement on Manuela, but the substance of his characterization of her as an androgynous figure is not new.

History versus Histories: *La esposa del doctor Thorne* as a New Historical Novel

Denzil Romero's critics defend the sanctity of a sacred, referential history. Although Romero is faulted for immorality, misuse of the Spanish language, and sloppy characterization and literary technique, the overarching transgression is violating the essence of Manuela Sáenz's historical being: "A life or an event can be fictionalized . . . as long as the essential is not disfigured" (Valero Martínez and Calderón Chico 127). Romero's crime is not only against the memory of Manuela but against Bolívar as well, whose greatness is tarnished by Romero's depiction of his lover's transgressive sexual conduct. In the words of Alfonso Rumazo González, who bemoaned the nymphomania of Romero's Manuela: "How could the Liberator be so blind, ignorant, and naïve during the last seven years of his life?" (53). The defense of a monological historical truth that *La esposa del doctor Thorne* has provoked underlines the relevance of a discussion of Romero's work in the context of what recent criticism has termed the "new historical novel," a genre of historical fiction that undermines official history.

Discussions of "new historical fiction" in contemporary literature invariably circle back to complex, theoretical debates about postmodernity and postmodernism, terms that have provoked much controversy and discussion in Latin American cultural studies. In order to understand the new historical novel, these slippery terms need to be defined, however generally and provisionally. In Europe and the United States postmodernity is understood as a period of accelerated, capitalist production that makes the construction of coherent, centered identities difficult (Hall 569–70). Postmodernism avails itself of the modalities of expression of the past to produce immanent and ironic art. This immanent art undermines the dominant scripts through which meaning has been expressed in the modern age, such as liberal humanism, nationalism, and the distinction between high and low culture. By rejecting these scripts, postmodern art decenters the subject and signals a new kind of alienation that corresponds to post–World War II capitalism (Harvey 66). Whereas modernist art and architecture was innovative in its own time, it remained beholden to a quest for wholeness, or to certain notions of unity and order, such as psychology (the unconscious) or utilitarianism (as in modern urban architecture). In contrast, postmodern art rejects such principles of structure, and as such, both amplifies and moves beyond modernism's innovations.[6]

In Latin America, the postmodern debate has taken on a life of its own as critics debate the differences between political and economic development in the developed world, which the foundational statements of postmodernism address, and in Latin America, the realities of which seem to demand a new way of defining postmodernism, or at least an amendment to or qualification of existing theoretical models. The problem is basically one of nomenclature: while most critics agree that Latin American culture at the end of the twentieth century was not the same as during the first half, or at mid-century, they disagree about how these differences should be theorized and framed in relation to debates in European and North American criticism (Lindstrom 49–50). Therefore, the term *postmodern* is unstable for discussions of Latin American culture, requiring a series of complex qualifications and shadings. At its simplest, however, we can assert that Latin American postmodernism in art and culture may be defined as both a symptom of the push and pull of late capitalism as well as a critical response to these circumstances. As such, Latin American postmodernism is characterized by hybridity, irony, and the critique of the ideologies of progress.

In the domain of literature, one of the salient expressions of postmodernism is what Linda Hutcheon has called "historiographic metafiction." Historiographic metafiction undermines the truth claims of official history in favor of a more provisional and indeterminate vision of historical experience (109–10). Theorists of contemporary historical fiction in Latin America, such as Fernando Ainsa, Seymour Menton, and Elzbieta Sklodowska, concur in arguing that contemporary historical novels respond to the political disenchantments of the present, highlighting the false nature of official histories through ironic and playful riffs on foundational historical periods and characters. This characterization echoes broader statements about postmodern fiction writ large, such as Julio Ortega's assertion that postmodern texts express "the implosive power of migrant cultures, of relativizing pastiche and popular kitsch, the insistent immediacy of oral forms and of sensual freedom" ("Postmodernism" 198). Juan Dávila's painting of Bolívar is an excellent illustration of this postmodern sensibility. As shown in the introduction, his vision of Bolívar erases everything that is essential and powerful about the hero of independence, leaving in its wake the notion that Bolívar is a fiction. What remains to be seen now is whether or not Romero's novel is as extreme an example of postmodern iconoclasm.

Denzil Romero has dedicated himself almost exclusively to the genre of new historical fiction, and is one of the most inventive and adventurous of its proponents. The subject matter of *La esposa del doctor Thorne*, like other novels by Romero, suggests distrust toward epic forms of historiography by avoiding a direct treatment of the mythical referent of Bolívar. In his historical fiction, Romero has skirted Bolívar at every turn: his novel *La tragedia del Generalísimo* (1983) is about Francisco de Miranda, one of Venezuela's early leaders of independence; and *La carujada* (1990) deals with Pedro Carujo, a would-be assassin of Bolívar. This choice of protagonists demonstrates willingness to foreground what has been eclipsed, subordinated, or vilified in epic forms of Venezuelan historiography and historical fiction. Further, this focus always treats Bolívar with a kind of sideward literary glance, as if the direct, fictional treatment of the hero belonged more to demagogy and historical apology than to the promise of fiction. In short, whereas in the cult of Bolívar the hero is always at the center of the frame, Bolívar is situated in the margins of Romero's fiction.

La esposa del doctor Thorne decenters official history by foregrounding bodies in sexual excess, and utilizing temporal and literary techniques that violate more conventional notions of narrative. The challenge to official history in Romero's treatment of Manuela Sáenz begins at the very outset with a title that defines Manuela as the wife of Dr. Thorne. The mythic title of La Libertadora del Libertador, which Manuela earned when she helped avert the assassination of Bolívar in 1828, is discarded in favor of a phrase that underscores the adulterous nature of her relationship with Bolívar. Moreover, to be the "wife of Dr. Thorne," and not "the lover of Bolívar" or

"Bolívar's woman," for example, emphasizes her life before Bolívar and downplays her public profile as heroine of independence. It should be no surprise then that an anthology of anti-Romero texts should be titled *In Defense of Manuela Sáenz, La Libertadora del Libertador*, thus recentering Manuela in epic history on the very title page (Valero Martínez and Calderón Chico). Thus, the title of Romero's novel self-consciously revokes the epic status of Manuela by refusing to name her outright as the historical referent (Manuela Sáenz, individual historical agent) as well as negating the prevailing mythical interpretation that has become equivalent to her very name (La Libertadora del Libertador). The protagonist is an entirely different woman, as the reader soon finds out; she is the lusty wife of Dr. Thorne. In defining Manuela in this manner, Romero has found the space in which to present a character that is capable of breaking with history and myth, rather than simply being a fictional supplement to it.

The new historical novel problematizes mythic origins. Romero's refusal to propose Manuela as an epic heroine in his title is but one example of this phenomenon. Romero also discards epic by representing Manuela as a character embedded in fashion, popular speech, and sexualized spaces. When Thorne and Manuela move to Lima, Manuela relaxes fashion requirements for elite women, promoting low-cut dresses, and dramatic makeup, including painting the lips in the shape of a heart, and adding birthmarks in various places (84–85). In addition to setting these trends among the elite, Manuela becomes a referent in more popular quarters: "There appeared restaurants, saloons, taverns, and party houses named 'Manuela,' 'La Manuela,' 'Manuelilla,' 'Manuelina,' Manuelita,' 'Manola,' 'Manoleta.' The whores of Arequipa street, and those of Tacna street, and those of the terrifying corner of Rufino Torrico, and Ocaña, and those moving until dawn between Quilca and Camaná, and those of Huacavelica, toward Unión Plaza or, in the opposite direction, toward the Rimac, began to take on these names. To distinguish themselves among each other they took the most extravagant variations: 'Manuela Hummingbird,' 'Manuela Star,' 'Manuela Lace,' 'Manuela Oasis.' . ." (86).

And the list goes on. The word *Manuela* thus marks Lima as a body of pleasure, as a space of freedom and excess, a place for food or drink, and a body through which pleasure is accessed. Her influence as a symbol of excess among the elite is iconoclastic, but her incorporation into popular culture is also subversive since it defines her currency as quotidian, urban, and corporeal, as opposed to exceptional, Homeric, and transcendental. The collapsing of the boundaries between high and low culture divorces Manuela from her own myth; at the end of his catalogue of prostitute names, Romero's narrative voice sums up by declaring that Manuela was "the most popular, the most spoiled, the most praised, the most vituperated, adored to the point of deification or denigrated to damnation, Manuela Sáenz, Manuela Sáenz of Quito, the wife of Dr. Thorne . . ." (87). In this passage, Romero flaunts his refusal to name Manuela as the Manuela Sáenz who is La Libertadora del Libertador; instead, she is the site of many names, and the richness of popular culture.

Intertextuality is also very much present in the novel. Romero freely quotes from canonical sources of knowledge about Manuela Sáenz, finding most of his inspiration from Rumazo González's celebrated biography. The theme of colonial, sexual corruption and Manuela's characterization as a manly woman to Rosa Campuzano's womanly woman are transparently reframed in the novel. At times, Romero seems to follow Rumazo González almost page by page, rewriting and lifting passages for his own use. However, Romero's preferred mode of intertextuality uses twentieth-century historical references, literary texts, and authors to frame the novel's external referents conspicuously as fictional or poetic. By invoking twentieth-century poets such as Pablo Neruda and César Vallejo, as well as his contemporary, the novelist Caupolican Ovalles, Romero situates his novel not within official history, but within literary history. Further, the use of twentieth-century literary voices and personages to populate the margins of his novel (Sebastian Salazar Bondy, Greta Garbo, Pancho Villa) powerfully underscores the artifice of his own narration, which in announcing itself as play challenges the self-important and sober discourse dictated by the epic mode of official history or more realistic and grandiloquent historical fiction. For example, in their performance of heterosexual romance, Manuela and her lover Rosita take on the identities of famous lovers past, present, and future, including Pancho Villa and La Adelita (the latter, of course, being the subject of the most famous song of the Mexican Revolution). Since the existence of Villa and La Adelita corresponds to a full century after the role-playing scene in the novel, both are referents that defuse the pretense of a historical accuracy in the text; the naming of Pancho Villa and La Adelita underscores the fictional character of the novel and reminds us that the text does not mimic the conventions and chronological imperatives of historical narration.

The detailed description of sexual acts in the novel, including sadomasochism and the ingestion of semen and urine, may be seen as an extension of how language becomes sensual and excessive in the novel. One critical analysis of the novel recognizes this parallelism and describes Romero's narrative as a body in crisis through the following hyperbole: "We are referring to, of course, verborrea or linguistic diarrhea. A profound proliferation inundates the diegesis and then, without remedy, the text suffers strong jolts and its bases stumble dangerously . . ." (Valero Martínez and Calderón Chico 120–21). Examples of this linking of corporeality to language abound in the novel, and demonstrate how language can mirror the quantitative and qualitative nature of Manuela's quest for pleasure. One example is the description of how Manuela's first male lover, Friar Bernardo Castillejo de Mejorada y Anzur, shares her with his fellow friars. The resulting passage is a masterful example of how repetition and sonorous words may be used to create a humorous effect: "When Manuela was not satisfied, the friar proposed the help of the strong brothers of his order: that of Friar Lorenzo de La Parrila and that of Friar Benito Morreo de Bejarano, that of Friar Francisco de Avellaneda and that of Friar Eulogio Valencia de Aragón, that of Friar Leocadio Cueto de Quiñones and that of Friar Lisandro Morgado de la Puerta, that of Friar Tancredo Flores Risuarte and that of Friar Fernando de Laguna, that of Friar Luis Medina de Miranda and that of Friar Torcuato Satiliano de Velasco y Falcón; that of the whole Dominican family of Quito and the surrounding settlements, from Tulcán past Loja . . ." (39). The catalogue of long-winded names becomes an apocryphal wordplay rather than a referential list of personages and emphasizes the excess of Manuela's sexual activity. The primary function of the names is to provide a measure of the extent to which Manuela was shared sexually. This is accomplished through a rapid succession of ornately respectable names that are as rich in their acoustic quality as they are multiple. In a later novel, *Amores, pasiones, y vicios de la Gran Catalina* (1995), Romero would pursue this strategy once again, by including an apocryphal bibliography to supplement his historical narrative.

In Romero's poetics, language is not at the service of epic or romance, but operates analogously to the body of pleasure. Romero endeavors to represent the correlation language-pleasure through a passage in which Manuela reacts to an anonymous note sent to her husband to reveal her infidelities with her old lover Friar Bernardo. Romero utilizes the principle of repetition to achieve his effect, as well as a weaving together of temporally disparate historical and cultural references.

Now Manuela laughs, laughs, laughs, like the poor Garrick de Nervo when he was on stage; like Bergson when he wrote *Laughter;* like Estefanía, of *Palinuro de México,* with her teeth full of sand, when

she was ten; like the painting *Jesus* tied to the Column in the Monas-
tery, in spite of the torture: laughing; and like the happy poets of
Darío: the great Anacreont, the great Ovid, Quevedo, Banville.
Laughed, Manuela laughed, then, like a hairy hyena, like a crazy
woman hallucinating, like a mad child. She laughed as if she were
being tickled or if she were in a comedy. She laughed dropping the
rag, putting up her hair, pulling on her hair, holding her chest. She
laughed stunned, uncaringly, all wrapped up, broken up, barefooting
herself, spilling herself, decomposing herself, until her stomach hurt,
until tears leapt from her eyes, until she let loose the stream of piss in
her own underpants. . . . (62)

The laugh is a space of sensual disarray that manifests itself through the
loss of bodily controls, and an unleashing of the creative potential of language itself, which folds onto itself as an ever-proliferating, expressive energy without a beginning and an end. In laughter, the boundaries between
happiness, sadness, mystical transport, truth, fiction, body, and soul are all
collapsed.[7] As illustrated here, Romero's language of the risible exploits
the expressive potential of language, unmooring it from determinism and
absolute terms. The sounds of Manuela laughing, and the contortions of
her body as it loses control of itself, are an apt emblem of Romero's brand
of new historical fiction. It would seem that the foregrounding of pleasure,
whether it be in the form of laughter or a diverse array of sexual practices,
makes the maintenance of static, essential definitions of identity difficult if
not impossible. Yet, the case of Bolívar in *La esposa del doctor Thorne* does
point to some limitations in what might otherwise be called a nihilist attack on official histories and their conventions.

Simón Bolívar, Romantic Subject

At first glance, Romero's novel does not occupy itself that much with
Simón Bolívar, but rather with the sexual escapades of Manuela Sáenz. In
this respect, *La esposa del doctor Thorne* removes Bolívar from center-
stage, as in other novels by Romero about the independence period. However, on a deeper level, Romero is indeed contemplating Bolívar throughout the novel. The framing device, out of which the story of Manuela is
reconstructed, suggests that the failure of Bolivarian republicanism is tied
to the fate of Manuela's unruly body. Moreover, Romero presents Bolívar's power over Manuela, and by extension the continent, as a function of
his fundamentally romantic and mythological nature. Manuela's discourse

of corporeal excess, which permeates the novel practically from beginning to end, is opposed to this idealized discourse of identity. Thus, Romero transposes the dyad spirit/body onto the relationship of Bolívar and Manuela, utilizing the repeated descriptions of transgressive sex acts to deflate the fictions of epic and sentimental, foundational love. The resulting representation is unsatisfyingly ambivalent as a critique of the cult of Bolívar. While Bolívar's body remains intact, Manuela's is exploited in the name of political critique. Moreover, in spite of the abstract quality of the character of Bolívar, Romero emphasizes his phallic power in very literal terms; Bolívar is so well endowed that his friends call him "the Tripod."

Romero begins his exploration of the meaning of Bolívar by suggesting that the story of Manuela's undisciplined body is in fact an allegory about the corruption of Bolívar's ideals in 1828. Bolívar's dictatorship represented the failure of a true republican agenda and furthered conservative policies that hearkened back to the ancien régime. In this period, Bolívar undermined the secular, liberal policies of the Congress of Cúcuta of 1821 by defending religious orders and privilege, enforcing anti-heresy laws, broadening the political and juridical influence of the military, and restoring the Indian tribute, which had been the cornerstone of the colonial policies toward Indians (Bushnell, "The Last Dictatorship" 45). As the novel opens, Bolívar has convened his new Council of State and is making a speech defending his Organic Decree. By having Bolívar project his speech toward "an imaginary multitude" from inside a luxuriously adorned, palatial room, Romero effectively illustrates the degradation of Bolívar's popular and ideological valence as a "Liberator" (11). Bolívar himself seems aware of his own defeat as well, feeling death and existential despair encircle him. The defeat of Bolivarian ideals is associated with another decision that Bolívar makes at this moment: Manuela Sáenz, his "whore," will now move into the palace with him. Bolívar's Organic Decree, like his ultimate possession of Manuela, represents his will to take control of an unruly and chaotic body politic. Now that the covenant of the republic is broken for all to see, Bolívar is free to dispense with appearances and other social covenants and put his lover at his side inside the presidential palace. The narrative is both triumphant and defeatist. The move into the palace represents conquest, yet it comes at a price. Unable to control competing interests in the body politic, Bolívar caves in to authoritarianism and turns his back on the republican ideal.

By its very nature, a narrative frame that encloses a story that culminates in the present, and which opens and closes the narrative that it contains, suggests that both texts are intimately related. The frame acts as a key for understanding the story that it contains, while the inner text is also instructive for a reading of the frame. In the case of *La esposa del doctor Thorne*, the Organic Decree and the failure of the republic is the context for reading Manuela's story of sexual adventure. What do these seemingly disparate stories have in common? The Organic Decree is a surrender of the republic in the name of order and against anarchy. Manuela's journey in the novel is a story of disorder defined by the collapse of high and low culture and Manuela's sexual excess (adultery, promiscuity, incest). Thus, Manuela's story allegorizes the chaos of a body politic that Bolívar must dominate at all costs, including the declaration of a dictatorship. In this light, the final scene in which Bolívar invites Manuela to move into the palace takes on a different meaning. By enclosing his "whore" in the palace, Bolívar restores order to his conquest (both America and Manuela).

Romero makes it clear, however, that Bolívar is not merely a strong caudillo willing to impose his will on Manuela's body and the body politic of the republic. His Bolívar is a sentimental being of great seductive power. Manuela will go to the palace at the end of the novel because she loves Bolívar. She has been conquered by a romantic who is capable of projecting his vision onto others. We first see evidence of Bolívar as a romantic visionary when he leafs through an edition of Goethe's *The Sorrows of Young Werther* and recognizes himself in an illustration of the protagonist. Alone and frustrated by the political turn of events that has precipitated his dictatorship, particularly the accusation that he is an American Napoleon, Bolívar seeks refuge in a fantasy of Manuela. For the first and last time, Manuela comes into focus as an idealized being, whose body is the site of regeneration and transcendence, rather than pleasure and transgression.

I will kiss your breasts. I will kiss them as if they were two blind and acid seeds. I will hold your waist to me until it flies like a word that loses itself in the air until transforming itself into a fruit. In the night I will make a clear sun for your flight, a circle of images that will ascend with that slowness of hours burnt in the rhythm of the heart. And your hands. Let them travel my body. Oh, your hands with roses! Your hands are more pure than roses. And from between the white leaves they rise like pieces of starlight, like butterfly dawns, like candorous silks. Did they fall unto you from the moon? Did they play in the blue spring? Are they of the soul? They have the vague splendor of otherworldly lilies; they emanate what they dream, they refresh what they sing. . . . I want to love you Manuela. Love, love, love, be more, be even more! To love inside of love, bask in the light! (23–24)

Readers are invited to see Manuela as an inspiration for Bolívar, and as a measure of the spiritual depth and sensitivity of his character. Its exultant quality and unabashed celebration of the sublimity of romantic love idealizes both Bolívar and Manuela as sentimental beings. The depth of Bolívar's sensitivity is highlighted while Manuela is constructed as an idealized object of desire. However, this moment is undermined throughout the novel as Manuela repeatedly engages in transgressive sex acts that belie transcendental categories, including romantic love. Moreover, while most of the novel is mediated through Manuela's association with carnality, the sanctity of Bolívar's body is not questioned. He remains a register of epic, myth, and sentimentality, and as such, maintains a measure of wholeness in the text. This power and wholeness, which explains Manuela's submission to him, is illustrated by the prodigious size of his penis, hence his nickname in the novel, "the Tripod."

Manuela's seduction by Bolívar is foreshadowed and clarified by her incestuous ménage-à-trois with her half brother José María, and her friend Rosita. The character of José María may be read as a double of Bolívar because he too is constituted as a romantic subject capable of entering into official history's epic modes of signification and myth making. A soldier in the patriot Numancia Batallion, José María is passing through Lima and is reunited with his half sister, who invites him to dine with her and Rosita. Drunk on many bottles of champagne, José María tells stories of his campaigns in the discourse of epic: the bloodthirsty cruelty of the Spanish king, the patriot struggle against the forbidding landscape, the catalogue of exotic and heroic battalion names, and the battles. In his drunken discourse on independence, José María briefly falls into the role of Bolívar himself: "For moments he is Bolívar deciding to put into practice the risky theory that to liberate Venezuela the war needs to be taken outward . . ." (149). Like Bolívar, José María is able to slip into romantic discourse and empower himself before Manuela. We learn that as an adolescent, José María's "imagination knew no limits and that he frequently play-acted characters from the classic sixteenth-century novels of Knight Errantry: Amadís of Gaul and Esplandián." José María's magnetism is thus a result of his imaginary hold over Manuela and Rosita, who find his discourse irresistible: "The two women are awed by the grace and fine speech of José María, what charm! What music! What virtuosity! What a way to narrate and describe!" (150). The flowing champagne becomes an image of the intoxication and seduction of language, and as the three lovers engage in desperate sex, the champagne becomes the image of male seed (159).

Romero repeatedly underlines the importance of Bolívar's idealism for his sexual persona, explicitly attributing Bolívar's ability to conquer a woman forever as an extension of his romantic persona (186). The description of how Manuela delights in Bolívar's tenderness and touch, through which he reveals and gives of himself, creating something new, suggests that his geopolitical power is really a function of his sensual power. Yet, Romero subtly undermines these idealized discourses of seduction by foregrounding their artificial construction. In particular, one of Romero's descriptions of Bolívar and Manuela's lovemaking underlines how the exceptionalist, heterosexual myth of foundational lovers is channeled through classical, literary models. The passage refers to the pairing of Bolívar and Manuela through the lens of myth, producing exceptional and foundational scenes.

> In "El Garzal" they make love in the manner of Virgil, it might be said with the specter of Publius Virgilius Marón protecting them, between familiar rivers and sacred fountains, luxuriating in the freshness of dank forests. . . . Bucolically, in the manner of Horace, they saw how the pig pleasured in acorns, and how the forest produced arbutus, and how with various fruits the autumn covered its floor . . . with the inhabitants they commemorated the festivals, and around the fire, they libated in honor of Bacchus with the flowered vase. . . . But it is then that the clarion resonated . . . the Liberator set off. And Manuela followed. In any rest along the way, or in the midst of combat, they made love again. Then, they made love Homerically, errantly blind, sponsoring the intervention of gods in the war. . . .
> (195)

The liaison between Manuela and Bolívar structures the landscape in three different ways of imagining the continent: pure nature, pastoral, and epic. By associating Bolívar and Manuela's lovemaking with these motifs, which are in turn associated with specific literary registers, Romero draws attention to how sexuality may be sublimated into different classical models. Instead of being defined as a singular act with one meaning, sex is presented as an opening up into different aesthetic formulations. While

the affirmation of this kind of amorous plasticity is not necessarily negative within Romero's commitment to multiplicity, excess, and the variability of identity, a more contextual look at how other sex acts are described in
the novel demonstrates that something more complex is at work. Whereas
Romero populates his novel with the geographical and cultural specifici-
ties of Latin America, and with references to Latin American authors and
historical characters (César Vallejo, Sebastian Salazar Bondy, Pablo Neruda, Pancho Villa), this one passage deterritorializes the American continent by presenting it as an extension of the world of Greece and Rome. All
three aesthetic models substitute history with classical primitivism, which
presents the landscape of the New World as a well delineated, stylized, and
subdued landscape. In contrast, Manuela's tempestuous and uncontained
world of desire is associated with the volcanic landscape of the New World,
and with its authors past and present and its popular culture. In falling
under the sway of Bolívar, Manuela enters into a distinctly artificial
reimagining of the continent. Bolívar's love paradoxically yokes Manuela,
and by extension the unruly continent she represents, to the foreign power
of classical literature. In short, rather than representing an emancipation,
as Bolívar's title of "Liberator" would seem to promise, this self-consciously mythic pairing negates native identity. Manuela's story of sexual
excess may be a distinctly Latin American story, framed by certain landscapes, cities, words, and references, but the mythic story of Bolívar and
Manuela as foundational lovers is distinctly foreign and rehearsed.

Unlike other narrators of the degeneration of the Bolivarian dream,
such as García Márquez, Romero does not dwell on the failure of the body
of the character of Bolívar to make his critique of Bolivarian mythology.
Instead, he self-consciously imagines Bolívar as a discourse that can be
ironized, undercut, and called into question through juxtapositions with
Manuela's quest for pleasure. In his romantic delusions about love, Manuela's body, and his own vision of himself, Bolívar is conjured up as an
Ariel-like character, while Manuela, whose life is centered around dramatic sex acts, may be read as Caliban. In order to understand what occurs
when Romero brings these two very different characters together, we need
to consider how Manuela's sexuality is represented in the novel.

Manuela and the Performance of Masculinity

La esposa del doctor Thorne has been vilified the most for its exploration
of Manuela's sexuality. The novel's treatment of gender is quite complex,

oscillating between the rejection of gender and the validation of its biological narratives. In other words, gender is both performative (contingent)
and biological (essential). The character of Manuela is presented as a per-
former of masculinity whose theatrical sexuality uncovers and undermines the conventions of masculinity and femininity. Yet, Romero remains wedded to the notion of phallic power, and attributes Manuela's
masculinity to the size of her clitoris. In a circular return onto itself, biological gender is broken only to be reconfigured as the reinscription of the
phallus on the sex of woman. Therefore, the resulting representation of
gender in the novel falls short as an indictment of the power of Bolívar.
Ultimately, if Manuela is masculine because of her phallus, she is made
woman again by the dominant phallus of Bolívar. The relational, corporeal
differences between them remain instrumental in plotting their relationship as man and woman.

In spite of this return to biology, Romero's depiction of Manuela's sexuality does raise some important questions about the gendered underpin-
nings of the cult of Bolívar, most particularly the mythic pairing of Bolívar
and Manuela. This is seen most clearly in her liaison with Rosita
Campuzano, when Romero establishes that because of the size of her clitoris, Manuela's body has to be read as the masculine, and therefore the
dominant: "Rosita understood it, and that's why she lay on the bed and
squeezed her breasts, one against the other, until joining them almost
completely, widelegged, and in a passive pose" (121). Once established that
Manuela will be the manly woman and Rosita the womanly woman the
couple embarks on a performance of several heterosexual pairings predicated on the identities of famous historical and literary figures, such
as Napoleon and Josephine, Marc Antony and Cleopatra, Hamlet and
Ophelia, Don Quijote and Dulcinea (although Romero interjects a question about where Sancho might fit in), Jesus Christ and Mary Magdalene,
Pancho Villa and La Adelita, and many, many more (125–26). Also, the
couple performs stock roles that relativize the singularity and conventionally considered transcendence of such mythical pairings; they play monk
and nun, doctor and nurse, animal tamer and tamed beast, grand gourmet
and waitress, "John" and prostitute, Creole man and *cholita* woman, all of
which are constituted through the power of one (the male) over the other
(the female) (125–27). This passage problematizes the possibility of seeing
Bolívar and Manuela as "great lovers," for they too dissolve in the textuality of performance, and lose their essential stability as singular referents. Instead of being "great lovers" they constitute another performance

of the dominant (the masculine) and the submissive (the feminine), no different than the pairing of Creole-cholita, doctor-nurse, and so on. The destabilizing of mythic, exceptional heterosexual pairings structurally destabilizes the gender identities of both Manuela and Bolívar as they enter into their union. If all great lovers are ultimately constructing gender through power, then essential forms of male or female identity formation are called into question. Although Bolívar's prodigious penis establishes that his masculinity is indeed rooted in the body, his status as a phallic male is also a function of his performative ability to create meaning by imagining Manuela and the continent she represents. The performative aspect of his power as a romantic subject is not absolute, but contingent on his ability to invent himself through the inscription of Manuela's body as an ideal object. In this register, gender is framed as artifice and establishes a logic of its own, in which if Bolívar's power is merely performative, it becomes accessible to Manuela as well, who may utilize it to constitute herself as the subject and Bolívar as the object.

Romero presents the relationship between masculinity and femininity in ambiguous ways in a scene in which Manuela objectifies Bolívar for her pleasure. Romero describes Bolívar exposing himself to Manuela so that she may masturbate as if before an image of Marilyn Monroe or Brigitte Bardot (188). However, at the same time, we are reminded of Bolívar's prodigious phallus: "He could expose himself naked, as he used to walk about his house naked, or rocking comfortably in his hammock, erect, with his well-formed member a bit out of proportion with his corporeal conformation and for which his closest friends called him the 'Tripod,' so that Manuela, at a distance and for the visual incentive, could masturbate . . ." (187–88). While Bolívar becomes the passive object of the gaze, Manuela takes on the persona of she who looks for pleasure. Although we also learn that Bolívar allows Manuela to engage in any and all sex acts possible between man and woman without any hint of defensive machismo, his status as a phallic male is referenced at the very same time that it is questioned. In his passive pose—and it is important to underline the provisionality suggested by the term "pose"—Bolívar is indeed an object of Manuela's desire. In that moment of objectification, or during Manuela's penetration of him, Bolívar is not a foundational father, but a body under Manuela's controlling gaze and touch. As in her sex games with Rosa, Manuela takes on the dominant role, play-acting her status as manly woman, while Bolívar's genitalia temporarily lose their referential hold on identity and permit his performance of submission.

I began my analysis of the politics of gender in *La esposa del doctor Thorne* with the argument that Bolívar, and his Organic Decree, both conquers and submits to the unruly body of Manuela Sáenz, which represents the anarchy of the New World. The image of the "Tripod" being penetrated by Manuela brings us full circle to that inaugural moment in the novel. Bolívar is conqueror and conquered at the same time. Moreover, the image of Manuela pleasuring herself by looking at and penetrating the body of Bolívar also may be read as a commentary on the adoration of the hero in the modern cult of Bolívar. This unruly, Latin American body, upon which the mechanisms and narratives of material and political progress have repeatedly failed, was supposed to be the obedient mistress of Bolívar's romantic vision of unity and progress. Instead, it has broken that vision while pleasuring itself through the symbolic body of Bolívar. In other words, the relationship America-Bolívar, like Manuela-Bolívar, is bound together by contradictory impulses: the breakdown of Bolívar's authority and its continual, seductive presence.

The Politics of Gender in *La esposa del doctor Thorne*

It would be easy to gloss over the complexities of gender and simply reduce *La esposa del doctor Thorne* to a subversive attack on Bolívar and gender norms, or a misogynist attack on Manuela Sáenz and women's sexuality. Within a novel that self-consciously undermines the referentiality of language and myth, the weaving in and out of conventional gender norms might suggest a feminist text, if not a queering of Bolívar and Manuela. By the same token, the reverential treatment of Bolívar's body invites us to see the novel as reactionary. Indeed, any conclusions about *La esposa del doctor Thorne* need to be mediated by awareness that it resists reductive readings. Like Manuela's laughter, this novel is an overflowing site of meanings that resists easy classification and description. To conclude this chapter, I trace the salient points of the ideology of gender in this complex text.

Romero clearly privileges the phallus in his novel. Bolívar's formidable penis and sexual prowess, both of which are foreshadowed by Manuela's brother, are linked to the ability to generate epic discourse and seduce Manuela, whose body doubles for that of the lusty and disordered continent that both resists and succumbs to Bolívar's seductive power. Manuela's performance of masculinity with Rosa is also constituted as a function of the phallus, as mediated through her genitals' simulacrum of the penis, but whereas Bolívar and José María's phallic masculinity enables them to generate transcendental knowledge, Manuela is only able to generate discourses of sexual submission through an extensive gallery of famous lovers and types. The scope of her power, as a subject endowed with her own miniature phallus, is limited to play-acting romance or sexual domination, while Bolívar and José María are privy to imagining independence.

The protection of the phallus in the novel leads to the related issue of how Romero is able to criticize the eclipsing of the Bolivarian, republican ideal without challenging the integrity of Bolívar's body. By framing Manuela's story within the context of the corruption of the Bolivarian ideal in August of 1828, and indicating that this is the beginning of the corruption of Bolívar's own body, Romero carnivalizes Manuela's body as a measure of the degeneration of the colonial period, which now doubles for the loss of the transcendental, emancipatory project of Bolívar. Manuela is placed in the conventional role of the feminized, degenerate body while Bolívar's status as an incorporeal visionary is preserved through the displacement of his failure upon Manuela's body. The paradigmatic nature of the Organic Decree theme demonstrates that the subversive aspects of the novel are deployed in defense of Bolívar's own body. The source of the novel's subversions of identity is the plundering of Manuela's body, while, by and large, Bolívar's corporeality is protected. Romero's critics were wrong in seeing *La esposa del doctor Thorne* as an affront to Bolívar; on the contrary, the novel preserves the integrity of Bolívar's incorporeality at the expense of Manuela's body.

La esposa del doctor Thorne is a dramatic intervention in the ambivalent histories of Manuela Sáenz as a protagonist of Latin American independence and the Bolivarian project. As a particularly able practitioner of the new Latin American historical novel, Romero is able to create a brilliant array of subversive effects in his writing, mainly by pleasuring in the parallel excesses of language and of the body, resulting in a kaleidoscopically complex reimagining of his subject that invites praise for its rejection of the conventions of official history. His controversial depiction of Manuela, however, demonstrates that he remains wed to one of the most important elements of the cult of Bolívar: the inviolable contours of the body of the patriarch. It is hard not to sense that the insatiability of Manuela's flesh in the novel is in part a function of the need to contemplate and identify with the prowess of Bolívar. After all, as Romero writes at the beginning of the novel, Manuela craves a man, a "man, yes, a man to make her live with her ominous flesh; a man that could calm her, that could cure her, that could corrupt her . . ." (37). Notwithstanding Bolívar's authoritarianism, the taming of so prodigious a woman is one of Bolívar's greatest triumphs in the novel, and as such, an indicator of the limitations of the novel's critique of the cult of Bolívar.

Although the masculinist overtones of *La esposa del doctor Thorne* are undeniable, so are its iconoclastic elements. Romero's novel daringly discloses the terrain of Bolívar's sexuality as a space where biological definitions of gender may be challenged. The outrageous descriptions of orgies, submission, and dominance break with the decorum of the foundational, Bolivarian narratives of identity. Moreover, lest we forget, the story of Manuela's sexual journey into the presidential palace is ultimately the story of the Organic Decree's break with democracy. Upon Manuela's body Romero maps the story of a continent that refuses to bend to the will of democratic progress, and which ends up being the concubine of a caudillo in the presidential palace. Manuela's lusty body is the defeat of the Bolivarian dream.

Solitude, Signs, and Power in
The General in His Labyrinth

I've become lost in a dream, searching for something that does not
exist. . . .
Gabriel García Márquez, *The General in His Labyrinth*

In his interviews with Plinio Apuleyo Mendoza, Gabriel García Márquez
remarks that the solitude of power entails a disconnection from the world.
García Márquez compares the solitude of fame to that of power and concludes that both are marked by an inability to represent and comprehend
reality accurately: "In the final analysis it becomes a problem of informa-
tion which isolates both the powerful and the famous from the fleeting and
changeable reality of the world. Fame and power raise the big question,
'Whom do you trust?' Taken to its bewildering conclusion this must lead
to the ultimate question, 'Who the hell am I?'" (Apuleyo Mendoza 90).
The links between power and alienation are explored in *One Hundred
Years of Solitude* (1967) through the rise and fall of Colonel Aureliano
Buendía, and in *The Autumn of the Patriarch* (1975) through the story of
a nameless protagonist who embodies all Latin American dictators past
and present. The thematic affinities shared by both novels are underscored
by García Márquez himself, who noted that if Colonel Aureliano Buendía
had taken the reigns of absolute power in *One Hundred Years of Solitude*,
the novel would have effectively transformed itself into *The Autumn of
the Patriarch* (Apuleyo Mendoza 105). In this light, *The General in His
Labyrinth* (1983) may be read as yet another variation on the theme of
solitary, powerful men whose separation from reality leads to the fracturing of the self, historical agency, and the promise of solidarity. In all three
novels, power operates as a wound upon the body of meaning, troubling
the ability of systems, models, and signs to represent their intended objects.

Despite the unflinching nature of his descriptions of the failure of Bolívar's infirm body in *The General in His Labyrinth,* García Márquez evokes
the hero with tenderness and compassion, and most importantly with
hope. This is hardly surprising, considering that from an early age García
Márquez had been taught to admire Bolívar by his grandfather, Nicolás
Márquez, one of the models for the character of Aureliano Buendía. "It
was my grandfather . . ." remembers García Márquez in his memoirs, "who
asked me to never forget that he [Bolívar] was the greatest man ever to be
born in the history of the world" (*Vivir* 105). Years later, when García
Márquez interrupted his studies to flee the rioting that engulfed Bogotá in
April of 1948 and arrived in Cartagena de Indias he was comforted by the
sight of the equestrian statue of the man that his grandfather had ordered
him to revere (*Vivir* 367–68). Far from Bogotá and his childhood home of
Aracataca, García Márquez discovers that Cartagena de Indias is not so
foreign after all; the equestrian statue binds him to memories of his grandfather and his childhood, and reminds him of the shared, Bolivarian patri-
mony of his homeland. Suddenly, the solitude of a stranger in a strange
city is broken by a familiar sight rich in personal and regional connotations. It is tempting to read *The General in His Labyrinth* as a fictional
mise-en-scène of this moment of recognition because the novel seeks to
overcome solitude and separation by transforming the monumental Bolívar, whose glory has made him hermetic to his heirs, into a recognizable
sign of unity and wholeness. Specifically, García Márquez achieves this
reinvention by reactivating the political charge of Bolívar's pan-Americanism.

The General in His Labyrinth is so full of disconnects between signifier
and signified that it is necessary to use this theme as a frame for reading
the novel's investment in Bolívar. First, there are misreadings based upon
the illusion of appearances. José Palacios, the General's valet, is mistaken
for his master because of the silver trimmings on his saddle and his gold
spurs, although his deferential service to his master "made any such confusion unthinkable" (39). Similarly, Colonel Wilson is misread as the
highest ranking officer in the General's coterie because of his blond good
looks and the trimmings of his uniform (43). The issue of attribution is
underlined several times, underscoring the impossibility of fixing meaning with certainty. When the General asks Palacios who had said the
phrase, "There is great power in the irresistible force of love," his valet
responds "Nobody," provoking the General to say playfully, "Then I said it

myself . . . but let's say it was Field Marshal Sucre" (58). In several instances, memory and perception are rejected as valid markers of meaning.
As the General's party approaches Zambrano, where Don Cástulo Campillo awaits to entertain them with the General's favorite *sancocho* dish,
the General and Palacios are disoriented, and cannot remember if sancocho
is the same as a Venezuelan *hervido* (119). Further, the General denies the
existence of the town of Mompox and confuses Caracas with Santa Marta
in a dream (102, 241). These are but a few examples of how the novel self-
consciously challenges the relationship between objects in the real world
and the words that are meant to represent them.[1] At the center of all the
confusion, however, is the most misunderstood referent of all, described as
the "greatest and most solitary soldier who ever lived" (81).

In the novel's opening scenes, when the General is shown drifting in his
bath "like a man no longer of this world," the General's connection to an
authoritative, historical myth of origin has been severed.[2] The infirm corporeality of the General calls attention to the fragility and vulnerability of
the transcendent narratives of identity that have historically centered on
the image of Bolívar. A less commented aspect of the novel is how the
protagonist's dying body also parallels the disruption of language and its
transparency in relation to the theme of the solitary nature of power.
García Márquez's Bolívar (the General) is not the source of the "word," the
originary moment of signification that makes identity possible, but the
victim of the arbitrariness and contradictions of representation, which tear
at his self-knowledge and paralyze his ability to create meaning as a historical agent. In this manner García Márquez challenges the privileged status of Bolívar as a coherent script of nationalist discourse. Unlike the
monumental Bolívar, the General is not an all-powerful creator whose
words and acts are full of mythological and disciplinary meaning but
rather a broken body unable to attune itself to language in a meaningful
way. For example, when José Palacios discovers his master trapped in a
delirium at the beginning of the novel, the fate of the suffering body is
linked to the question of coherence in expression: "He heard him utter
disconnected phrases that all fit together into one: 'Nobody understood
anything.' His body burned in a bonfire of fever, and he was farting stony,
foul smelling gas" (10). The array of phrases that "fit together into one" is
a powerful metaphor for the General's disintegrating body, which is
threatened with dissolution. The emphasis on misunderstanding in the

passage relates the problem of incoherence (both bodily and linguistic) to the problem of understanding Bolívar. By making the General a mouth-piece for his own pan-American views, and the intimate rendering of his protagonist's death, García Márquez frees him from contradiction and leads him out of the "labyrinth," reconciling his life with the possibility of meaning. Thus, the novel both negates and affirms the political potential of Bolívar, destroying his official, symbolic body while trying to resuscitate it through the stripped-down, essential vision of the hero as a messenger of pan-Americanism. In short, *The General in His Labyrinth* is an elegiac text that rediscovers Bolívar as a principle of lost wholeness that can help mend a solitary continent.

Ultimately, García Márquez's novel is one of the most forceful of all literary attempts to exorcise the cult of Bolívar in the name of Bolívar himself. This paradox points to the disjunction between the cult of Bolívar, which is associated with political corruption, demagoguery, and a lack of the political imagination, and the man who many perceive to be the real Bolívar: an original thinker and a courageous statesman whose life and example are as current today as during the Wars of Independence. Once we accept this caveat, García Márquez's novel is a brilliant diagnosis of how the mythic Bolívar is enmeshed in the partisan language of myth and de-traction, passing into history as the shell of a former self. The nostalgia for this lost, original Bolívar adds emotional power to the novel but also points to the redefinition of the hero as a principle of identity. García Márquez makes this elegiac treatment of Bolívar a mournful analysis of Latin American identity, which has become alienated from itself, incoherent, and confused by divisions and corruption. In the Bolívar that has been lost, García Márquez recognizes a lost dream of plenitude that is the inherit-ance of the continent itself. In the pages to follow, I explore this nuanced vision of Bolívar. Moreover, I demonstrate how other texts by García Márquez, such as *One Hundred Years of Solitude*, *The Autumn of the Pa-triarch*, the Nobel lecture "The Solitude of Latin America" (1982), and se-lected essays and short stories help illuminate *The General in His Laby-rinth* as a text that is as much about Bolívar's unfulfilled promise as about his solitude.

Bolívar/General

> A famous name is a grave responsibility.
> **Gabriel García Márquez**

García Márquez stakes his interest in exploring the limits of representation by distancing his protagonist, the conspicuously and generically named "General," from the mythic referentiality of "Bolívar," who is named as such only once by the narrative voice. The disconnect between the glorious and exceptionalist associations of "Bolívar" and the negative associations of calling the hero of Latin American independence "General," liberates Bolívar from the weight of his own mythology and allows fiction to free itself from the demands of historiography and epic. Although this transaction would seem to indicate the conversion of Bolívar into the archetype of the fallen Latin American dictator, García Márquez is engaged in a more complex meditation on how the true identity of Bolívar has become opaque. The anonymity of the name "General" discloses how "Bolívar" marks a contradictory and ultimately fruitless site of meaning and historical action. In other words, to read, write, and utter the word "Bolívar" is to enter into a repetitive and self-referential terrain of martial and political superlatives that has nothing to do with the man it is intended to represent, ultimately stripping him of his humanity and meaning. The mythological nature of the cult of Bolívar, with its falsifications of history and its inflated claims, has driven a wedge between the man and the image and estranged the General from himself and from his symbolic descendants.

The first chapter is particularly effective in demonstrating how the General is alienated by his own identity as "Bolívar." The cult of Bolívar operates as a barricade that makes the General's credibility and his authenticity as a subject inaccessible to those around him, isolating him from others as well as from himself. The novel opens with a flurry of temporal and narrative juxtapositions that underline the General's failure in making his illness and resignation from power believable to the people of Bogotá. José Palacios, the General's valet, is himself unsure as to how to interpret the General's dramatic assertion: "Let's go . . . as fast as we can. No one loves here" (3). Having heard it so many times before, Palacios cannot bring himself to believe in the finality of the statement, since at other times the General had tried to feign departure for political ends (14). García Márquez then weaves in elements of the cult of Bolívar to demonstrate the futility of the General's discourse of departure, defeat, and death, effectively explaining the political graffiti of those who had scrawled "He won't leave and he won't die" on the palace walls (13). The General's renunciation of power had been a staple of his political discourse from the very beginning of his presidency, particularly in the case of the failed conspiracy to assassinate him in September of 1828. He declared that there would be no investigation, no prosecution, and that he would leave Colombia forever. The outcome, however, was quite different: "Nevertheless, the investigation took place, the guilty were judged with an iron hand, and fourteen were shot in the main square" (15). And so he remained in power. The General's health and "moribund appearance" is also unconvincing, or illegible as a faithful measure of his health, as proven by many previous (and inaccurate) announcements of his death, the most dramatic being the mythically famous anecdote about the hero's death agony in Pativilca, in which he declared to a visitor: "Go and tell the world how you saw me die covered with chicken shit on these inhospitable sands" (16). Trapped in the labyrinth of the myth of Bolívar, the General is unable to claim disillusionment, resignation, and death as his own and live out his final days in peace.

In his memoirs, García Márquez writes that his childhood fascination with his ancestor's sonorous names (such as Tranquilina, Wenefrida, Argemira) led him to believe that the characters in his novels could not be truly independent unless they had a name that resonated with their manner of being (*Vivir* 60). In this light, it is significant to observe that the protagonist of *The General in His Labyrinth* is referred to as "Bolívar" only once. Julio Ortega suggests that this reticence is an attempt to situate the novel's protagonist outside of the labyrinth of Bolivarian literature that so encircles and torments his protagonist at the outset of the novel ("Lector" 171–72). García Márquez's long-standing interest in people's names, and in the problem of relating a person's self to one name and not another, supports this claim. In a brief column titled "El problema de llamarse Jorge" [The Problem of Being Named George], published in the newspaper *El espectador* in 1955, García Márquez told the story of George Washington of Key West, Florida, whose lack of a driving license catapulted him to the front page of the news because of a simple traffic accident. With characteristic chagrin, García Márquez observes that carrying a famous name is analogous to carting another's statue around the world. "Anyone has the right to kill himself driving at unheard of speeds. If his name is George Washington he is obligated to observe all rules precisely, because the only accident that was permitted of him in his life already took place at baptism" (*Entre cachacos* 396–97). A famous name represents the script of authority, the discourse of structure and assigned meaning, pressing upon freer and less predictable forms of identity formation (that is, reckless driving, accidents, and so on). In an earlier article titled "Hay que parecerse al nombre" [The Need to Look Like One's Name], published in *El heraldo* in 1952, García Márquez states that linking the referent to the self is crucial to the creation and maintenance of one's status as a subject. Not looking like one's name is a calamity analogous to being unknown to oneself, to not recognizing one's own portrait (*Textos costeños* 716). The dilemma of the General in *The General in His Labyrinth* is this separation of the self from its purported signifier, "Bolívar." By recovering the more anonymous connotations of the name "General," García Márquez humanizes his subject and recovers him for fiction, as opposed to the depleted Bolivarian discourses of biography, epic, or demagoguery.

The resistance to naming Bolívar directly in the novel may be read in relation to García Márquez's identification with the Caribbean coastal regions of Colombia, comprising Magdalena, Bolívar, Córdoba, César, Sucre, and Guajira (Williams 87). García Márquez privileges *lo costeño* (the coastal) over *lo cachaco* (the highland), rejecting cachaco conceptions of the *costa* as a provincial and underdeveloped cultural zone. In an early article, García Márquez defended the Caribbean cultural zone by writing that "Colombia's literary provincialism begins at two thousand meters above sea level" (*Textos costeños* 44.) The single mention of the name "Bolívar" by the narrative voice in *The General in His Labyrinth*, which takes place as the General departs Bogotá into his final exile, may be read as yet another example of this rejection of the canonical, writerly discourse of the highland in favor of the more sensuous and corporeal zone of the coast: "It was the end. General Simón José Antonio de la Santísima Trinidad Bolívar y Palacio was leaving forever. He had wrested from Spanish domination an empire five times more vast than all of Europe, he had led twenty years of war to keep it free and united, and he had governed it with a firm hand until the week before, but when it was time to leave he did not even take away with him the consolation that anyone believed in his departure" (37). With the phrase "it was the end" García Márquez marks the end of Bolivarian narrative, defined as epic and nationalist, and the beginning of his own tale, which will distance itself from the conventions of that discourse. The utterance of Bolívar's name is also spatially important, for it takes place in the former capital of his political career, "the same city he had loved more than any other and had idealized as the center and reason of his life and the capital of half the world" (41). As he leaves Bogotá, and the ruins of his political designs, Bolívar enters into the anonymity of a death-march along the Magdalena River toward the Caribbean. In other words, the General's story is driven by his journey toward García Márquez's beloved costa, where the telos of linear history and narrative are substituted with forgetfulness, waking dreams, and the sensations of the body.

The General, Critical Reader

García Márquez's rejection of the cult of Bolívar as a paradigm through which to read the life of the General is manifested in his playful insistence in making his protagonist a critical reader of his own cult, in a move reminiscent of Cervantes's humorous representation of Don Quixote encountering Avellaneda's unauthorized version of himself in Book II of his adventures.[3] One of the most dramatic readings carried out by the General is that of a letter from interim Colombian president Caycedo, which provokes the General by using the term *liberal* to describe his enemies, the Santanderistas: "I don't know where the demagogues got the right to call themselves liberals. . . . They stole the word, pure and simple, just as they steal everything they lay their hands on. . . . The Truth is, the only two parties here are those who are with me and those who are against me, and you know that better than anyone. . . . And although they may not believe it, no one is more liberal than I am" (73). The General struggles to control the political terminology, which threatens to legitimate his enemies and alienate him from a political process that associates liberalism with progress. The insertion of this outburst in the novel problematizes the usefulness of conventional political categories to understand Bolívar nonreductively; we may term Bolívar a liberal or a conservative, depending on the historical context or frame of reference. As David Bushnell has suggested, Bolívar's final dictatorship of 1825–1830 was characterized by the defense of church privilege, militarism, and colonial tithing practices ("The Last Dictatorship" 65–66). Although in this register Bolívar would not be classifiable as a liberal, the arc of his career, his political and philosophical readings, and his commitment to an international vision would define him as a liberal statesman. Which version is true? The General's anger derives from the fact that an otherwise transparent term, *liberal*, has become a site of illusory contradictions that makes it useless as a label. García Márquez shares his frustration, and ultimately clears the conceptual clutter surrounding Bolívar by reinventing him along pan-Americanist lines.

The General's difficulties in knowing himself as "Bolívar" are underlined again when he becomes his own archivist and investigates a supposed romance between him and a young woman of Tenerife. The General has no recollection of romancing this woman, and cannot find evidence of her ever having existed (127). The sense of estrangement from the mythical version of himself is reminiscent of another passage, which also coincides with the General's arrival in Tenerife: the General sees a steamboat named *The Liberator* going the opposite direction on the river, to which he responds: "To think I'm that man!" (126). Whether as a lover or as a liberator, the General is unable to recognize himself as the legendary Bolívar. Whereas the General drifts down the Magdalena toward death, stripped of everything except his ailing body and confused memories, his legend travels upriver, into the future, to the former seat of his power. Bolívar the man is no more, what remains is the vessel of his fame, *The Liberator*. This alienation of the self is further developed in scenes that emphasize the General's inability to inhabit the intertwined roles of lover and liberator that are associated with Bolívar. The first is the Queen María Luisa story, in which the General remembers the seduction of a beautiful "mulatta in the flower of her youth and with the profile of an idol" (41). After taking the virginity of the slave girl, the General declares that love has made her free, describing her deflowering as a liberation, but María Luisa declines his offer to exercise her newfound freedom and chooses to stay at the plantation (51). María Luisa is reminiscent of García Márquez's famous creation Eréndira, who appears in *One Hundred Years of Solitude* and "The Incredible and Sad Tale of Innocent Eréndira and Her Heartless Grandmother." Like Eréndira, who accidentally burned down her grandmother's house and was forced into prostitution to pay her back, María Luisa is engaged in a power struggle with her grandmother, who seeks to control her movements: "She too was naked, for her grandmother, who slept in the same room, took her clothes to keep her from going out to smoke . . ." (50). The General, like Eréndira's lover, is unable to take complete possession of her; like Eréndira herself, who flees from the lover who helps her escape her prison, María refuses the General's offer of freedom. In another passage, the General sleeps beside a naked, undernourished adolescent, unable to take her virginity (182). The peculiar story of a young Bedouin-like girl completely covered with down whom the General tries to possess forever through the "sacramental act" of shaving her from head to toe also under-scores the protagonist's fundamental impotence as a liberator (213); the hair will grow back and the girl will thus recover her hairy virginal state once again. In the same manner that he is unable to posses the virginal bodies that he claims, the General is historically impotent, and unable to maintain or reinitiate his glory as the Latin American Liberator. This is why the General is right when he declares that he does not exist (141).

The difficulty of knowing and defining reality is also underlined through questioning writing and memory (Alvarez Borland 443–44). The General's projected memoirs are delayed until it is too late, and memoirists and memoirs are criticized as unreliable.[4] Moreover, the critique of memory and representation is emphasized by the fact that the General cannot disentangle his memories and dreams from reality. García Márquez thus reminds us that memoirs and memories are not vessels of truth, but deeply personal forms of fiction that can lay claim to a person's past and give it meaning. This is why he opens the first volume of his memoirs, *Vivir para contarla* (2002) with the epigraph "La vida no es la que uno vivió, sino la que uno recuerda y cómo la recuerda para contarla" [Life is not what one lived, but what is remembered and how one remembers it to tell it]. In this context, the General's inability to articulate his memories into a coherent whole, and his failure to produce any memoirs, underscores his alienation from his identity as "Bolívar," and the erasure of his self. In short, the General cannot fashion a story capable of giving life to the life that he has lived.

The Barricades of Power and Military Impotence

One of the least commented aspects of *The General in His Labyrinth* is the protagonist's troubled relationship to the men under his command. Not only is the reader a witness to the bodily degeneration of the General, but also to the degeneration of one of the most extraordinary military opera-tions in Western history. Once again, García Márquez explores this disin-tegration in terms of the solitude that alienates the powerful from others, from reality, and from the ability to act in the world. The most explicit instance of this theme is how the General is continually deceived about the fact that his troops are suffering from an epidemic of gonorrhea, which doctors and military authorities have been unable to check. Because of the deception surrounding the outbreak, the General is helpless to act upon reality and affect any kind of change. When he finally learns of the epidemic, the General breaks through the misinformation and silence that encircles him and reclaims his historical agency by simply imposing a quarantine on the men under his command (238). In this one instance, the General is able to care for his subordinates by directing them, by exercising his authority to structure acts and movements.

The novel as a whole, however, underlines the erasure of the General as an effective leader of his military subordinates. What most alarms his men is the lack of a sense of purpose, "which became more and more unbearable the more he continued to slog his way through this endless journey to nowhere" (163). García Márquez suggests that the dynamic at work here is a filial one. Although the General may be read as an absent father with regard to all of his military subordinates, including José María Carreño and José Laurencio Silva,[5] this association seems most accurate in relation to the younger men of his entourage, namely Colonel Wilson, Agustín de Iturbide, Fernando Bolívar, and Field Marshal Sucre. For all of these men, the General is a father figure who directs their lives and destinies, yet the relationship each one has with his symbolic father is fraught with failure and disappointment. Colonel Wilson's resentful and tense relationship with the General is expressed through the game of *ropilla*. Wilson desperately wants the approval of the General, whom he has overhead criticizing him for being inexperienced (62). Through the game of ropilla, Wilson vents his anger by continually defeating the General, whose political and military powerlessness is illustrated by his rising frustration over being defeated by Wilson. The presence of the Mexican Agustín de Iturbide in the novel results in another father-son set piece with the General, whose life as the mythic "Bolívar" resonates with the tragic story of Iturbide *fils*, who was also a tragic liberator. The General dispenses fatherly advice to young Iturbide, warning him against solitude and insisting that he return to Mexico at any cost, to avoid a fate of perpetual exile like his own (224). Rather than a moment of hope and renewal, it is a ghostly scene in which the phantom of Iturbide's vanquished father returns to warn the son of the same fate. Finally, the General's nephew Fernando is a disappointment who will not carry on Bolívar's work into posterity like the young Field Marshal Sucre, whose life was cut short by assassins intent on wounding Bolívar and his cause. In depriving the General of viable heirs, García Márquez intensifies the solitude of his protagonist, who moves toward the most solitary and anonymous of deaths.

In contrast, the characters of Silva and Carreño personify the paralysis and hopelessness that the patriarch's inertia has brought down upon what was formerly a purposeful and directed military organization. Both of these men evoke two minor characters in García Márquez's "A Very Old Man with Enormous Wings," the story of an old man with wings who is washed onto a muddy beach near a small village during a storm. Two villagers, Salvador and Elizenda, put the Old Man on display in a chicken coop and charge a fee to the crowds of visitors eager to see the outlandish being in the flesh. Because the Old Man is perceived as an angel, pilgrims and invalids, such as the insomniac obsessed with undoing everything he does during the day and a man fixated on counting his own heartbeats, come seeking the Old Man's "miracles." Like the Old Man, the General is a mythical being who elicits the hopes of his solitary followers but is incapable of delivering the miracles that are expected of him. In this register, Silva and Carreño evoke the insomniac and the man of the heartbeats, respectively. Silva is an insomniac who builds cabinets at night without any apparent explanation. When he learns that the General has recommenced a military campaign out of Venezuela, his response underscores his solitary, alienated state: "Idleness is also a war . . . I'll stay here" (198). In turn, Carreño's penchant for counting the stars echoes the obsession of the pilgrim who wanted to count his own heartbeats; both obsessions are predicated on enumerating elements that are not quantifiable.

When the General temporarily revives and plans the reintegration of the continent, his body becomes recalcitrant and his movements begin to be determined by his failing health rather than any political or military will (235). The failure of the body is accompanied by a breakdown in the communications that are central to restarting the epic, Bolivarian enterprise. García Márquez notes that the General has fallen prey to deceptive, hermetic codes of meaning that are key to his own military enterprise. For example, in his reflections on the Santanderista press responsible for spreading lies about him, the General muses that such "slanted reporting" had been a part of his own intelligence strategy during the war, a strategy that was now, ironically, turned against him (113–14). The General does not receive the news he requires and the news he does receive is misread because of its baffling encryption (218, 238). As his body deceives him, making him less and less the master of his destiny, distracting him from his ambitious designs, the General is deceived by his imperfect apprehension of the world around him, corrupting his plans and hopes for political and military action. Without the will of the General, the organizing force behind the plan to reinitiate the epic of independence vanishes and pushes the possibility of recovering the heroic identity of Bolívar further away.

Solitary Soldiers and Broken Signs

"Yes, I believe it: in general, a writer only writes one book," García Márquez declared to Plinio Apuleyo Mendoza, "although that book appears in
many volumes with diverse titles" (77). Although *The General in His
Labyrinth* demands to be read in relation to the monumentalist Bolívar of
official history, the novel's protagonist coherently emerges from out of
García Márquez's previous writings, suggesting that the General belongs
as much to the orbit of the author's fiction as to Latin American history.
The intertwined failures of the body and the sign appear in García Márquez's other novels, most notably *One Hundred Years of Solitude* and *The
Autumn of the Patriarch*. Colonel Aureliano Buendía, the Patriarch, and
the General may be read as variants of the same character: the solitary
soldier unmoored from reality and from the expressive and transitive potential of the sign. Although Aureliano Buendía is a composite of García
Márquez's grandfather, Nicolás Márquez, and the famous liberal soldier
Rafael Uribe Uribe, there are some revealing similarities to Bolívar as
well.[6] The most concrete example of this is when Buendía escapes one of
many failed assassination attempts by changing hammocks with his friend
Magnífico Visbal, who is assassinated in his place (García Márquez, *Solitude* 228), echoing the circumstances of the death of Bolívar's friend Felix
Amestoy in Jamaica in 1815. Aureliano Buendía, like the General, is larger
than life and estranged by his own fame. Drunk on his own "unbelievable"
triumphs, Aureliano becomes a stranger to himself and to everyone else
(272). In particular, the accelerated rate of his continual military triumphs,
in direct opposition to the decelerated rate of news transmission, makes a
realistic definition of his person impossible, effectively transforming him
into a supernatural being: "That was how the legend of the ubiquitous
Colonel Aureliano Buendía began. Simultaneous and contradictory infor-
mation declared him victorious in Villanueva, defeated in Guacamayal,
devoured by Motilon Indians, dead in a village in the swamp, and up in
arms again in Urumita" (142). The alienating effect of the legend is predicated on its inability to convey meaning in a convincing, believable manner. Ultimately, Aureliano is like a film character in Bruno Crespi's Macondo movie venture, which fails miserably because the town's inhabitants
cannot accept the death of an actor in one film and his subsequent reap-
pearance in another (339).

    The distancing of Aureliano Buendía from himself, others, and reality
itself is clearly expressed through the image of the circle of chalk, which is

meant to seal him within his own power (272). Although Aureliano becomes an arbiter of all things big and small within his circle of chalk, he becomes lost in nothingness, set adrift by the fear and obedience of his followers: "There was always someone outside the chalk circle. Someone who needed money, someone who had a son with whooping cough, or someone who wanted to go off and sleep forever because he could not stand the shit taste of the war in his mouth and who, nevertheless, stood at attention to inform him: 'Everything normal, colonel.' And normality was precisely the most fearful part of that infinite war: nothing ever happened" (181). In this state of separation, Aureliano's relationship to his own power and authority changes; rather than being the director of his own affairs and of his own political program, his power begins to speak for him, becoming as it were a third entity between him and his military organization. For example, a political foe is assassinated by his followers in spite of his refusal to give an overt order to that effect (180). Aureliano does recognize that he is responsible, however, because his lieutenants had anticipated the order, "misreading" his inflammatory comments against his enemy. The sense of displacement created by this paradoxical separation from his own authority stirs up mistrust between him and those under his command. As refracted through his circle of chalk, the reality that surrounds Aureliano becomes deceptive and uncertain; he cannot distinguish between adulating crowds and those that celebrate the enemy and he becomes convinced that he is being misled (181). Aureliano has shifted from being a revolutionary and a potential statesman into being a dictator; he is no longer interested in fighting for anything other than the preservation of the same alienating power that encircles him and closes him off from the world (185).

The strongest connection that can be drawn between Aureliano Buendía and the General, however, lies in how the solitude of power is described as a distinctly corporeal dissolution of meaning. The breakdown of Aureliano Buendía's wartime designs, which will ultimately result in his isolation in Melquiades's library where he casts and melts gold fishes until death, is described as both a breakdown of the body, and as a blurring of lines, points, and words, as if reality itself were losing its cartographic tethers to legibility: "At first those exchanges would determine the course of a flesh and blood war, the perfectly defined outlines of which told them at any moment the exact spot where it was and the prediction of its future direction. . . . Little by little, however, and as the war became more intense and widespread, his image was fading away into a universe of reality. The characteristics of his speech were more and more uncertain, and they came together and combined to form words that were gradually losing all meaning. . . . What in other times had been a real activity, an irresistible passion of his youth, became a remote point of reference for him: an emptiness" (175–76). The preservation of the body and its contours is associated with direction, purpose, and the signifying capacity of language. In Aureliano's decadent state, the very body of the sign has been corrupted, barring the way to any kind of historic agency. It is hardly surprising, then, that when the colonel revives for one final revolt, he only does so when he rejects abstract labels and referents, fighting merely to finish what he has started (279). Aureliano recognizes that the war, and Colombian politics as a whole, works as a system of signs that is completely ineffectual in implanting meaning in a stable fashion: "The certainty that finally he fought for his own liberation, and not abstract ideals, for slogans that politicians could play around with according to circumstance, imbued him with great enthusiasm" (185).

Colonel Aureliano Buendía may be read as a testing ground for some of the themes of García Márquez's challenging *The Autumn of the Patriarch*, the story of a Latin American dictator whose excesses are narrated through a kaleidoscopic combination of multiple points of view and temporal frames, repetition, and its scarcely interrupted narrative flow. The theme of the broken sign of identity is repeated here through the image of the unrecognizable body of the Patriarch, in the rubble of his palace, which has been overrun by cows: "Only when we turned him over to look at his face did we realize that it was impossible to recognize him, even though his face had not been pecked away by vultures, because none of us had ever seen him, and even though his profile was on both sides of all coins, on postage stamps, on condom labels, on trusses and scapulars, and even though his engraved picture with the flag across his chest and the dragon of the fatherland was displayed at all times in all places, we knew that they were copies of copies of portraits that had already been considered unfaithful . . ." (4). The nameless narrators that discover the body cannot trust its significance; like the General, the Patriarch has died before, only to resuscitate miraculously. His first death is that of Patricio Aragonés, his double, who literally enacts the Patriarch's disconnection from himself by governing in his place for many years until he is poisoned. This previous death, in combination with the overproliferation of the Patriarch's image, which is no longer moored to a stable, visible original, makes the Patriarch's ultimate death difficult to accept. In the words of one of the text's voices: "We knew that no evidence of his death was final, because there was always another truth behind the truth" (43). In the realm of the Patriarch, the solitude of power has fed off illusion, deception, and trickery, to the point that even truths lose their absolute footing and become texts with a provisional claim on reality.[7] The Patriarch himself suffers the consequences of this textualization of his identity, as he writes and rewrites his name, Zacarías, until he can no longer tell if the name is related to him or not (129).

García Márquez establishes that one of the conditions and causes of the Patriarch's alienation is his mistrust toward his own military organization. One passage in particular confirms the continuities between this novel, *One Hundred Years of Solitude*, and *The General in His Labyrinth:* "And they saluted him all's well general sir, everything in order, but he knew that it wasn't true, that they were dissembling from habit, that they lied to him out of fear, that nothing was true in that crisis of uncertainty which was rendering his glory bitter . . ." (21). Ruled by fear and mistrust, and controlled by circumstances that never are what they seem, the dictator's military apparatus is unable to cohere as a unit, and unable to fix itself to the source of all authority, the Patriarch. A case in point would be the passage about the Patriarch's fixed lottery, which echoes Buendía's ambivalent relationship to his own authority. The Patriarch institutes a fraudulent lottery in which children are used to pick the winning numbers. Since the children are witnesses to the fraud, they are kidnapped by the authorities and imprisoned. Eventually, when most of the nation's children have been captured and hidden away, the Patriarch is faced with the decision of "how to dispose of them." When the order to place them all in a ship and blow them up is carried out, and his men promoted and honored, the Patriarch flies into a rage and orders them executed for carrying out his own inhumane order (113). The Patriarch is hopelessly deadlocked within himself, and in this solitary state unable to make his own power echo his will and his person. Like the General, who is plagued by misinformation, the Patriarch cannot administer his authority because he is relegated to the self-sufficient, symbolic status of his power. This is why, when the Patriarch declares, "I am the government," the director of his secret police, José Ignacio Sáenz de la Barra, corrects him: "You aren't the government, general, you are the power . . ." (213).[8]

The protagonist of *The General in His Labyrinth*, and his encirclement by the solitude of power, as expressed by the image of the labyrinth, is not a new character or theme in García Márquez's fiction. Like Aureliano Buendía and the Patriarch before him, the General cannot separate himself from the fiction of his own identity, a condition that results in the estrangement of the self and the fracturing of language as a reliable vehicle for representation. García Márquez's commitment to analyzing militarism in particular emerges again through the General, who is plagued by an isolation that deadens reality and places it out of reach. In these contexts, all three of these characters are one and the same. In Aureliano Buendía's case, the solitude of power is presented in the context of a caudillo that eventually slips out of the game of civil war and political engagement. The Patriarch, as García Márquez himself has suggested, explores the fate of Buendía if he had taken the reigns of absolute power and not let go. Finally, *The General in His Labyrinth* adds another layer to García Márquez's exploration of power, militarism, and defeat through the tale of the exile and death agony of the fallen caudillo, statesman, dictator, and founder. Perhaps García Márquez's treatment of Bolívar is also a variation on how the death of Aureliano Buendía is narrated, as suggested by his description of how he finally killed Buendía in *One Hundred Years of Solitude:* "One day I said:'Today he gets fucked!' . . . I have always wanted to write a story that describes in detail every moment of a person in a day like any other, until he dies. I tried to give that literary solution to the death of Colonel Aureliano Buendía, but I found that if I followed that path, the book changed completely" (E. García Márquez 615).

Reviving Bolívar

One of the most touching passages of *The General in His Labyrinth* takes place when the feverish General sees a small boy watching him through a window, whispering: "Bolívar, Bolívar. . . . Do you love me?" The General assents with a tremulous smile (135). The dreamlike quality of the incident poignantly underlines the difficult relationship between the General and the name "Bolívar," but also, in the General's affirmative answer to the boy, provides a redemptive view of the hero's place in Latin American history. So far, I have shown that García Márquez intertwines the fate of the body with the fate of language and representation; the corruption of the General's body enacts the deconstruction of reductive mythical and political signifiers. Now what remains to be seen is how García Márquez scripts the failure of the body and of the representation in a constructive fashion, in search of a way to revive and reimagine a body that has been buried and deadened under its own iconicity. The novel's defense of pan-Americanism provides a "way out" of the labyrinth, demonstrating how García Már-quez's views on language, representation, and colonialism rescue Bolívar from chaos. One key passage illustrates the push and pull between the novel's view of Bolívar as a lost referent and its investment in rescuing Bolívar for the future.

> "I know I'm ridiculed because in the same letter, on the same day, and to the same person I say first one thing and then the opposite, because I approved the plan for monarchy, or I didn't approve it, or some-where I agreed with both positions at the same time." He was accused of being capricious in the way he judged men and manipulated his-tory, he was accused of fighting Fernando VII and embracing Morillo, of waging war to the death against Spain and promoting her spirit, of depending on Haiti in order to win the war and then considering Haiti a foreign country in order to exclude her from the Congress of Panamá, of having been a mason and reading Voltaire at Mass but of being the paladin of the Church, of courting the English while woo-ing a French princess, of being frivolous, hypocritical, and even dis-loyal because he flattered his friends in their presence and denigrated them behind their backs. "Well, all of that is true, but circumstantial," he said, "because everything I've done has been for the sole purpose of making this continent into a single, independent country, and as far as that's concerned I've never contradicted myself or had a single doubt." And he concluded in pure Caribbean: "All the rest is bull-shit!" (202–3)

The passage contrasts the particularistic, which entangles Bolívar as an incoherent site of meaning, with the universal, which recovers a sense of wholeness and redemptive purpose. The novel mostly takes place in the first, alienating register, constituting the labyrinth referred to in the title, which manifests itself at the level of the General's loss of power and direc-tion, his confusion, and the decline of his body. García Márquez has un-doubtedly written a critique of the official Bolívar, but few have noted that his novel also comments upon the extraordinary, contradictory, and ever-proliferating industry of Estudios Bolivarianos (Bolivarian Studies), which moves the hero further and further out of reach, placing him deeper in a labyrinth of academic and patriotic discourse. The archive of heroics, politi-cal intrigues, and philosophical theories that have proliferated since Bolívar's death is rejected in favor of the simplest of formulations, through which we may come to know Bolívar coherently: pan-Americanism. Ultimately, the stakes of this issue do not pertain to Bolívar alone, but to the political future of the continent.

Before exploring how García Márquez appropriates Bolívar for pan-Americanism, it is useful to step back and consider some historical particulars regarding Bolívar's geopolitical thought. During his career as the Liberator, Bolívar was primarily driven by a commitment to the Republic of Gran Colombia, which comprised the Captaincy General of Venezuela, the Viceroyalty of New Granada, and the Audiencia of Quito. Bolívar's association with Gran Colombia won him the distrust of Venezuelan elites between 1825 and 1830, who resented the authority of Bogotá, the republic's capital, over their affairs. In 1826, Bogotano interests were troubled by rumors that Bolívar was intent on creating an Andean federation comprised of Gran Colombia, Perú, and Bolivia, under the authority of a conservative constitution he had written for Bolivia. Thus, in an immediate sense, Bolívar's military and political career was not driven by continentalism, but by smaller geopolitical units, such as Gran Colombia and the Andean federation.

Yet it is clear that Bolívar's political and military thought was informed by continentalism. The identification of Bolívar with pan-Americanism has two legitimate sources: his classic document, the "Letter of Jamaica" (1815) and a proposed league of American nations which met at the Congress of Panamá in 1826. In the "Letter of Jamaica," Bolívar demonstrates an awareness of how the Latin American Wars of Independence were taking place in lands bound together by a shared history, culture, and democratic destiny. Although he thought that it was a "grandiose" idea to create a single, Latin American republic, Bolívar conceded that the wounds of the ongoing Wars of Independence and competing regional interests would make such a union impossible (Bolívar, *Selected Writings* 115–16, 118). Bolívar also gauged the contradictory, postcolonial reality represented by the Creole movement for independence, noting that "though Americans by birth we derive our rights from Europe, and we have to assert these rights against the rights of the natives, and at the same time we must defend ourselves against the invaders" (110). Bolívar's eloquent diagnosis of the continent's ills and his speculations about its future and potential did much to canonize him as a prescient founder of modern pan-American thought in Latin America. Yet, the cult of Bolívar, in all of its manifestations has downplayed one of the most important arguments in the "Letter of Jamaica": the notion that the continent needs the guidance and protection of a liberal nation (such as England) to cultivate the ability to truly consummate the civilized, republican ideal (122).

Ten years after writing the foundational "Letter of Jamaica," Bolívar began to channel his ideas about the shared destiny of the Latin American republics toward a more practical end. First and foremost on his mind was the belief that only an independent continent could guarantee the security of its individual republics, including Gran Colombia. Secondly, Bolívar believed that British intervention in the Wars of Independence could ensure a quicker victory over Spain, and political and social stability in the republican era to follow. To these ends, Bolívar convened the Congress of Panamá (1826), a league of nations that would prominently include a representative of the British government. A draft of Bolívar's plans for the congress reveals the utopian reach and paradoxical dependence upon England of his idea for a pan-American federation:

> The Congress of Panama [sic] will bring together representatives from all the governments of America and a diplomatic agent of the government of his Britannic Majesty. This congress seems destined to form the vastest league, the most extraordinary and the strongest which has ever appeared on earth. The Holy Alliance will be inferior in power to this league, if England consents to take part in it. The human race would give a thousand thanks for this league of salvation, and America and England would receive manifold benefits from it.
>
> A code of law to regulate the relationship between political bodies would be one of its benefits.
>
> 1. The new world would take shape in the form of independent nations, all joined by a common law which would control their foreign relations and would offer them the stabilizing force of a general and permanent congress.
>
> 2. The existence of these new states would obtain new guarantees.
>
> 3. Spain would make peace because of the presence of England among her foes, and the Holy Alliance would grant recognition to these nascent countries.
>
> 4. Internal order would be preserved among these countries and within each of them.
>
> 5. No one of them will be weak in respect to any other; no one will be stronger.

6. A perfect equilibrium would be established in this truly new order of things.

7. The strength of all would come to the aid of any one which might suffer from the aggression of a foreign enemy or from anarchic factions within.

8. Differences in origin and in color would lose their meaning.

9. America would no longer fear this tremendous monster which has devoured the island of Santo Domingo, nor would it fear the numerical preponderance of the indigenous inhabitants.

10. Social reform, finally, would be achieved under the holy auspices of liberty and of peace—but England necessarily must hold in her hands the balance of this scale. (Belaunde 265–66)

In this vision, utopian considerations about "the vastness" of the proposed league, and the equality, order, and equilibrium that it would spread throughout the Americas, is tempered by the strategic importance of having Great Britain chaperone this project, and ultimately ensure its success. When the congress actually convened, it accomplished little (only the delegates of Perú, Colombia, Guatemala, and Mexico attended) but its underlying idea resonated deeply on a symbolic level, establishing Bolívar as a foundational pan-Americanist. Thus, in modern Bolivarian thought, the Liberator's pan-Americanism has been removed from its original military and political context and cleansed of its British predicate to emerge as an illuminated celebration of continental unity, democracy, and social justice. In *The General in His Labyrinth*, García Márquez weds this pan-Americanist definition of Bolívar with his belief that Latin American reality and its expression need to be defended against foreign interpretive models.

García Márquez develops his ideas about Latin American autonomy and hermeneutics in his Nobel lecture, "The Solitude of Latin America" (1982). In it, García Márquez argues that the solitude of the continent results from an inability to represent reality in ways that are conventionally "realistic." This estrangement is summarized by the memorable image of an early explorer's wondrous description of a llama, which deforms it into an extraordinary beast by describing it as a composite of Old World animal parts, including the body of a camel, the legs of a deer, and the ears of a mule. As seen through the rationalist, Enlightenment lens of Western civilization, Latin American reality becomes fantastic, aberrant, or excessive, instead of local and familiar. Solitude results from a disconnect between representational codes and the reality they are intended to represent, from "the lack of conventional means to render our lives believable" (89). As a step to overcome this disjunction, García Márquez urges the Old World to check its impulse to measure the New World by the same standards it measures itself or to script the continent after its own desires and experiences. Instead, he recommends that the New World be viewed as a work in progress like the Roman Empire or the city of London before they became symbols of political and cultural influence. Moreover, underlying this analysis is an anti-colonialist call against Cold War interventionism: "Why think that the social justice sought by progressive Europeans for their own countries cannot also be a goal for Latin America, with different methods for dissimilar conditions? No: the immeasurable violence and pain of our history are the result of age-old inequities and untold bitterness, and not a conspiracy plotted three thousand leagues from our home. But many European leaders and thinkers have thought so, with the childishness of old-timers who have forgotten the fruitful excess of their youth as if it were impossible to find another destiny than to live at the mercy of the two great masters of the world. This, my friends, is the very scale of our solitude" (90). In short, García Márquez concludes, Latin America has the right to achieve the same measure of praise for originality in the arena of social change that is accorded to it for its works of the imagination.[9] To a certain degree, this argument echoes some of the ideas that underpin Bolívar's Congress of Panamá; García Márquez wants to protect Latin American republics from foreign invasion and subjugation, and to allow them the political autonomy they deserve as members of a community of independent nations. And like many pan-Americanists before him, García Márquez describes the Latin American continent as an exceptionalist force for global renewal; whereas the "developed" world holds the power of nuclear destruction in its hands, Latin America holds the power of life and regeneration: "to oppression, plundering and abandonment, we respond with life" (90).

The relationship between the Nobel lecture and the novel is pertinent in light of the General's encounter with extraordinary animals not unlike those described by Antonio Pigafetta, the explorer whose description of a llama resulted in a fantastic and monstrous image. Along the shores of the Magdalena River, the General's entourage discovers tracks "that seemed to be those of a bird as large as an ostrich and at least as heavy as an ox, but this seemed normal to the oarsmen, who said there were men roaming that desolate place who were as big as ceiba trees and had the crests and claws of roosters" (94–95). The image of tracks in the mud models the very act of writing, through which traces of different referents, in this case "ostrich," "ox," "ceiba trees," and "rooster crests and claws," are combined to create an extraordinary monster.[10] The composite and therefore fantastic contours of the beasts who left the tracks by the river also relate to the intertwined questions of representation, violence, and freedom that are central to the Nobel lecture. The General's entourage rescues a German from an island where he had been abandoned by his own oarsmen for beating them. The German claims to be an astronomer and a botanist on a mission to capture the mythical men with rooster claws, which he has seen with his own eyes. This shady character wants to parade the rooster men around Europe "as a phenomenon comparable only to the Spider Woman of the Americas, who had caused such a sensation in the ports of Andalusia a century before" (95). The mysterious and fantastic nature of the men with rooster claws, who like Pigafetta's llama, have not found a realistic measure in the vocabularies of the Old World, now condemns them to be hunted for the purposes of displaying them for profit in Europe as monsters. The solitude of representation results in the threat of violence, extraction, and possession.

The projected fate of the men with rooster claws as similar to that of the Spider Woman of the Americas is a useful one, if we are to take seriously the evidence of the short story "A Very Old Man with Wings," in which the Spider Woman first appears. At the end of the story, after the village loses interest in the anomalous being, the stranger takes flight. Whereas the Old Man with Wings resists easy interpretation, falling out of favor as an attraction because he does not conform to expectations, the Spider Woman that comes through the village with a circus is a big hit, precisely because the meaning of her outlandish body conforms to a pre-established cultural narrative: the Spider Woman was a disobedient little girl who was transformed into a spider by a punitive lightning bolt. "A spectacle like that, full of so much human truth and with such a fearful lesson," García Márquez writes, "was bound to defeat without even trying that of a haughty angel who scarcely deigned to look at mortals" (Collected Stories 208). The fantastic shape of the Spider Woman's body is made believable, transformed into a "human truth" because it is plotted in a moralizing tale about obedience and God's personal stake in dramatically punishing individuals for their moral failings. Although García Márquez does not elucidate in The General in His Labyrinth on how the German explorer would narrativize the men with claws once he captured them and transported them to Europe, the encounter with difference represented by the German's quest to possess the rooster-men underlines how the interpretation and classification of different realities can result in violation and violence.

Much in the same manner that García Márquez alludes to well-intentioned and bad-intentioned European "rational interests" in his Nobel lecture, *The General in His Labyrinth* contrasts the German stranger, whose intentions are portrayed in a negative light, with Alexander von Humboldt, the German explorer whose account of his New World journeys, *Voyage de Humboldt et Bonpland aux régions équinoxiales de nouveau continent, fait en 1799* (1805–1834), helped to disseminate botanical, geographical, and sociological knowledge about the New World, and critically assessed its problems on the eve of the Wars of Independence. Humboldt's rich tract mapped out Latin American realities with sensitivity, and Bolívar, who had known Humboldt during one of his French sojourns, drew from it in his "Letter of Jamaica." While the General describes the nameless German as a "motherfucker" who "isn't worth a single hair on Humboldt's head" (96), Humboldt is praised for opening the General's eyes (97). Thus, the interlude about the German operates as a complex, and balanced, meditation on two types of European contact with Latin American reality.

The most transparent restaging of García Márquez's Nobel lecture takes place at the Zambrano banquet in which Don Cástulo Campillo treats the General to a special sancocho. During the meal, an arrogant Frenchman named Diocles Atlantique provokes the General. Atlantique's resemblance to King Neptune and his name alert the reader to the character's association with transatlanticism, and as the General finds out, to the most damaging kind of international relations. Atlantique pontificates on a variety of subjects: the deciphering of Egyptian hieroglyphs, "experimental proof of the influence of celestial bodies on disease," cats in ancient Greece, and the true origins of corn (121). All of these claims are characterized by an arrogant confidence in reason and science for explaining everything, from the quotidian to the cosmological. When the two men come around to talking about politics, Atlantique suggests that the model of Bonaparte is a good one for Latin America, and queries the General about his rumored monarchism. The General denies it and declares that "Europeans believe that only what Europe invents is good for the entire universe, and anything else is detestable" (122). The label of "monarchist" proposed by Atlantique, like that of "liberal" and "conservative," is discarded as a foreign referent, with little heuristic value for interpreting the General's actions and motives. In this light, the General's praise of the Abbot Pradt position that "policy depends on where and when it is formulated" (123) asserts the historical specificity of the continent against foreign interpretive models, defining it as a history in flux that should not be subordinated to European formulas. Echoing the Nobel lecture, the General goes on to cite the bloody history of Europe, chastising Atlantique and his interventionist views: "So stop doing us the favor of telling us what we should do. . . . Don't attempt to teach us how we should be, don't attempt to make us just like you, don't try to have do well in twenty years what you have done so badly in two thousand" (124).

The General's final moments, marked by an awareness "of the final brilliance of life that would never, through all eternity, be repeated again" (268) recast the theme of the particularity of Bolívar, the continent, its history, and its people outside of the impoverishing simulacra that estrange identity from itself in a solitary and paralyzing encirclement. The decay of the General's body is thus the decay of the continent, wounded by its marginalization from the very discourses that define it. In the final scenes of the novel, after accompanying the General on his final journey, the reader is able to experience Bolívar's death intimately, as a comment on the wonderment of life's frailty and fleeting nature. García Márquez successfully sheds layer after layer of historicity and iconicity in his narrative, leading his protagonist out of the labyrinth through the clairvoyant truth and pathos of death. The General examines the room in which he is soon to die, surrendering to the truth of his impending end. He crosses his arms, listening to the radiant song of the slaves in the mills, contemplating Venus, and "the new vine whose yellow bellflowers he would not see bloom on the following Saturday . . ." (267). As Julio Ortega observes, the final scene recovers elegy by surrendering the protagonist to the singularity of life and death: "Death no longer occurs in the discursive stage of romanticism but in the most sober and quotidian account of objects, which acquire the value of transitive signs, humanized, as in a poem by César Vallejo, by their quotidian nature. The future takes place outside of his life, from his past; separated from time, that last fluttering confirms his uniqueness, impossible to repeat" ("Lector" 176). The catharsis of the final images of the General's life affirms that beneath all the discourse, beyond the contradictory decrepit body of an icon, lies another body, joined to an American world of sounds, sensations, and renewal.

The Handsomest Liberator in the World

What is to become of the Bolívar that emerges at the moment of death is not spelled out in the novel. However, another of García Márquez's short stories, "The Handsomest Drowned Man in the World," provides some insight into the foundational promise of a body freed from reductive, rationalistic, and self-consciously mythic referents. The story takes place in a seaside village tenuously connected to history and place, where there "was so little land that mothers always went about with the fear that the wind would carry off their children and the few dead that the years had caused among them had to be thrown off the cliffs" (*Collected Stories* 231). A beautiful drowned man of great proportions is washed on shore, provoking much speculation about his provenance and powers. The drowned man comes to represent the promise of a better life; the villagers believe that this man "would have put so much work into his land that springs would have burst forth from among the rocks so that he would have been able to plant flowers on the cliffs" (232). The majesty of this mysterious figure, in contrast to the meager village, might very well have been disassociated from the villagers if an old woman had not simply declared "He has the face of someone called Esteban" (232). It is significant that the mythical Lautaro (the name of an Auracanian leader who defeated Pedro de Valdivia in sixteenth-century Chile) is discarded in favor of a name that is spontaneous and that reflects the drowned man's countenance. By rejecting the discourse of myth ("Lautaro") and embracing the quotidian ("Esteban"), the villagers construct a foundational discourse that is familiar and spontaneous, not alien or artificial. With "Esteban" in place as a cornerstone of their myth of origin, they are free to reimagine and reconstruct their physical reality: "They also knew that everything would be different from then on, that their houses would have wider doors, higher ceilings, and stronger floors so that Esteban's memory could go everywhere without bumping into beams . . ." (236) The villagers paint their houses in color to memorialize Esteban and work with renewed zeal to make the land fertile and productive. They have all, in effect, become as big as Esteban the giant.[11]

In the case of Bolívar's death in 1830, things were not different "from then on." In the wake of Bolívar's life, the vast continental vision he embodied shrunk into narrow nationalisms and regionalisms, destructive civil wars between liberals and conservatives, grotesque crimes against humanity, the sorrows of exile, imperial interventions, the economic paralysis of debt, and the continuing presence of disease, poverty, and hopelessness. Rather than treating this warrior of independence as someone familiar, Latin America has made him a myth, and as such, distant and confusing. The name of Bolívar does not suit the person anymore, and much less his memory, which is muddled by the abundant and contradictory connotations of his myth. In daring to rediscover Bolívar through the anonymity of death, García Márquez casts the hero's body onto the shores of the world again, inviting us to rediscover his humanity and the promise of pan-American unity all over again.

Afterword

Bolivarian Self-Fashioning into the Twenty-First Century

"I Swear in the Name of the God of My Parents"

In 1850, the Colombian historian Manuel Uribe Angel visited Simón Bolívar's renowned childhood tutor and friend, Simón Rodríguez, in Quito. The elderly Rodríguez was poor and disillusioned after a string of failures in implementing his radical educational ventures in Latin America. Uribe asked the elderly man about his memories of Bolívar. Rodríguez recalled that when he and Bolívar had visited Rome in August of 1805, they climbed the Monte Sacro, where Bolívar was overcome with emotion. Rodríguez described how the twenty-two-year-old Bolívar became inspired and vowed to liberate his homeland from Spanish tyranny. After invoking the faded glories of the classical world, Bolívar declared: "I swear before you; I swear in the name of the God of my parents; I swear upon them; on my honor and my homeland, I swear that I will not let my arm rest, nor give my soul repose, until I have broken the chains that oppress us by order of the Spanish authorities" (Bolívar, *Doctrina* 4). Rodríguez's second-hand account of Bolívar's vow on the Monte Sacro has become one of the cornerstone texts of the myth of Bolívar. The Venezuelan painter Tito Salas immortalized the scene on one of the frescoes of the National Pantheon in Caracas; the elegant young Bolívar is portrayed with the soft nimbus of a white cloud hovering around his figure, his right arm outstretched toward the future and the other resting on a fallen column, while the awestruck and proud teacher Rodríguez looks on from a seated position. In truth, as Susana Rotker has observed, we cannot be sure of the details of this scene or of Bolívar's exact words. The so called "Oath of Rome," deprived of the framing devices that indicate that Bolívar's words are being represented through the memory of another person, has entered into the canon of Bolivarian literature as Bolívar's first proclamation. "If this did not happen," Rotker declares, "it does not matter: *it should have happened*" (42; emphasis in original). Indeed, as an emblem of Bolívar, and of his iconicity as a national and pan-American symbol, the "Oath of Rome" faithfully represents a foundational scene of Latin American identity.

Fast forward to December 17, 1982. A captain in the Second Regiment of Venezuela's Parachute Division decides to formalize his plans for a revolution against the Venezuelan state. He and two fellow officers inaugurate their secret political cell, the Movimiento Bolivariano Revolucionario-200, by restaging Bolívar's Roman oath. They take turns declaring: "I swear in the name of the God of my parents; I swear on my homeland that I won't give peace to my soul until I have seen broken the chains that oppress my people, by order of the powerful. Popular election, free men and lands, horror to the oligarchy." Captain Hugo Chávez Frías had decided to fashion himself after Bolívar and his spectacular journey. He was self-consciously surrendering himself to history by beginning with a thinly veiled reenactment of Bolívar's oath. It was a gamble, but if his plans were to come to fruition, Chávez knew that his oath would recreate the iconic image of Bolívar and secure his place in Venezuelan mythology as a true heir to the hero of independence. And as extraordinary as it might seem in retrospect, Chávez's self-important bid to "be like" Bolívar did produce results, and shook Venezuela to its foundations. Eighteen years after his oath, and after a failed coup and two years in prison, Hugo Chávez ascended to the Venezuelan presidency and embarked on an ambitious plan to transform Venezuela radically.

At the time of this writing, in January of 2003, President Hugo Chávez has survived one coup and is facing a month-long national strike that has paralyzed oil production and resulted in massive protests and violence on the streets. Although the years to come will provide the necessary hindsight better to understand his presidency and its outcome, it is not too bold to say that Chávez embodies the most dramatic instance of Bolivarian nationalism in twentieth-century Venezuela. Like most of the writers discussed in this study, Chávez diagnoses the failure of Bolivarian nationalism and proposes a reinvention of the hero of independence. His version of Bolívar is predicated on a rejection of neoliberalism, economic dependency, and political corruption. Moreover, Chavismo is sustained by the conceit that it is desirable and possible to erase a century of liberal constitutionalism and restart history through the recovery of an original Bolivarian ideology. Chávez himself assiduously cultivates the notion that he is the true heir to Bolívar, to the point of fashioning himself after Bolívar. It is fitting, then, to close my study of Bolivarian iconoclasm with a postscript on Hugo Chávez, whose tumultuous political career is predicated on a populist reconstruction of the institutionalized cult of Bolívar and a pointed rejection of the traditional formulas of liberal progress. Chávez's brand of Bolivarian self-fashioning provides us an opportunity to offer some final reflections on the Bolivarian monumentalism that has been the subject of this study.

"I Alone Shoulder the Responsibility for This Bolivarian Military Uprising"

Hugo Chávez Frías was born in the town of Barinas in 1954, where his parents, both school teachers, struggled to make ends meet. To supplement his parents' meager salaries, Hugo Chávez sold fruit and sweets out of a cart on the streets of his town (G. García Márquez, "Enigma"). If family funds were limited, however, a wealth of historical memory bound the family to Venezuela's martial history. Apart from their nationalist devotion to Bolívar, the Chávez Frías family could trace its ancestors to two caudillos, Colonel Pedro Pérez Pérez, who fought during the Guerra Federal of the nineteenth century, and Pedro Pérez Delgado, known as Maisanta, who resisted the dictatorship of Juan Vicente Gómez in the first quarter of the twentieth century.

In 1971, the seventeen-year-old Hugo Chávez enlisted in the Venezuelan military and began his life as an ambitious and independent-minded career soldier. From early on, Chávez questioned the integrity of the counterinsurgency campaigns of the Venezuelan armed forces against Marxist guerillas.[1] In the 1980s Chávez began to network with close friends in the armed forces and formed the Movimiento Bolivariano Revolucionario-200 (MBR-200). The conspirators rejected the democratic state as corrupt and incapable of representing the interests of the masses. They were alarmed by increasing poverty and the state's growing commitment to neoliberal policies that exacerbated the living conditions of the poor. Inspired by the example of other populist military leaders, such as General Raul Velasco of Perú and Omar Torrijos of Panama, they believed that the armed forces could be a force for progressive, social change. They were willing to wait for the right moment to strike, when they had moved up the ranks, and when the popular sector might be drawn into the struggle (Gott 42).

The window of opportunity came on February 27, 1989, when Caracas erupted into riots over the price of public transportation. When the government raised oil prices, the cost of bus fares for the thousands of people who commuted from outlying communities into the capital every day doubled within twenty-four hours. However, if the price of oil set off the riots, long-standing resentment of a lingering economic crisis and the state's inability to address it had set the scene for the violent outburst. A state of siege was declared and the armed forces killed hundreds if not thousands of protesters (Gott 47). Despite the indignation of the members of Chávez's cell, they were caught unprepared and could not act. The riots, known as the Caracazo, intensified the conspiratorial activities of the MBR-200.

Three years later, on February 4, 1992, the MBR-200 attempted its coup. Tank divisions entered the city and attacked the defense ministry, the military airport of La Carlota, the presidential palace of Miraflores, and the president's private residence of La Casona. Plans to capture President Carlos Andrés Pérez and high-ranking officials of the military failed in the face of miscommunication and limited resources. In a chase worthy of fiction, the president escaped his enemies at Maiquetía International Airport, at La Casona, and at Miraflores. Chávez realized he had missed his chance and appeared on television to call for his men to surrender; in the process he became a hero to many in the country. His words transfixed a populace that was deeply distrustful of a political establishment and deserve to be quoted in their entirety.

> First I want to say "good morning" to all the people of Venezuela, but this Bolivarian message is directed specifically to the courageous soldiers of the parachute regiment of Aragua and the tank regiment of Valencia.
>
> Comrades: unfortunately, for the moment, the objectives that we had set for ourselves have not been achieved in the capital. That's to say that those of us here in Caracas have not been able to seize power. Where you are, you have performed well, but now is the time for a rethink; new possibilities will arise again and the country will be able to move definitively toward a better future.
>
> So listen to what I have to say, listen to comandante Chávez who is sending you this message, and, please, think deeply. Lay down your

arms, for in truth the objectives that we set ourselves at a national level are not within our grasp.

Comrades, listen to this message of solidarity. I am grateful for your loyalty, for your courage, and for your selfless generosity; before the country and before you, I alone shoulder the responsibility for this Bolivarian military uprising. Thank you. (Gott 70–71)

Chávez caught the popular imagination by taking personal responsibility for the failed coup, and by defiantly uttering the phrase *por ahora* (for the moment) while acknowledging the failure of his plans (Gott 71). The Bolivarians of MBR-200, Chávez seemed to be saying, had lost the battle, not the war.

In an astonishing series of twists and turns, President Carlos Andrés Pérez was impeached for corruption in 1993, Chávez was pardoned in 1994, and elected president in 1999. Chávez's MBR-200 had been reborn as the Movimiento Quinta República, and its central political mission was summed up by its name: to convene a constitutional congress to rewrite the Venezuelan constitution and found the fifth Venezuelan republic. When he was being sworn in as president, Chávez swore upon the "moribund constitution" that he would lead the nation to a new and improved Magna Carta. Protests from old party horses, intellectuals, and the Supreme Court of Venezuela were pushed aside. A referendum on whether or not to convene a constitutional congress was overwhelmingly approved by the public and the majority of delegates from the Movimiento Quinta Republica were voted into the assembly. The new constitution created by the assembly was approved by yet another popular referendum and Venezuela was officially renamed the Bolivarian Republic of Venezuela. By 2001, however, Chávez lost national and international political capital by antagonizing the opposition, unions, the oil industry, and the press.

Chavez's opponents see his regime as a throwback to the paternalistic, military dictatorships of the past. The distinguished historians Manuel Caballero, Elías Pino Iturrieta, and Inés Quintero, among others, decried Chávez's manipulative and excessive appeals to Bolivarian nationalism, his bid to militarize the government, and his initiative to rename the nation. The well-known novelist Mario Vargas Llosa published an editorial in *El universal* in August of 1999 calling Chávez a demagogue, an autocratic populist, a felon, and a traitor to his constitution and his uniform. Indeed, Chávez's words and acts give some credence to the criticism that he is autocratic. In his presidential acceptance speech before the congress and foreign dignitaries, Chávez declared that he aspired to be a much better "commander" than before (Chávez, "Discurso de toma de posesión"). Later on that same day, in a speech at the Paseo de los Próceres, he referred to his new title as president in a distinctly martial pitch: "this president will be the first soldier on the battlefield" (Chávez, "Discurso paseo de los próceres"). Indeed, one of the defining characteristics of the Chávez presidency has been the symbolic and political prominence of the military in the new state. Not only has Chávez named military officers to important government posts, but he has also promoted plans to use the armed forces in social services, education, and public works.[2]

As president, Chávez wanted to become a continental leader capable of counteracting the hegemony of the United States in the hemisphere by reviving Bolivarian pan-Americanism.[3] On inauguration day, in his speech at the Paseo de los Próceres, Chávez said: "Venezuela from this moment onward declares itself standard bearer of Latin American and Caribbean unity." Chávez's close friendship with Fidel Castro, and his friendly state visits to China and Iraq have given him ample opportunity to disseminate his conviction that the United States should not be the only arbiter of foreign affairs in the world. For example, he refused U.S. requests for permission to fly over Venezuelan airspace to pursue drug war missions over Colombia. Further, he defied Latin American dependency upon the United States by proposing a NATO-like organization for Latin America, as well as a common currency for the entire continent. Compared to his neoliberal predecessors, who presided over bureaucracies that were viewed as inherently corrupt, Chávez broke the mold of the modern Venezuelan foreign diplomacy through a combative, pan-American stance.

"Now Is When Venezuelans Will Listen to Me Speak of Bolívar . . ."

No other president since Antonio Guzmán Blanco has promoted the image of Bolívar as effectively as Hugo Chávez. Although Venezuela is historically steeped in the cult of Bolívar, Chávez's populism has intensified Bolivarian ritual and discourse. As tempting as it might be to think of Chávez as yet another demagogue taking advantage of the symbolic capital of a century and a half of Bolivarian nationalism, a closer look reveals that this president is engaged in a more complex transaction. As president, Chávez is attempting to preserve the critical dimensions of oppositional nationalism from within the state. For Chávez, Bolívar is not a trophy for consolidating national pride, but rather a call to arms to remake a nation marred by what he calls "a moral cancer" (Chávez, "Discurso de toma de posesión"). His Bolívar is not the monument, but a spirit of renewal in an age of crisis. As such, Chávez engages the Bolívar question on two related fronts: on the one hand he criticizes the static and self-congratulatory discourse of official identity, while on the other he tries to mobilize a more dynamic and politically transformative version of Bolívar. In the process, Chávez cultivates parallels between himself and the hero of independence, suggesting that his authority springs directly from Bolívar himself.

A survey of Chávez's presidential acceptance speech (herein "Discurso de toma de posesión") may provide some insight into how his new Bolivarian nationalism is defined. Chávez's speech is gregarious and dynamic, and underscores his optimistic populism. At one moment, he cites Walt Whitman, an apt choice considering how Chávez strives to contain multitudes in his discourse. Alongside Whitman, and repeated references to the spirit of Bolívar, Chávez invokes Galileo, José Martí, Miguel Angel Asturias, Pablo Neruda, Pedro Mir, Pope John Paul II, Gabriel García Márquez, and Chinese proverbs. From within this multitude of voices, Chávez negotiates a discourse of crisis, in which Venezuela is the victim of a catastrophe, and a providential discourse of renewal, in which Venezuela faces a glorious and epic struggle to reinvent itself. An example of the discourse of crisis: "Our homeland is wounded in the heart, we are in a kind of human grave." The discourse of renewal: "this day, which is not just another day . . . is the first passing of the torch to a new epoch . . . the opening of a door onto a new national existence." Chávez calls for a collective mea culpa, and for reconciliation. He assails neoliberalism as a savage ethos and rejects the statist models of governance, proposing a third way, a balance between the invisible hand of the market and the protective presence of the state. The symbolic axis for these ambitious plans for reconstructing Venezuela is the spirit of Bolívar.

Early on in his speech, Chávez tells a revealing anecdote about Bolivarian nationalism in Venezuela that underscores his commitment to separate himself from the institutionalized cult of Bolívar: "Why Bolívar? It's not about the forced protocol of repeating any obscure phrase of Bolívar, just to speak of Bolívar, like I remember one of the soldiers in my tank platoon did on one occasion several years ago. It was his responsibility to gather the company every day, and every day it was his task and obligation to begin the announcement of the day's orders with a thought of the Liberator that he would read in the patio; and he had a book from which to take the thoughts and pick any one of them. One day he lost the book and when we were about to form ranks and formally read the orders of the day, the corporal invented a maxim: 'Let us care for the trees for they are life.' Simón Bolívar." Chávez's tale of the Bolívar of protocols rejects the notion of Bolívar as a random compendium of parables and dictums. The story also reveals a sense of disillusionment with Bolivarian identity in general, which has become dislodged from the Venezuelan self, like a foreign and meaningless object that serves no idealistic purpose. The solution to this dispersal of Bolivarian meaning is a return to the kind of Bolívar celebrated by José Martí and Pablo Neruda. Their Bolívar was a Bolívar of the people and for the people, stirring into life every time that the masses lift themselves up to struggle for liberty. This linking of Bolívar to internationalist social justice is not new in and of itself, but the endorsement of this vision by a Venezuelan president signals the legitimation of a rich tradition of Marxist interpretations of Bolívar that have existed on the margins of official culture in Latin America.[4]

The most striking deployment of Bolívar, however, takes place when Chávez restages the present as a repetition of the Wars of Independence, with himself playing the role of Bolívar. Standing before a hostile congress, Chávez anticipates resistance to his plans to do away with the old constitution, and preemptively attacks his critics by suggesting that Venezuela is at the same symbolic crossroads it was at when independence was being debated in 1811. Resistance to change, argues Chávez, is analogous to the position of those who defended the legitimacy of the Spanish Crown, while support for the immediate transformation of the Venezuelan political system is the equivalent of the cause of independence. In 1811, Bolívar had argued for the new Venezuelan polity to remain united in its commitment to independence, and Chávez interjects this call for unity of purpose into the present, calling for the congress to join his Bolivarian revolution. Echoing Bolívar's condemnation of the foes of independence in 1811, Chávez terms those who would resist his agenda traitors: "Today gentlemen, to join those who want to conserve things as they are now, to seek consensus with those who oppose those changes that are necessary, I say today like Bolívar: it is a betrayal!"

Chávez presents himself as a celestial messenger, telling the congress and the nation the big truths that need to be spoken. In one of his most grandiloquent moments, Chávez suggests that he is the incarnation of Bolívar by referencing another mythic scene of the life of Bolívar, the 1825 ascent of the highest peak of the Andes, Ecuador's Mount Chimborazo. After his ascent Bolívar composed a short text called "My Delirium on Chimborazo," in which he describes being swept up in the sublimity of the divine realm and its providential direction. Despite convincing evidence that Bolívar's ascent of Chimborazo did not take place, and that "My Delirium on Chimborazo" is apocryphal, the scene has been canonized as another foundational moment attesting to Bolívar's providential leadership (Rotker 41–42). In his speech, Chávez juxtaposes God's command to Bolívar upon Chimborazo to speak the truth to the people with his own dramatic pronunciations about the painful truth of Venezuela's present crisis. "The truth is this," declares Chávez, "Venezuela is wounded in the heart; we are on the edge of a sepulchre." By heeding the voice of the same God that spoke to Bolívar on Chimborazo, and to Chávez in the present, the nation will be resurrected.

"An Embrace for All and Thank You Very Much for Your Attention . . ."

Chávez's Bolivarian self-fashioning underscores the enduring power of Bolivarian mythology, which continues to be rewritten in politics as well as in art into the twenty-first century. Throughout this study, I have underlined how Bolívar belongs to two distinct yet intertwined realms of experience: the failures of the present and the promise of tomorrow. This combination of utopia and dystopia also marks the discourse of Chávez, and might explain his emergence as one of the most controversial presidents in Venezuelan history. For his supporters, Chávez represents a break with corrupt political traditions and infrastructures; for his critics, however, his Bolivarian self-fashioning signifies a return to the manias and delusions of Latin American dictators of the past. Which version is real? In the words of Gabriel García Márquez, from his insightful essay on Chávez, Chávez is a bewildering man who could very well save his country or pass into the annals of history as yet another despot ("Enigma").

What is certain is that Chávez's Bolivarian ideology topples the static and ossified monument of Bolívar and replaces it with a version of Bolívar that signals the conceit that an original, pure, and unquestionable Bolivarian truth can be identified and harnessed for reimagining the nation. Yet, in a deeper sense, Chávez recreates the dominant poses of the monumentalist Bolívar. Bolívar continues to be the organizing principle of a teleology that promises the realization of the ideal of "progress." Although Chávez rejects the discourse of neoliberalism, he maintains that political, social, and economic regeneration are predicated on the sanctity of Bolívar. The patrilineal dimensions of the cult are also reified and strengthened, with celestial commands descending from God onto Bolívar and finally, through Chávez, to the people of Venezuela. The authority of the father remains intact. Finally, Chávez underscores the inviolable nature of his brand of Bolivariana. Bolívar is more than a symbol of tomorrow, and of the authority of the father; he represents an authoritative horizon of meaning, the last word. For Chávez, the sign of Bolívar is univocal and irrevocable; it does not admit contradiction, interpretation, or challenge. Chávez's rhetoric may have a critical dimension to it, but in the end, he conjures up the tried and true icon of Bolívar as the embodiment of absolute power.

This discussion of Hugo Chávez's Bolivarian self-fashioning invites us to reflect on the underlying dynamic between crisis and plenitude that has been at the center of most modern revisions of Bolívar since the end of the nineteenth century. Bolivarian nationalism began in the early national period as a refashioning of religious paradigms; Bolívar was to be the overseeing spirit of a harmonious national unity predicated on reverence for his words and example. Yet, as soon as Bolivarian identity acquired monumental visibility as an ideology of the state, it became available to intellectuals as an ambiguous symbol. In the face of the failures and contradictions of liberal progress, these observers questioned whether or not the true spirit and mission of the original Bolívar was being served by official culture. Thus framed, the monumental Bolívar ceased being an authoritative symbol equal to the spirit of Bolívar and became a false idol.

Manuel Díaz Rodríguez, Teresa de la Parra, Gabriel García Márquez, as well as Chávez, seek to topple the false idol and replace it with a new vision of the hero of independence, one that is more commensurate with his true meaning. Between the push and pull of disenchantment and hope, these modern Bolivarians did not take the monumental Bolívar for granted; they interrogated it in the name of refashioning it in the name of tomorrow. Others who have meditated on the cult of Bolívar and who have been included in this study, such as Juan Dávila and Denzil Romero, are more pointed in their questioning of Bolivarian monumentalism. Rather than resurrecting a Bolivarian spirit through their critique, their representations question some of the very premises of idealizing and mythologizing history and its protagonists. Although some artists will undoubtedly continue questioning Bolívar in this deeply iconoclastic vein, the currency of Bolívar in Latin American political and popular culture will continue being constructive, rather than destructive. Bolívar will be a banner and a call to arms, not a word in quotation marks or a question mark. The cult of

Bolívar will remain and continue to adapt to changing historical conditions, in a continuous process of symbolic resurrection. It will continue to feed off the vast reservoir of wonder and affection that Latin Americans have for their quixotic hero of independence.

The continuing power of the cult of Bolívar as an ideological mechanism continually readapted to a changing present, and flexible enough to accommodate the extremes of the political right and left, raises the question of whether or not Bolivarian identity in the twenty-first century is a handicap or a new horizon of possibility. The very repeatability of monumentalist definitions of Bolívar in politics and art lends credence to Luis Castro Leiva's pessimistic assessment of the limitations of Bolivarian political discourse. If identity begins and ends with Bolívar, in a continuous repetition of the same iconic scenes, regardless of the ideology that frames their utterance, political discourse is impoverished and reduced to hollow formulas. More troubling is the fact that the commitment to constructing identity through the image of a single man validates political personalism. If it is accepted that Bolívar was a genius, a giant among men, and the authorizing principle for the construction of nations and political movements, then his providential leadership must be accepted as well, along with the corollary that in times of crisis such a man might need to assume all powers in the name of a greater good. In short, the embeddedness of caudillismo within the cult of Bolívar is an affront to democracy, dialogue, and new political solutions to two centuries worth of civil war, economic and cultural dependency, and political oppression. Regardless of who Bolívar the man was in actuality, and of whether he is celebrated or vilified in political and popular culture, the only way to overcome the hollowness of the monumentalist Bolívar is to move beyond Bolívar and the personalist definition of identity. What makes this challenge so daunting is that it assails modern nationalism itself, which is predicated on mythic narratives in general.

Whatever the course of future events on the political scene and in the arts, Bolívar will continue to play center stage in discussions of Latin American identity for the simple reason that his quest for political independence and a modern, postcolonial Latin America continues to be relevant. The wounds of independence have not healed. The unfulfilled promise of a truly "new" world has not been achieved. In spite of the eternal return of Bolivarian monumentalism and its authoritarian narratives, there is an alternative model of Bolívar to consider. Rather than an essential being with a providential, predetermined historical meaning, this

Bolívar might be conceived as a metaphor for questions left unanswered across two centuries, and an invitation to dialogue about the unfinished business of modern Latin America in the twenty-first century. Why not honor Bolívar's memory by seeking answers to the same questions that he tried to answer through his dramatic political and military career? Only then would Bolívar, atop his horse on a pedestal in the Plaza Bolívar, transcend monumentalism and the disillusionment that has accreted on his body of bronze like a patina. Such an impetus would move the continent forward rather than backward in a remembrance of the unfinished nature of his journey, opening up history to the promise of answers that have yet to be found.

Notes

Introduction: Dominant Poses, Iconoclastic Gestures

1. Diamela Eltit suggests that Dávila's carnivalized image exorcizes, in a refracted manner, the image of the bodies of the victims of the military regime (Richard 192–93).

2. For a succinct overview of the ideology of progress in Latin America, see E. Bradford Burns's *The Poverty of Progress*. "The more the capital city architecturally resembled Paris," writes Burns about nineteenth-century urban development in Latin America, "then ipso facto the greater degree of progress that particular country could proclaim" (20).

3. For a discussion of monuments and iconoclasm in Eastern Europe, see Katherine Verdery's *The Political Lives of Dead Bodies: Reburial and Postsocialist Change*.

4. In "Pintura e indiferenciación de los sexos," published in *La nación* on August 12, 1994, Justo Pastor Mellado writes, "Everyone knows that in the current political lexicon we speak of 'lowering one's pants' or of arriving to a meeting with 'tin underpants.' They are phrases that frequently circulate in the environment of businessmen. Dávila's painting is thus sustained by the notion of penetration" (26).

5. The indexical gesture as the exercise of power or moral superiority may be seen in the painting *St. Paul before Felix the Roman Governor* by Hogarth, or *St. John the Baptist* by El Greco (Critchley 111).

6. Carrera Damas establishes that representations of Bolívar function as ideologically transitive phenomena, capable of affecting social reality. He writes: "In a given historical moment ideological representations can correspond . . . to different historical periods and nonetheless retain the condition of real and active historical factors . . ." (27).

7. In my use of "abundance" and "lack" I am indebted to the work of Julio Ortega. In "El lector en su laberinto," Ortega summarizes these concepts as follows: "The discourse of abundance . . . is based on a proliferating economy of signs, on a genetic historicity, on a circular temporality that constitutes the process-oriented nature of representation. The second model is the discourse of lack . . . history is here conceived

critically, as deterioration . . ." (168). Also see Ortega's "The Discourse of Abundance."

Chapter 1. Bolívar and the Emergence of a National Religion

1. An important commentator of the cult, Luis Castro Leiva, demonstrates that the liturgical impetus of this new, civic religion sought to recreate independence within the transcendental realm, substituting religious codes with new, patriotic ones: "'Liberty' and 'Patriotism' offered . . . two intellectual contexts within which one could experience the passion and absolutes demanded by both Catholicism and republicanism, all of it from the horizon of meaning of an Enlightenment, ethical-political discourse" (148).

2. The roots of Colombian animosity toward Bolívar may be traced back to the failure of Bolívar's second republic, which had been sponsored by the United Provinces of Nueva Granada. Upon his return to Tunja after the loss of Caracas in 1814, Bolívar was recriminated for his defeat and accused of excessive cruelty (Liévano Aguirre 138–39). David Bushnell makes the case that after the creation of Gran Colombia, Bogotano interests viewed the Venezuelan military, which was associated with Bolívar, with distrust and prejudice (*The Santander Regime* 256–57).

3. As Antonio Cussen has shown in his study of Bello and Bolívar, the currency of the term *Augusto* (August, Augustan) in the first quarter of the century was contingent on the existence of a legitimate, higher power that justified "the dividing line between the powerful and the powerless, the rulers and the ruled" (Cussen 10).

4. This passage is from the poem "Colombia constituida, poecia [*sic*] compuesta por un español americano, impresa en Paris" and is contained in the *Gaceta de Colombia*, August 18, 1822. For more examples of this early Bolivarian literature, see the following poems in the *Correo del Orinoco*: "Gratitud nacional" (January 15, 1820), "La Campaña de Bogotá" (February 19, 1820), "Epístola patriótica" (March 25, 1820), "El pabellón Colombiano" (August 5, 1820), "Himno patriótico" (December 15, 1821), "Elojio" (May 11, 1823), and "Oda" (November 3, 1829). In the *Gaceta de Colombia*, see "La fidelidad" (January 4, 1820) and "El Libertador en Popayán" (February 15, 1829). Also, see Leonardo Altuve Carrillo's *Genio y apoteosis de Bolívar en la campaña del Perú*, which contains a wealth of Bolivarian poetry from the era of independence.

5. For a detailed discussion of the reception of "La victoria de Junín," see my article "Gender, Revolution, and Empire in 'La victoria de Junín.'"

6. The quoted passage from "Catón en Utica" is from Emilio Rodríguez Demorizi's *Poetas contra Bolívar: El Libertador a través de la calumnia* (69). Other poems similar to "Catón en Utica" may be found in Rodríguez Demorizi's anthology, such as "Soneto" (133) and "Fábula" (141).

7. Lander wondered what would have happened if Bolívar had harshly punished José Antonio Páez for supporting Venezuelan secession in 1827. If Páez had been imprisoned or executed for disagreeing with Bolívar, Lander argued, then Venezuela

would not have counted with Páez's invaluable services during the Guerra de Reformas of 1835 (González Guinán 2:446).

8. One passage of the play reads: "What sublime patriot/does not praise you about the vast regions with enthusiasm?/What *caraqueño* does not lift hurrahs/ When your resplendence in the frost/arrives with the most beautiful aurora/entwined with morning rays?" (Gómez 11).

9. Bolívar married María Teresa del Toro in 1801 and maintained a lifelong friendship with her father, the Marqués del Toro, Fermín's uncle.

10. Toro was editor of *El correo de Caracas* in 1839 and *El liceo Venezolano* in 1842. Toro's poetry, published in different magazines during and after his lifetime, includes "A la zona torrida" and "Hecatonfonia." Toro's most famous costumbrista sketches are "Costumbres de Barullópolis" (1839) and "Un romántico" (1842). "Europa y América" (1839), "Ideas y necesidades" (1842) and the book-length *Reflexiones sobre la Ley 10 de Abril de 1834* (1845) constitute Toro's most important work as a political thinker. His novel *Los mártires*, which is set in England, was serialized in 1842.

11. In *Crowds and Power* Canetti describes and defines several crowd symbols, such as fire, forests, rivers, and seas. Canetti argues that these symbols are synoptic codes that describe the nature of crowds. About the sea crowd symbol, he writes: "The sea is multiple, it moves, and it is dense and cohesive. Its multiplicity lies in its waves; they constitute it. They are innumerable. . . . They are never entirely still. . . . The dense coherence of the waves is something which men in a crowd know well. It entails a yielding to others as though they were oneself, as though there were no strict division between oneself and them" (80).

12. A prior essay, "Europa y América" (1839), shows that Toro's earlier conception of the problem of continuity in Venezuelan history was quite different. The essay is a scathing attack on civilized Europe's emerging "industrial feudalism" (a term Toro borrows from Simonde de Sismondi) and its negative repercussions on liberty, social justice, and human dignity. In the essay, Toro views the wartime caudillos so central to the necessary destruction of Spanish colonialism and the creation of new forms of government as men whose times and patriotic tasks have passed. The age of postwar reconstruction is the domain of a new generation of peacetime, enlightened, republican patriots: "the generation that destroys is never the one that builds; and it is not its fault that the heavens do not confer upon the same hands the two missions" (67). In this earlier assessment, Bolívar is incapable of transcending the era of destruction, and thus descends into tyranny. After liberating a whole world, Bolívar's "formidable arm, not knowing where to put the bolt in his right hand, began to strike against the work of his own creation" (67). Toro's attack on Bolívar was clearly a response to the *Reformistas* and their claim to political authority in early national Venezuela. These were not heroes, Toro suggests through the example of Bolívar, but warriors of the past incapable of leading a constitutionalist and civilian Venezuela.

13. Early on in his career as a journalist, Larrazábal underlined this commitment to religion as a modernizing, republican force in 1845, when he reprinted an article on religious education from the French paper *L'Université Catholique*. In the translated article, "Influencia de la educación religiosa en sus relaciones con el desarollo de la inteligencia de la juventud," M. D. Hermite argued that Catholicism formed good citizens, shaping youth into accepting sacrifice, obedience, and discipline: "Those peoples whose genius is only exercised over purely terrestrial affairs will not be able to maintain their political existence for very long: disdained by all, they fall prisoner of barbarians and their science dies with them, while societies with a culture in harmony with faith will continue their march full of glory and destiny for centuries." A decade later, when he was asked to prepare a history of clerical seminaries to serve as a tract for Catholic pedagogy in Venezuela, Larrazábal echoed Hermite's emphasis on the centrality of religion to social life. In *Historia de los seminarios clericales* (1856), he wrote that the church serves to shape a society's moral constitution, without which the common good and the state cannot exist. Once again, the operative word is "order"; without the subjective conditions implanted by the institution of the church, "torrents" of "uncontrolled" passions and "factions" will go uncontained and tear asunder the very fabric that holds a modern society together (23–24).

14. In the following passage from the introduction to the life of Bolívar, for example, Larrazábal echoes his writings on the use of the Bible in seminary by way of the specific use of the word "doctrine": "My readers will find in the correspondence . . . a copious source full of inexhaustible, timely reflections: of thoughts full of juice and doctrine, precious documents of experience, and of moral and political teachings, with which men can be formed for public life" (*Correspondencia* xix–xx). The passage emphasizes the public uses of the study of Bolívar's writings and reiterates Larrazábal's conception of sacred writing as an essentially combative and transitive phenomenon; in his treatment of seminary education, the Gospels are equated with spiritual armories that will supply humanity with the weapons necessary for edifying social mores and aiding in the establishment of ordered societies (*Historia* 50).

Chapter 2. Monumentalism and the Erotics of National Degeneration

1. In 1755, Governor Felipe Ricardo complained that the arcades served to concentrate urban undesirables in the center of the city. In 1809, Caracas's last governor, Vicente Emparán, envisioned moving the street vendors from the plaza and creating a more sophisticated, garden-like space with benches, railings, and fountains (Zwiska 78).

2. In 1825, the Municipality of Caracas named the Plaza Bolívar but did not have the resources to place a statue. Attempts to place a statue also failed for lack of funds in 1842, 1845, and 1869 (Clemente Travieso 35).

3. In the words of one commentator: "It is the eminent duty of love, admiration and gratitude of all civilized societies to pay homage in solemn acts to their benefactors, whom living or dead, deserve to have their names consigned with golden pen to

the sacred book of history. Moreover, the history of great men does not only appear in books. Statues and monuments also attest to coming ages, to feats, merits and the illustrious virtues of those who, with their lofty and transcendental acts, came to conquer an idea, or to seal the peace of nations" ("28 de octubre: La estatua del Libertador").

4. About Guzmán Blanco, one journalist wrote: "For him there are no difficulties; and if there are, his greatest effort is to defeat them. This time, the confidence that he breathes is communicated, it is transmitted as always, it contaminates brave and patriotic hearts, and the enterprise of tearing the stolen treasure from the ocean is resolved in minutes, is organized in hours and gives its felicitous results in very few days" ("¡Salvada!"). The reference to "difficulties" in relation to Guzmán Blanco echoes Bolívar's nickname, *el hombre de las dificultades* (the man of the difficulties), a rubric that communicates the Liberator's infallibility in the face of setbacks and difficulties.

5. Here I am citing Benedict Anderson's well-known definition of the nation: "It is imagined because the members of even the smallest nation will never know most of their fellow members, meet them, or even hear of them, yet in the minds of each lives the image of their communion . . . it is imagined as a community, because, regardless of the actual inequality and exploitation that may prevail in each, the nation is always conceived as a deep, horizontal comradeship. Ultimately it is this fraternity that makes it possible, over the past two centuries, for so many millions of people, not so much to kill, as willingly to die for such limited imaginings" (15–16).

6. See my "Monumental Space and Corporeal Memory: *Venezuela heroica* and the Cult of Bolívar in Nineteenth-Century Venezuela" for more on monumentalism in Blanco's writing. For further discussion of Blanco and his historical and cultural context, see "Fundar el estado/narrar la nación (*Venezuela heroica* de Eduardo Blanco)" by Beatriz González Stephan.

7. In 1892, General Joaquín Crespo came to power in Venezuela. In 1899, General Cipriano Castro took his place. It is difficult to say with certainty who precisely the "Venezuelan Caesar" is; Díaz Rodríguez was probably thinking in terms of the modern caudillo presidency, which was founded by Antonio Guzmán Blanco.

8. Sommer writes that the Latin American national romances "are all ostensibly grounded in 'natural' heterosexual love and in the marriages that provided a figure for apparently nonviolent consolidation during internecine conflicts at mid-century. Romantic passion . . . gave a rhetoric for the hegemonic projects in Gramsci's sense of conquering the antagonist through mutual interest, or 'love,' rather than coercion. . . . The rhetoric of love, specifically of productive sexuality at home, is notably consistent, taken for granted in fact, despite the standard taxonomies that distinguish novels as either 'historical' or 'indigenist,' 'romantic' or 'realist'" (6).

9. My analysis is indebted to *The Nationalization of the Masses: Political Symbolism and Mass Movements in Germany from the Napoleonic Wars through the Third Reich* by George Mosse. Mosse highlights the nationalist, liturgical dimensions of monumentalism (15, 74).

Chapter 3. The Promise of Bolivarian Paternity

1. This anecdote is from the *Diario de Bucaramanga* by Luis Perú de Lacroix, one of Bolívar's secretaries. Lacroix paraphrases Bolívar's conversation in the following manner: "that he alone has not had descendants, because his wife died early, and that he had not married again, but it should not be assumed that he is sterile or not fecund, because he has proof to the contrary" (132). Luis Subieta Sagárnaga's *Bolívar en Potosí* claims that Bolívar elaborated on these comments to Lacroix, with the following comment: "Potosí holds three memories for me: there I shaved off my moustache, there I dressed for a dance, and there I had a son" (98–108).

2. Lesser-known cases include those of the children Socorro Bolívar (1812), Inés Berbesí (1813), Angel Bolaños (1822), and María Josefa Cuero (1829) (Cacua Prada 215–24).

3. *Las aventuras de Simón Bolívar* has been reprinted several times since its original publication in 1972. The 1976 edition includes an official document from the Ministry of Education that says that the president personally approves it as a textbook for use in the school system.

4. For a history of education in modern Latin America, see Carlos Newland's "La educación elemental en hispanoamérica: Desde la independencia hasta la centralización de los sistemas educativos nacionales" and "The Estado Docente and Its Expansion: Spanish American Elementary Education, 1900–1950."

5. Blanco writes, for example: "There are places marked by events of such transcendence that it is not possible to pass them by with indifference, unless to make one's refined stoicism or crass ignorance evident" (*Venezuela heroica* 37).

6. The philosophical context of this crisis was presciently noted by Key Ayala decades before the consolidation of poststructuralist notions of language: "It is the hour in which words no longer represent ideas" (193).

7. The most detailed and suggestive account of Parra's links to the Venezuelan politics of her time may be found in Garrels (81–103). Garrels distinguishes between links to the dictator Gómez and Parra's fundamentally anti-positivist ethos. For more on Parra's ideology, also see Velia Bosch (149).

8. González Boixó's reading of Blanca Nieves's father and her cousin, Juancho, are unpersuasive. He presents the authority of the father in the novel as an uncomplicated fact, despite his relative absence and irrelevance in the narrative, in comparison to the mother, Juancho, and his employees Vicente Aguilar and Daniel, whose talent for subverting the authority of the patrón is clear. In the case of Cousin Juancho, González Boixó glosses over the sympathy with which the narrative voice considers this character, and conflates him with the very politics that the novel critiques.

Chapter 4. "A Whore in the Palace": The Poetics of Pornodetraction

1. A fine example of the kinds of stories that circulate about Bolívar's *donjuanismo* (seductiveness, from Don Juan) may be found in Ricardo Palma's "The Liber-

ator's Three Et Ceteras," in which women are equated with Bolívar's power to secure Latin American independence.

2. For a discussion of Boussingault's memoirs, which were published between 1889 and 1903, and their veracity, see Pamela Murray's "'Loca' or 'Libertadora': Manuela Sáenz in the Eyes of History and Historians, 1900–1990" (292–93).

3. The exact birth year of Manuela is the subject of some debate. See Mogollón Cobo and Narváez Yar (24).

4. This translation is by Helen Lane, from "The Protectress and the Liberatrix," which appears in the manuscript of the new English translation of Palma's *Peruvian Traditions*.

5. The notion of Manuela's sensations disrupting her body is used throughout the novel. Her skin is variously described as swollen, prickling, burning, and tender to the brush of her clothes and to the bathtub ministrations of her maidservant Jonatás (Aguilera Malta 17, 28, 37).

6. About postmodernism, David Harvey writes: "I begin with what appears to be the most startling fact about postmodernism: its total acceptance of the ephemerality, fragmentation, discontinuity, and the chaotic that formed the one half of Baudelaire's conception of modernity. But postmodernism responds to the fact of that in a very particular way. It does not try to transcend it, counteract it, or even to define the eternal and immutable elements that might lie within it" (44).

7. Manuela's laughter should remind us of Mikhail Bakhtin's *Rabelais and His World* and its description of medieval laughter as a subversion of power: "It was the victory of laughter over fear which most inspired medieval man. It was not only a victory over mystic terror of God, but also a victory over the awe inspired by the forces of nature, and most of all over the oppression and guilt related to all that was consecrated and forbidden ("mana" and "taboo"). It was the defeat of divine and human power, of authoritarian commandments and prohibitions, of death and punishment after death, hell and all that is more terrifying than the earth itself" (90–91).

Chapter 5. Solitude, Signs, and Power in *The General in His Labyrinth*

1. On the subject of attribution, Miranda Lyndsay guesses that a poem by the General is by Napoleon (81). Upon returning to Bogotá from his Andean campaigns in 1825, the General similarly errs when he mistakes one of his ministers for another (16). When Colonel Wilson declares to the General that "I don't know anything anymore, General . . . I'm at the mercy of a destiny that isn't mine," the General responds, "That's what I should be saying" (67). In his reflections upon the Santanderista press responsible for spreading lies about him, the General muses that such "slanted reporting" (113) had been a part of his own intelligence strategy during the war, a strategy that was now, ironically, turned against him (114). Similarly, the military custom of encrypting messages bewilders the General, who misinter-

prets an innocuous message about a political favor for a communication about his plans for a counterrevolution (238).

2. As González Echeverría writes: "Afloat like a fetus or a drowned man, Bolívar is exiled from the world and from temporality; he's a castaway sailing without direction. In this kind of test tube or time capsule, the hero lacks all telos. Like Cortázar's axolotl, he is a monster floating toward infinity in a transparent pool . . . this is the labyrinth of the General" ("Archival Fictions" 73).

3. Critics have been quick to observe the similarities between the General and Don Quixote. Ortega writes: "Like another Quixote, this Bolívar travels in defeat as an exile of his own discourse; and like Don Quixote, who recovers his strength when he proposes to Sancho that they become shepherds (that is, that they assume a new discourse), Bolívar recovers his strength when the promises of utopia, the promise to do it all over again, allow for the illusion of a new beginning" ("Lector" 167–68). Also see González Echeverría ("Archival Fictions" 72).

4. Before his departure from Bogotá, the General intends to write his memoirs, but he is distracted by the dawn on the savannahs near the manor that is on loan to him (23). On another occasion, he calls memoirs dead men making trouble (201), and during his Jamaican interlude in 1815, he and his lover Miranda Lyndsay pass "close to the sugar plantation where Sir London Lyndsay was writing the memories that no one but him would remember" (78). In describing O'Leary, his own, most famous memoirist, the General calls written memoirs a particularly dangerous thing (154). The General's hope that his nephew Fernando would write his memoirs "as an act of love" to pass on to future generations of the Bolívar family ends in disaster because Fernando would "live to the age of eighty-eight without writing anything more than a few disordered pages, for fate granted him the immense good fortune of losing his memory" (265). When the General triumphantly goes to rhetorical battle against the petty and arrogant views of the Frenchman Diocles Atlantique, what should have been a particularly "memorable" event is lost to history as the chronicler to whom Wilson reports the incident "did not take the trouble of recording it" (125).

5. In the words of José María Carreño, the General has orphaned his men (165).

6. Aureliano Buendía's request that his doctor mark the place of his heart for the purposes of committing suicide invokes the extraordinary suicide of the modernista poet José Asunción Silva.

7. Apart from the use of Aragonés as a double, the coterie of the Patriarch make use of a ventriloquist, misinformation, and the total seclusion of the dictator to perpetuate him in power.

8. The distinction between power and government is illustrated by the scene in which the Patriarch's creditors, eager to get compensation for his Leticia Nazareno's shopping sprees, overcome their fear of the insubstantial, God-like Patriarch, and gain access to the government to stake their financial claims. The creditors are shown a footprint of the Patriarch, which stirs in them a sense of the mystery, power,

and solitude of the dictator (185). The government is within reach; the power ostensibly directing it is mysterious and unseen.

9. Fourteen years before, the first chapter of *One Hundred Years of Solitude* effectively illustrated García Márquez's point about how foreign models and categories can generate alienation and solitude. The idyllic village of Macondo, which measured wealth through access to the sunlight and the water of the river, and the profusion of beautiful, caged songbirds, is shattered by the arrival of the gypsies, whose outside marvels create an awareness of underdevelopment in the mind of José Arcadio Buendía, the patriarch of Macondo (10). What has been a world of plenty is now transformed into a world of lack, as Buendía restlessly seeks to overcome the inadequacy of his shrunken world through several frustrated schemes, which include alchemy and the journey to "civilized lands of the north." Frustrated by his inability to break through to civilization, and his discovery of the sea, Buendía vents his frustrations in a solitary, cartographical interpretation of his journey, one that propagates for years the misconception that Macondo is a peninsula (13).

10. The notion of fantastic creatures living near the Magdalena River, and their significance as models of interpretive confusion or collage, is rooted in one of García Márquez's memories of traveling down the river in his youth. "One big-mooned night we were awakened by a heart-rending lament from the shore. Captain Climaco Conde Abello, one of the greatest ones, gave the order to search for the source of those cries with searchlights, and it was a female manatee that had been entangled in the branches of a fallen tree. . . . It was a fantastic and touching being, in between a woman and a cow, almost four meters long. Her skin was livid and tender, and her torso with its large teats was that of a biblical mother. It was the same captain Conde Abello whom I heard saying, for the first time, that the world was going to end if the killing of the animals of the river continued, and prohibited any shooting from his ship" (*Vivir* 210).

11. The story of Esteban relates to the *Autumn of the Patriarch* in interesting ways. The plotting of the Patriarch in his own official story is quite similar to the story of the drowned "Esteban": "the descriptions made by his historians made him very big and official schoolboy texts referred to him as a patriarch of huge size who never left his house because he could not fit through the doors, who loved children and swallows . . ." (*The Autumn of the Patriarch* 46). The Patriarch and Esteban are adrift in their own power, unconscious of their own myth, but they contrast in one important respect: in the case of Esteban, myth works to build solidarity, identity, and prestige, whereas in *The Autumn of the Patriarch*, the "official story" is an act of erasure and disempowerment that turns the nameless republic into a veritable wasteland.

Afterword: Bolivarian Self-Fashioning into the Twenty-First Century

1. In his 1999 conversation with Gabriel García Márquez, Chávez told the story of how he had stopped the torture of captured guerillas only to be disciplined for his

actions later on by his superiors. Chávez went on to describe his first existential crisis as a result of helping mortally wounded soldiers off a helicopter after a skirmish with guerillas. As Chávez told it, he held a wounded soldier in his arms, listening helplessly to the poor man's pleas for help. After witnessing these scenes, Chávez was racked by doubts: "What am I here for? On the one hand peasants dressed like soldiers tortured *guerillero* peasants, and on the other, *guerillero* peasants killed peasants dressed in green" (G. García Márquez, "Enigma").

2. As Jennifer McCoy writes, Chávez has rejected the militarist model of direct control (military dictatorship) as well as the concept of the armed forces as puppet master of civil society and democratic institutions, and seems "to be introducing a new model of open military participation in a civilian government" (74).

3. In his conversations with García Márquez, Chávez described a seminal moment in his life that illustrates his faith in Bolivarian internationalism, another key aspect of his aspirations as president. Chávez told the story of how he had been detained by a Colombian border guard in Arauca and accused of being a spy because of the maps, photographs, papers, and guns he was carrying. Chávez was carrying the materials because he was researching and retracing the movements of his great-grandfather Maisanta, but the border guard did not believe him. Chávez noticed the iconic image of the heroic Bolívar on a horse on one of the walls of the room where he was being detained. "Look, my captain, at what life is," Chávez finally said, "almost a century ago we were in the same army, and he who is gazing at us from that painting was the leader of both of us. How can I be a spy?" (G. García Márquez, "Enigma"). The border guard was won over by this statement and the two men spent the rest of the night drinking Colombian and Venezuelan beers at a cantina before parting ways as friends.

4. Marxist Bolivarianism is generally characterized by the interpretation of Bolívar as a class-conscious, anti-imperialist revolutionary who fought against the Spanish Empire and against oligarchy in general. For a sampling of Marxist essays on Bolívar, see *Interpretaciones y ensayos marxistas acerca de Simón Bolívar*, edited by Max Zeuske; *Simón Bolívar* by Iosif Romual'dovich Grigulevich, and *Bolívar visto por los marxistas*, edited by Jerónimo Carrera.

Works Cited

"Advierten sobre falta de transparencia en FONDART." In *El caso "Simón Bolívar."* Compiled by Nelly Richard. Spec. section of *Revista de crítica cultural* 9 (1994): 30. First published in *El mercurio,* August 14, 1994, n. pag.

Aguilar, Lilian. *Un hombre, una nación, un ideal.* Turmero, Venezuela: Departamento de Materiales Educativos del Centro de Capacitación Docente "El Mácaro," 1975.

Aguilera Malta, Demetrio. *"Manuela, la caballeresa del sol": A Novel.* Contemporary Latin American Classics. Carbondale: Southern Illinois University Press, 1967.

Agustini, Delmira. "La estatua." In *Antología crítica de la poesía modernista hispanoamericana,* edited by José Olivio Jiménez. Madrid: Hiperión, 1994.

Ainsa, Fernando. "La nueva novela histórica latinoamericana." *Plural: Revista cultural de excelsior* (September 1991): 82–85.

———. "La reescritura de la historia en la nueva narrativa latinoamericana." *Cuadernos americanos* 4, no. 28 (1991): 13–31.

Aldrete, Gregory. *Gestures and Acclamations in Ancient Rome.* Baltimore: Johns Hopkins University Press, 1999.

Alexander, George. "The World, the Flesh, and Dávila." *Art and Text* 30 (1988): 84–88.

Alonso, Carlos. "The Mourning After: García Márquez, Fuentes, and the Meaning of Postmodernity in Spanish America." *MLN* 109, no. 2 (1994): 252–67.

Altuve Carrillo, Leonardo. *Genio y apoteosis de Bolívar en la campaña del Perú.* Barcelona: Herder, 1979.

Alvarez Borland, Isabel. "The Task of the Historian in *El General en su laberinto."* *Hispania* 76, no. 3 (1992): 439–45.

Anderson, Benedict. *Imagined Communities: Reflections on the Origin and Spread of Nationalism.* London: Verso, 1983.

Anderson-Imbert, Enrique. *Spanish American Literature: A History.* Detroit: Wayne State University Press, 1969.

"Apoteosis de Bolívar, 7 de Noviembre, Boletín Oficial." *La opinión nacional,* November 2, 1874.

Apuleyo Mendoza, Plinio. *The Fragrance of Guava*. Translated by Ann Wright. London: Verso Editions, 1983.

Arratia, Alejandro. *Etica y democracia en Fermín Toro*. Caracas: Monte Avila Editores Latinoamericana, 1993.

Austria, José de. *Bosquejo de la historia militar de Venezuela: Estudio preliminar por Héctor García Chuecos*. Biblioteca de la Academia Nacional de la Historia 29–30. Caracas: Academia Nacional de la Historia, 1960.

Bakhtin, M. M. *Rabelais and His World*. Bloomington: Indiana University Press, 1984.

Belaunde, Victor Andrés. *Bolívar and the Political Thought of the Spanish American Revolution*. New York: Octagon Books, 1967.

Bell, Steven, Albert Le May, and Leonard Orr, eds. *Critical Theory, Cultural Politics, and Latin American Narrative*. Notre Dame: University of Notre Dame, 1993.

Bellini, Giuseppe. *Historia de la literatura hispanoamericana*. Madrid: Editorial Castalia, 1997.

Bhabha, Homi K., ed. *Nation and Narration*. London: Routledge, 1990.

Blanco, Eduardo. "Las noches del panteón, homenaje al gran mariscal de Ayacucho, Antonio José de Sucre en su primer centenario." Caracas: Tipografía El Cojo, 1895.

———. *Venezuela heroica*. Caracas: Monte Avila, 1979.

Bolívar, Simón. *Doctrina del Libertador*. Caracas: Biblioteca Ayacucho, 1985.

———. *Selected Writings of Bolívar*. Edited by Harold A. Bierck Jr. Translated by Lewis Bertrand. New York: Colonial Press, 1951.

Bosch, Velia. "*Las memorias de la Mamá Blanca* en la historia personal de la autora en su momento histórico-político." In *Las memorias de la Mamá Blanca. Edición Crítica*, edited by Velia Bosch, 137–56. Colección Archivos. Madrid: CSIC, 1988.

Bravo-Villasante, Carmen. "La literatura infantil francesa." *Cuadernos hispanoamericanos* 76 (1968): 771–75.

Bretos, Miguel Americo. "From Banishment to Sainthood: A Study of the Image of Bolívar in Colombia 1826–1883." Ph.D. diss., Vanderbilt University, 1976.

Brett, Guy. "Montage as Mestizaje." *Juanito Laguna: Exhibit by Juan Dávila*. London: Chisenhale Gallery, 1994.

Briceño Perozo, Mario. *Historia bolivariana*. Caracas: Ministerio de Educación Departamento de Publicaciones, 1970.

———. *Reminiscencias griegas y latinas en las obras del Libertador*. Caracas: n.p., 1971.

Burns, E. Bradford. *The Poverty of Progress: Latin America in the Nineteenth Century*. Berkeley: University of California Press, 1980.

Busaniche, José Luis. *Bolívar visto por sus contemporáneos*. Mexico City: Fondo de Cultura Económica, 1960.

Bushnell, David. "The Last Dictatorship: Betrayal or Commitment?" *Hispanic American Historical Review* 63, no. 1 (1983): 65–105.

———. *The Santander Regime in Gran Colombia*. Newark: University of Delaware Press, 1954.

Butler, Judith. *Gender Trouble: Feminism and the Subversion of Identity.* New York: Routledge, 1990.

Cacua Prada, Antonio. *Los hijos secretos de Bolívar.* Santafé de Bogotá, D.C., Colombia: Plaza and Janés Editores, 1992.

Calle, Manuel J. *Leyendas del tiempo heroico.* Biblioteca de la juventud hispanoamericana. Madrid: Editorial America, 1918.

Canetti, Elias. *Crowds and Power.* New York: Farrar Straus Giroux, 1984.

Carbonell, Diego. *Psicopatología de Bolívar.* Paris: Librería Franco-española, P. Rosier, 1916.

Carilla, Emilio. "Introducción" to *Poesía de la Independencia.* Edited by Emilio Carilla. Caracas: Biblioteca Ayacucho, 1992.

Carlyle, Thomas, et al. *On Heroes, Hero-Worship, and the Heroic in History.* Edited by Thomas Carlyle. Berkeley: University of California Press, 1993.

Carreño, Manuel Antonio. *Manual de urbanidad y buenas maneras.* México: Editora Nacional, 1979.

Carrera, Jerónimo. *Bolívar visto por los marxistas.* Caracas: Fondo Editorial Carlos Aponte, 1987.

Carrera Damas, Germán. *El culto a Bolívar: Esbozo para un estudio de la historia de las ideas en Venezuela.* 1969. Reprint, Caracas: Grijalbo, 1989.

Castro Leiva, Luis. *De la patria boba a la teología bolivariana: Ensayos de historia intelectual.* Caracas: Monte Avila Editores, 1991.

Castronovo, Russ. *Fathering the Nation: American Genealogies of Slavery and Freedom.* Berkeley: University of California Press, 1995.

Chávez, Hugo. "Discurso paseo de los próceres, 2 Febrero 1999." February 22, 2001 <http://www.analitica.com/bitblioteca/hchavez/los_proceres.asp>.

————. "Discurso de toma de posesión, 2 Febrero 1999." February 22, 2001 <http://www.analitica.com/bitblioteca/hchavez/toma.asp>.

————. "Programa de Gobierno. Presentado en el Hotel Caracas Hilton el 22 de mayo de 2000." February 22, 2001 <http://www.analitica.com/bitblioteca/hchavez/programa2000.asp>.

Clemente Travieso, Carmen. *Las esquinas de Caracas: Sus leyendas, sus recuerdos.* Caracas: Editorial Ancora, 1956.

Colas, Santiago. *Postmodernity in Latin America: The Argentine Paradigm.* Post-Contemporary Interventions. Durham, N.C.: Duke University Press, 1994.

"Colombia constituida, poecia [*sic*] compuesta por un español americano impresa en París." *Gaceta de Colombia,* Aug. 18, 1822, n. pag.

Conde, Juan José. "Prólogo" to *Proclamas del Libertador Simón Bolívar.* Caracas: Imprenta de "El Venezolano," por M. J. Rivas, 1842.

Conway, Christopher. "Gender, Empire, and Revolution in 'La victoria de Junín.'" *Hispanic Review* 69, no. 3 (summer 2001): 299–317.

————. "Monumental Space and Corporeal Memory: *Venezuela heroica* and the Cult of Bolívar in Nineteenth-Century Venezuela." In *La Chispa '97 Selected Proceedings.* Edited by Claire J. Paolini. New Orleans: Tulane University, 1997.

Cordero Ceballos, J. J. *Entrevista al Libertador en el bicentenario de su nacimiento.* Caracas: Comite Ejecutivo del Bicentenario de Simón Bolívar, 1984.

Critchley, Macdonald. *Silent Language.* London: Butterworths, 1975.

Cussen, Antonio. *Bello and Bolívar: Poetry and Politics in the Spanish American Revolution.* Cambridge: Cambridge University Press, 1992.

Darío Suárez, Ramón. *Genealogía del Libertador.* 1970. Reprint, 2d ed. Mérida, Venezuela: n.p., 1983.

Díaz, Gonzalo, Eugenio Dittborn, and Arturo Duclos. "Pueblo chico, infierno grande (Declaración de la Escuela de Santiago)." In *El caso "Simón Bolívar."* Compiled by Nelly Richard. Spec. section of *Revista de crítica cultural* 9 (1994): 26–31. First published in *La epoca,* August 21, 1984, n. pag.

Díaz Rodríguez, Manuel. *Idolos rotos.* Caracas: Monte Avila Editores, 1981.

Donoso, Claudia. "Tu comodidad es mi silencio." In *El caso "Simón Bolívar."* Compiled by Nelly Richard. Spec. section of *Revista de crítica cultural* 9 (1994): 28. First published in *Revista caras,* August 22, 1994, n. pag.

Douglas, Mary. *Purity and Danger: An Analysis of the Concepts of Pollution and Taboo.* London: Routledge, 1992.

Dunham, Lowell. *Manuel Días Rodríguez, vida y obra.* Mexico City: Ediciones de Andrea, 1959.

Durkheim, Emile. *Moral Education: A Study in the Theory and Application of the Sociology of Education.* New York: Free Press, 1973.

Filippi, Alberto, and Alberto Gil Novales. *Bolívar y Europa en las crónicas, el pensamiento político, y la historiografía.* Caracas: Ediciones de la Presidencia de la República Comité Ejecutivo del Bicentenario de Simón Bolívar, 1986.

Franceschi González, Napoleón. *El culto a los héroes y la formación de la nación venezolana: Una visión del problema a partir del estudio del discurso historiográfico venezolano del período 1830–1883.* Caracas: Litho-Tip, 1999.

Franco, Jean. *An Introduction to Spanish American Literature.* Cambridge: Cambridge University Press, 1996.

———. *Plotting Women: Gender and Representation in Mexico.* Gender and Culture. New York: Columbia University Press, 1989.

Garcia Márquez, Eligio. *Tras las claves de Melquíades: Historia de "Cien años de soledad."* Edited by Roberto Burgos. Bogotá: Grupo Editorial Norma, 2001.

García Márquez, Gabriel. *The Autumn of the Patriarch.* Translated by Gregory Rabassa. New York: Harper Perennial, 1991.

———. *Collected Stories.* New York: Harper Perennial, 1984.

———. "El enigma de los dos Chávez." *Revista cambio,* December 18–25, 2000. March 12, 2001 <http://www.cambio.com.co/web/interior.php?idp=8&ids=40&ida=236>.

———. *Entre cachacos.* Compiled by Jacques Gilard. 2 vols. Buenos Aires: Editorial Sudamericana, 1988–1989.

———. *The General in His Labyrinth.* Translated by Edith Grossman. New York: Alfred A. Knopf, 1990.

———. *Obra periodística: De Europa a América (1955–1960)*. Vol. 3. Compiled by Jacques Gilard. Madrid: Mondadori, 1992.

———. *Obra periodística: Textos costeños*. Vol. 1. Compiled by Jacques Gilard. Narradores de hoy. Barcelona: Bruguera, 1981.

———. *One Hundred Years of Solitude*. Translated by Gregory Rabassa. New York: Alfred A. Knopf, 1995.

———. "The Solitude of Latin America." In *Gabriel García Márquez and the Powers of Fiction*, by Julio Ortega, 88–91. Austin: University of Texas Press, 1988.

———. *Vivir para contarla*. New York: Alfred A. Knopf, 2002.

García Silva, Emilio. *Simón Bolívar en las escuelas y colegios*. Quito: Imprenta de la Escuela de Artes y Oficios, 1938.

Garrels, Elizabeth. *Las grietas de la ternura: Nueva lectura de Teresa de la Parra*. Caracas: Monte Avila Editores, 1985.

Geertz, Clifford. *The Interpretation of Cultures: Selected Essays*. London: Fontana, 1993.

Gil Fortoul, José. *Historia constitucional de Venezuela*. 3 vols. Caracas: Ministerio de Educación Dirección de Cultura y Bellas Artes Commisión Editora de las Obras Completas de José Gil Fourtoul, 1953.

———. *Pasiones*. Paris: Garnier, 1895.

Gilard, Jacques. "Prólogo." In *Obra periodística: Textos costeños*. By Gabriel García Márquez. Barcelona: Bruguera, 1981.

"El gobierno chileno se excusa por el controvertido retrato de Simón Bolívar." In *El caso "Simón Bolívar."* Compiled by Nelly Richard. Spec. section of *Revista de crítica cultural* 9 (1994): 28. First published in *La epoca*, August 17, 1994, n. pag.

Gómez, José. *Drama patriótico en elogio y recuerdo del glorioso día 19 de abril de 1810 y de los triunfos inmortales del primer caudillo de la libertad sudamericana*. Caracas: Imprenta de Manuel Marquis, 1840.

González, Aníbal. *La novela modernista hispanoamericana*. Madrid: Gredos, 1987.

González, Juan Vicente. *El Venezolano*, November 2, 1841, n. pag.

González Boixó, José Carlos. "Feminismo e ideología conservadora." In *Las memorias de la Mamá Blanca. Edición Crítica*, edited by Velia Bosch, 231–43. Colección Archivos. Madrid: CSIC, 1988.

González Echeverría, Roberto. "Archival Fictions: García Márquez's Bolívar File." In *Critical Theory, Cultural Politics, and Latin American Narrative*, edited by Steven Bell, Albert Le May, and Leonard Orr, 183–207. Notre Dame: University of Notre Dame, 1993.

———. "*Cien Años de Soledad:* The Novel as Myth and Archive." *MLN* 99, no. 2 (1984): 358–80.

———. *Myth and Archive: A Theory of Latin American Narrative*. Durham: Duke University Press, 1998.

González Guinán, Francisco. *Historia contemporánea de Venezuela*. 15 vols. Caracas: Tipografía El Cojo, 1909.

González Stephan, Beatriz. "Fundar el estado/narrar la nación (*Venezuela heroica* de Eduardo Blanco)." *Revista iberoamericana* 63, no. 178–79 (1997): 33–46.

Gott, Richard. *In the Shadow of the Liberator: Hugo Chávez and the Transformation of Venezuela.* London: Verso, 2000.

Graf, Fritz. "Gestures and Conventions: The Gestures of Roman Actors and Orators." In *A Cultural History of Gesture*, edited by Jan Bremmer and Herman Roodenburg. Ithaca: Cornell University Press, 1991.

Grases, Pedro. *Los papeles de Bolívar y Sucre (manuscritos y ediciones).* Caracas: Fundación de Promoción Cultural de Venezuela, 1985.

Grigulevich, Iosif Romual'dovich. *Simón Bolívar.* Moscow: Editorial Progreso, 1982.

Hall, Stuart. *Modernity: An Introduction to Modern Societies.* Cambridge: Blackwell, 1996.

Harvey, David. *The Condition of Postmodernity.* Oxford: Blackwell, 1989.

Harwich Valenilla, Nikita. "La génesis de un imaginario colectivo: La enseñanza de la historia de Venezuela en el siglo XIX." *Boletín de la Academia Nacional de la Historia* 61 (April–July 1988): 349–87.

"Hay simbologías que enaltecen y no agravian." In *El caso "Simón Bolívar."* Compiled by Nelly Richard. Spec. section of *Revista de crítica cultural* 9 (1994): 33. First published in *La tercera*, August 26, 1994, n. pag.

Hermite, M. D. "Influencia de la educación religiosa en sus relaciones con el desarollo de la inteligencia de la juventud." *El patriota*, August 23, 1845, año 1, num. 23, +2.

Hobsbawm, E. J. *Nations and Nationalism Since 1780: Programme, Myth, Reality.* Cambridge: Cambridge University Press, 1992.

Horace. *The Complete Odes and Epodes with the Centennial Hymn.* Translated by W. G. Shepherd. London: Penguin, 1983.

Huelepega, la ley de la calle. Directed by Elia Schneider. Centro Nacional Autónomo de Cinematografía, 1999.

Hutcheon, Linda. *Poetics of Postmodernism: History, Theory, Fiction.* New York: Routledge, 1988.

Jiménez, José Olivio, ed. *Antología crítica de la poesía modernista hispanoamericana.* Madrid: Hiperión, 1994.

Jordanova, Ludmilla. "Gender and the Historiography of Science." *British Journal for the History of Science* 26 (1993): 469–83.

Key Ayala, Santiago. *Vida ejemplar de Simón Bolívar.* Caracas: Ediciones EDIME, 1955.

Larrazábal, Felipe. *Correspondencia general del Libertador Simón Bolívar; enriquecida con la inserción de los manifiestos, mensages, exposiciones, proclamas, &, &. publicados por el héroe colombiano desde 1810 hasta 1830 (Precede a esta colección interesante la vida de Bolívar).* 2 vols. 1865. Reprint, New York: Eduardo Jenkins, 1875.

———. "De la Biblia considerada bajo un punto de vista literario." In *Obras literarias.* Caracas: Imprenta de Jesus María Soriano, 1862.

————. "Del sublime." In *Obras literarias*. Caracas: Imprenta de Jesus María Soriano, 1862.

————. *Historia de los seminarios clericales*. Caracas: Tipografía de Salvador Larrazábal, 1856.

————. *Obras literarias*. Caracas: Imprenta de Jesus María Soriano, 1862.

Lazo, Raimundo. *Historia de la literatura hispanoamericana*. Mexico: Editorial Porrúa, 1988.

Leal, Ildefonso, ed. *Ha muerto el Libertador: Homenaje de la Universidad Central de Venezuela en el sesquicentenario de su muerte*. Caracas: Ediciones del Rectorado de la UCV, 1980.

Lecuna, Vicente. *Cartas del Libertador*. Caracas: Lit. y Tip. Del Comercio, 1929.

Liévano Aguirre, Indalecio. *Bolívar*. 1956. Reprint, Nueva ed., Caracas: Ministerio de Educación Dirección General Departamento de Publicaciones, 1974.

Lindstrom, Naomi. *The Social Conscience of Latin American Writing*. Texas Pan American Series. Austin: University of Texas Press, 1998.

Lombardi, John V. *Venezuela: The Search for Order, the Dream of Progress*. Latin American Histories. New York: Oxford University Press, 1982.

Ludwig, Emil. *Bolívar: The Life of an Idealist*. Translated by Mary H. Lindsey. New York: Alliance Book Corp., 1942.

Magallanes, Manuel Vicente. *Historia política de Venezuela*. 3 vols. Colección letra viva. Caracas: Monte Avila Editores, 1975.

Martí, José. *La edad de oro*. Mexico City: Fondo de Cultura Económica, 1992.

Masur, Gerhard. *Simon Bolivar*. Albuquerque: University of New Mexico Press, 1948.

McCoy, Jennifer. "Chavez and the End of 'Partyarchy' in Venezuela." *Journal of Democracy* 10, no. 3 (1999): 64–77.

Menton, Seymour. *Latin America's New Historical Novel*. The Texas Pan American Series. Austin: University of Texas Press, 1993.

Mijares, Augusto. *El Libertador Simón Bolívar*. 1964. Reprint, [Caracas]: Academia Nacional de la Historia de Venezuela, 1994.

Miliani, Domingo. "Fermín Toro." In *Fermín Toro*. Edited by Domingo Miliani. Caracas: Academia Venezolana de la Lengua, 1977.

Misle, Carlos Eduardo. *Sabor de caracas*. N.p., 1981.

Mogollón Cobo, María, and Ximena Narváez Yar. *Manuela Sáenz: Presencia y polémica en la historia*. Quito: Corporación Editora Nacional, 1997.

Mosse, George. *The Nationalization of the Masses: Political Symbolism and Mass Movements in Germany from the Napoleonic Wars through the Third Reich*. New York: Howard Fertig, 1975.

Mumford, Lewis. *The Culture of Cities*. New York: Harcourt Brace and Company, 1938.

Murray, Pamela. "'Loca' or 'Libertadora': Manuela Sáenz in the Eyes of History and Historians, 1900–1990." *Journal of Latin American Studies* 33, no. 2 (2001): 291–310.

Naranjo, Helena. *Un niño de nombre Simón*. Valencia: Vadell Hermanos, 1992.

Newland, Carlos. "La educación elemental en hispanoamérica: Desde la independencia hasta la centralización de los sistemas educativos nacionales." *Hispanic American Historical Review* 71, no. 2 (1991): 335–64.

———. "The Estado Docente and Its Expansion: Spanish American Elementary Education 1900–1950." *Journal of Latin American Studies* 26, no. 2 (1994): 449–67.

Olmedo, José Joaquín. *Epistolario*. Mexico: J. M. Cajica, 1983.

———. *Poesías completas*. Mexico City: Fondo de Cultura Económica, 1947.

La opinion nacional, November 7, 1874, n. pag.

Ortega, Julio. "The Discourse of Abundance." Translated by Nicolas Wey Gómez. *American Literary History* 4 (1992): 369–81.

———. *Gabriel García Márquez and the Powers of Fiction*. Austin: University of Texas Press, 1988.

———. "El lector en su laberinto." *Hispanic Review* 60, no. 2 (1992): 165–79.

———. "Postmodernism in Latin America." In *Postmodern Fiction in Europe and the Americas*. Edited by Theo D'Haen and Johannes Willem Bertens. Amsterdam: Rodopi, 1988.

Osorio, Nelson. "Contextualización y lectura crítica de *Las memorias de la Mamá Blanca*." In *Las memorias de la Mamá Blanca. Edición Crítica*, edited by Velia Bosch, 245–57. Colección Archivos. Madrid: CSIC, 1988.

Páez, José Antonio. "Proclama." In *Ha muerto el Libertador: Homenaje de la Universidad Central de Venezuela en el sesquicentenario de su muerte*, edited by Ildefonso Leal. Caracas: Ediciones del Rectorado de la UCV, 1980.

Palma, Ricardo. *Peruvian Traditions*. Edited by Christopher Conway. Translated by Helen Lane. New York: Oxford University Press, 2004.

Parra, Teresa de la. "Influencia de las mujeres en la formación del alma americana." In *Obras completas*. Caracas: Editorial Arte, 1965.

———. *Mama Blanca's Memoirs. Critical Edition*. Edited by Doris Sommer. Translated by Harriet de Onís and revised by Frederick H. Fornoff. Pittsburgh: University of Pittsburgh Press, 1993.

———. *Las memorias de la Mamá Blanca. Edición Crítica*. Edited by Velia Bosch. Colección Archivos. Madrid: CSIC, 1988.

———. *Obras completas*. Caracas: Editorial Arte, 1965.

Pastor Mellado, Justo. "Pintura e indiferenciación de los sexos." In *El caso "Simón Bolívar."* Compiled by Nelly Richard. Spec. section of *Revista de crítica cultural* 9 (1994): 26. First published in *La nación*, August 12, 1994, n. pag.

Perú de Lacroix, Luis. *Diario de Bucaramanga: Vida pública y privada del Libertador Simón Bolívar*. Madrid: Editorial America, 1924.

Pineda, Rafael. *Simón Bolívar's Monuments Throughout the World*. Translated by Jaime Tello. Caracas: Centro Simón Bolívar, 1983.

Pino Iturrieta, Elías. "Bolívar, Santo de Vestir." *Revista bigott* July–August 1999, 16–43.

————. *Las ideas de los primeros venezolanos*. Caracas: Monte Avila Editores Latinoamericana, 1993.

Pividal, Francisco. *Bolívar, pensamiento precursor del antimperialismo*. La Habana: Casa de las Americas, 1977.

Polanco Alcántara, Tomás. *Simón Bolívar: Ensayo de interpretación biográfica a través de sus documentos*. Caracas: EG, 1994.

Proclamas del Libertador Simón Bolívar. Caracas: Imprenta de "El Venezolano" por M. J. Rivas, 1842.

Quintero, Inés. "Bolívar de derecha y Bolívar de izquierda." Unpublished ms., 2001.

Renan, Ernest. "What Is a Nation?" In *Nation and Narration*, edited by Homi Bhabha. London: Routledge, 1990.

Richard, Nelly. *Residuos y metáforas: Ensayos de crítica cultural sobre el Chile de la transición*. Providencia, Santiago, Chile: Editorial Cuarto Propio, 1998.

Rivas, Angel V. "Madrecita del Alma." *El Correo del Presidente*, December 1, 1999, sec. "El Correo de los Niños": 4.

Rivas Rivas, Jorge. *Carta de Manuela Sáenz a su pornodetractor*. Caracas: Universidad Central de Venezuela, 1990.

Rivera, Nelson. "Bolívar Sex Show." In *El caso "Simón Bolívar."* Compiled by Nelly Richard. Spec. section of *Revista de crítica cultural* 9 (1994): 27. First published in *El nacional de Caracas*, August 14, 1994, n. pag.

Rodríguez Demorizi, Emilio, ed. *Poetas contra Bolívar: El Libertador a través de la calumnia*. Madrid: Gráficas Reunidas, 1966.

Rohter, Larry. "Caracas Journal; Salutes, Some Skeptical, as Schools Go 'Bolivarian.'" *New York Times*, November 9, 2000, final ed.

Rojas, Arístides. *Leyendas históricas de Venezuela*. Caracas: Impr. de la Patria, 1890–1891.

Romero, Denzil. *Amores, pasiones, y vicios de la Gran Catalina*. Caracas: Grijalbo, 1995.

————. *La carujada*. Caracas: Planeta, 1990.

————. *La esposa del doctor Thorne*. 1983. Reprint, Barcelona: Tusquets, 1988.

————. *La tragedia del Generalísimo*. Barcelona: Argos Vergara, 1983.

Romero Martínez, Vinicio. *Las aventuras de Simón Bolívar: Autobiografía del Libertador*. 1976. Reprint, 5th ed. Caracas: Servicio Grafico Editorial, 1982.

Rondón Márquez, Rafael Angel. *Guzmán Blanco, "el autócrata civilizador": Parábola de los partidos políticos tradicionales en la historia de Venezuela (datos para cien años de historia nacional)*. Caracas: Tipografía Garrido, 1944.

Rotker, Susana. "El evangelio apócrifo de Simón Bolívar." *Estudios revista de investigaciones literarias y culturales* 6, no. 12 (1998): 29–45.

Rumazo González, Alfonso. *Manuela Sáenz: La Libertadora del Libertador*. Buenos Aires: Almendros y Nietos, 1945.

Sagredo Baeza, Rafael. "Actores políticos en los catecismos patriotas americanos, 1810–1821." *Historia* 28 (1994): 273–98.

Salas de Lecuna, Yolanda. *Bolívar y la historia en la conciencia popular.* Caracas: Universidad Simón Bolívar Instituto de Altos Estudios de América Latina, 1987.

———. *Ideología y lenguaje en la narrativa de la modernidad.* Estudios. Caracas: Monte Avila Editores, 1992.

Salcedo-Bastardo, J. L. *Bolívar, un hombre diáfano.* Colección juvenil de biografías breves, vol. 14. 2d ed. La Paz: Biblioteca Popular Boliviana de "Ultima Hora," 1981.

"¡Salvada!" *La opinión nacional,* October 19, 1874, n. pag.

Sarmiento, Domingo Faustino. *Facundo: Civilización y barbarie.* Letras Hispánicas. Madrid: Cátedra, 1999.

Schael Martínez, Graciela. *Historia de la estatua del Libertador en la Plaza Bolívar.* Caracas: n.p, 1974.

Silva Beauregard, Paulette. *Una vasta morada de enmascarados: Poesía, cultura, y modernización en Venezuela a finales del siglo XIX.* Caracas: Ediciones La Casa de Bello, 1993.

Sklodowska, Elzbieta. *La parodia en la nueva novela hispanoamericana (1960–1985).* Purdue University Monographs in Romance Languages, vol. 34. Amsterdam: J. Benjamins Pub. Co., 1991.

Smith, Anthony D. *The Ethnic Origins of Nations.* Oxford: B. Blackwell, 1987.

Sommer, Doris. *Foundational Fictions: The National Romances of Latin America.* Latin American Literature and Culture, vol. 7. Berkeley: University of California Press, 1991.

———. "'It's Wrong to Be Right': Mama Blanca on Writing Like a Woman." In *Mama Blanca's Memoirs. Critical Edition,* edited by Doris Sommer, translated by Harriet de Onís and revised by Frederick H. Fornoff, v–xxviii. Pittsburgh: University of Pittsburgh Press, 1993.

———. "Mirror, Mirror, in Mother's Room: Watch Us While We Tell and Groom." In *Mama Blanca's Memoirs. Critical Edition,* edited by Doris Sommer, translated by Harriet de Onís and revised by Frederick H. Fornoff, 162–82. Pittsburgh: University of Pittsburgh Press, 1993.

Subieta Sagárnaga, Luis. *Bolívar en Potosí.* Potosí, Bolivia: Tipografía "Artística" de S. Sivila, 1925.

Taussig, Michael T. *The Magic of the State.* New York: Routledge, 1997.

Toro, Fermín. "Europa y América." In Toro and Miliani, 11–81.

———. "Honores a Bolívar." In *Ha muerto el Libertador: Homenaje de la Universidad Central de Venezuela en el sesquicentenario de su muerte.* Edited by Ildefonso Leal. Caracas: Ediciones del Rectorado de la UCV, 1980.

———. "Ideas y necesidades." In Toro and Miliani, 83–92.

———. *Los mártires.* Caracas: Centro de Estudios Universidad Central de Venezuela, 1966.

———. *Reflexiones sobre la Ley de 10 de abril de 1834 y otras obras.* Caracas: Ministerio de educación nacional, Dirección de cultura, 1941.

————. "Un romántico." In *Antología de costumbristas venezolanos del siglo xix*, 42–46. Caracas: Monte Avila, 1980.

Toro, Fermín, and Domingo Miliani. *Fermín Toro*. Caracas: Academia Venezolana de la Lengua, 1963.

Tosta, Virgilio. *Fermín Toro, político y sociólogo de la armonía*. Caracas: Imprenta Juan Bravo, 1958.

"28 de octubre: La estatua del Libertador." *La opinión nacional*, October 20, 1874.

Valero Martínez, Arturo, and Carlos Calderón Chico. *En defensa de Manuela Sáenz: La Libertadora del Libertador*. [Ecuador]: n.p., 1988.

Vargas Tejada, Luis. "Catón en Utica." In *Poetas contra Bolívar: El Libertador a través de la calumnia*, edited by Emilio Rodríguez Demorizi, 65–69. Madrid: Gráficas Reunidas, 1966.

Vázquez de Knauth, Josefina. *Nacionalismo y educación*. 2d ed. Mexico City: Colegio de México, 1975.

Vega Aguilera, Ciro. *El corazón del libertador: Destino final de una inapreciable reliquia histórica*. Caracas: n.p., 1977.

Verdery, Katherine. *The Political Lives of Dead Bodies: Reburial and Postsocialist Change*. New York: Columbia University Press, 1999.

White, Hayden. *Tropics of Discourse: Essays in Cultural Criticism*. Baltimore: Johns Hopkins University Press, 1978.

Williams, Raymond Leslie. *The Colombian Novel: 1844–1987*. Austin: University of Texas Press, 1991.

Worcester, Donald Emmet. *Bolívar*. Boston: Little Brown, 1977.

Zeuske, Max. *Interpretaciones y ensayos marxistas acerca de Simón Bolívar*. Berlin: Akademie-Verlag, 1985.

Zwiska, Leszek. *Breve historia de los jardines en Venezuela*. Caracas: Oscar Todtmann Editores, 1990.

Index

192   Index

Christopher B. Conway is assistant professor of Hispanic studies at Brown University. He is the editor of *Peruvian Traditions* by Ricardo Palma (2004) and has published articles on Latin American literature in *Hispanic Review, Revista de Crítica Literaria Latinoamericana,* and other journals.